UNDERWATER IRELAND

Guide to Irish Dive Sites

Second edition

COMHAIRLE Fó-THUINN
Irish Underwater Council

78A Patrick Street, Dun Laoghaire,
Co. Dublin, Ireland.

Published by:
The Irish Underwater Council – Comhairle Fó-Thuinn (IUC/CFT)
78A Patrick Street, Dun Laoghaire, Co. Dublin, Ireland

Tel. 01 2844601 Fax. 01 2844602 E-mail scubairl@indigo.ie

Web site: http://www.indigo.ie/scuba-irl

Printed in Ireland by:
Colour Books Ltd, 105 Baldoyle Industrial Est., Dublin 13

IUC/CFT is affiliated to:
Confederation Mondiale des Activities Subaquatiques (CMAS)

ISBN 0 948283 02 5 (Paperback)
0 948283 03 3 (Hardback)

Contents

About this guide 1
Acknowledgments 2
Diving in Ireland 3
Dive centres 6
Advertisers in SubSea 12
Irish laws which affect diving 15
Weather and tide times 18
Irish Tourist Offices 20
The meaning of Irish place names 23
Books of interest 27
Map of Ireland 29

Dive Sites

Dalkey Island and the Muglins 37
Wicklow Head 40
Hook Head, Co. Wexford 43
The Saltee Islands, Co. Wexford 45
Waterford 48
South Cork 52
West Cork 55
Roaring Water Bay, Co. Cork 58
Mizen Head, Co. Cork 63
Dunmanus Bay, Co. Cork 67
Bantry Bay, Co. Cork 71
Derrynane, Co. Kerry 74
Skelligs, Co. Kerry 76
St Finan's Bay, Co. Kerry 79
Valentia Island, Co. Kerry 82
Dingle and the Blaskets, Co. Kerry 93
The Maharees, Co. Kerry 96
Kilkee, Co. Clare 99
North Clare 104
Aran Islands, Co. Galway 109
South Connamara, Co. Galway 112
North-west Connemara, Co. Galway 115
Killary Harbour, Co. Galway 117
Inisbofin, Co. Galway 119
Clare Island, Co. Mayo 123
Achill Island, Co. Mayo 133
Belmullet, Co. Mayo 136
North Mayo 138
North Sligo 141
South Donegal 145
Malinbeg, Co. Donegal 148
Aranmore, Co. Donegal 151
North Donegal 154
Malin Head, Co. Donegal 159
Rathlin Island, Co. Antrim 162
Antrim's wrecks 165
Stangford Lough, Co. Down 172
Lambay Island, Co. Dublin 179

DISCLAIMER

This book is not intended as an invitation or prospectus to members of the public or other interested parties to dive on any of the sites that are mentioned in the text, and anyone intending to do so should take appropriate advice with regard to the safety and viability of their proposed actions.

About this Guide

In this second edition we have added over one hundred dive sites and we now include the Skelligs, Valentia and Achill Islands, and have up dated other relevant information. We have removed accommodation listings, lifeboat stations and gardaí phone numbers. Even so, because an area is not mentioned in this Guide, it does not mean that area is uninteresting, but only that no information was available on going to press. Also the sites described in any given area are only a sample of the type of diving in that area and there may be many more sites to be explored. Visitors wishing to access some of the more difficult sites would be well advised to obtain local knowledge or use the nearest dive centre.

The maps in this guide show only the outline of the site, it is assumed that any diving group would equip itself with proper maps and charts of the area in which it intends to dive. For this reason, Admiralty chart numbers, which include the area, are given as are those of the appropriate Ordinance Survey maps. The Irish OS 1:126,720 (½" to 1 mile) scale maps show submarine contours for the 5 (9m) and 10 (18m) fathom depths, the 1:50,000 maps shows the tidal area. The latter map series which is more up to date, gives very detailed information of roads and access points and is recommended. Where the GPS position of a site or wreck is known it is given. Unfortunately, many divers and dive centre operators regard GPS positions as commercially valuable and are not willing to release them.

A summary of Irish law as it affects divers is included. With the development of the European Union (EU) many of our laws are being brought into line with those of our European partners but there are some notable differences, e.g. diving for shellfish. The operation of portable compressors in many locations is now also forbidden.

A short guide to Irish place names is included to help resident and visitor alike to understand how places came to be named. We hope this will be of interest to you all.

Finally, if you have knowledge of other dive sites, or find a serious error in one of those herein, please let us know and we will include them in our next edition.

While every effort was made to supply accurate information IUC/CFT cannot be held responsible for any errors or omissions. Nevertheless we hope this guide will be useful to you and wish you good safe diving!

John Hailes.
Editor

Acknowledgments

The Irish Underwater Council–Comhairle Fó-Thuinn (IUC/CFT) gratefully acknowledges the efforts following people who have contributed to this dive guide.

Editor:
John Hailes

Editorial team:
Eddie Bourke
Bernard Kaye
Nigel Motyer

Production Assistants:
Padear Farrell
Norma Hailes
Sarah Lyle

Design and Layout:
Bernard Kaye

Photography:
Nigel Motyer
John Collins
Eddie Dunne
John Costelloe

Contributors to second edition:
Ivan Donoghue
Micheal Duggan
Mick Egan
Ronnie Fitzgibbon
Nic Gotto
Nigel Kelleher
Des Lavelle
Frank McRory
Mick Moriarty
Billy Nott
Jerry Smith
Peter Steele
Caroline Steele
Jerry Smith
Aidan Walshe
Gerry Stokes
Roy Stokes
Jim Corrigan
Don McGlinchey

Diving in Ireland

Ireland, being an island on the western edge of Europe and on the continental shelf, is perfectly suited for the sport of SCUBA diving. Our waters provide dive sites of various qualities and standards to encompass all individual requirements. Because of its small size it is relatively easy to travel from one part of the country to another, giving divers the opportunity to travel for one or more days diving.

The dive season generally starts around March and ends around October. It is possible of course, to dive outside of this, but due to adverse weather and sea conditions it is not appealing.

Diving officially started in Ireland in the early 1950s with the founding of the Belfast Branch of the British Sub Aqua Club. Before then a few adventurous individuals overcame considerable difficulties to make short dives in shallow depths in remote locations. In those days equipment was very much the deciding factor on the duration and depth of a dive. Today it is much easier and more comfortable, but as a result we are now more exposed to various physical and physiological dangers.

From those early divers, we learned all about the sites they visited, the good and bad, where to go, what to see and what to do. Much of this information was passed by word of mouth and through club newsletters.

In the early 1960s the independent Irish diving clubs formed the Irish Underwater Council / Comhairle Fó-Thuinn (IUC/ CFT). The Council, a voluntary body, regulates all aspects of diving for its members and represents Ireland at Confederation Mondiale Des Activités Subaquatiques (CMAS).

Today, our magazine "SubSea" is the main source of information for the Irish diver on local dive sites, the Council and diving related activities. This publication is the second edition of our dive site guide bringing together this accumulated knowledge of many popular Irish dive sites. It is for both the experienced and inexperienced diver alike. It is for the visitor who wishes to get a taste of what Ireland has to offer.

Our waters never cease to frustrate, annoy, amaze and delight Irish divers. Our weather and somewhat exposed position have a lot to do with this, but many sites are continually visited over and over again. It may be said that no dive is the same as the last one on the same site.

Some sites are known only to the chosen few because they wish to return and find it as they left it, undisturbed. Most divers respect a unwritten code of practice whereby a site is left as one would wish to find it, and we would wish you to do the same. Please remove all litter, shut all gates and, most important, operate compressors with consideration for others (see Irish laws which affect Irish diving).

IUC/CFT clubs are grouped into regions. For information about a club in any particular region contact:

The Irish Underwater Council,
Comhairle Fó-Thuinn,
78A Patrick Street,
Dun Laoghaire,
Co. Dublin.
Tel. 01 2844601
Fax. 01 2844602
E-mail scubairl@indigo.ie

Regional Listing of IUC/CFT Diving Clubs

Dublin North
Alpha Dive
Aer Lingus Divers
Belvedere College
Drogheda
Garda
Irish
Omega
Portmarnock

Dublin South
Army
Bray Divers
Gill Dara
Curragh
Dalkey Scubadivers
Naas
Nautilus Divers
Seal Bay Divers
Trident
UCD SAC
Wicklow
Wild Seals

Dublin West
Aquamarine Divers
Aquarius
Aquatec
Atlantis
Gemini
Kish
Marlin
St. Kevin's College
Viking
Waverley

Midlands
Athlone
Dolphin
Longford
Lough Ree
Mullingar
Strokestown

South East
Hook
Kilkenny
Waterford Harbour
Wexford

North
City of Derry
Donegal Bay
Inishown
Monaghan
Mullaghmore
Omagh
Sheephaven
Sligo
Sligo RTC
Strabane

South
Anglesea
Blackwater
Cork
Daunt
Discovery
Kinsale Museum
Sovereign Divers
UCC
West Cork

West
Achill
Atlantic Divers
Galway
Grainne Uaile
Jolly Mariner
Pucan
Shellfish
U.C.G.

South West
Aughinish
Banna Scubadivers
Buccaneer Divers
Burren
Ennis
Inbher Sceine
Kilkee
Limerick
Lough Derg
Tralee
Valentia Island

Diving Cylinders

The IUC/CFT operates a Visual Inspection Programme (VIP) conforming to BS 5430 which ensures that diving cylinders are visually inspected every two years and proof tested every four years. Inspected cylinders carry a VIP sticker showing the month and year by which time the cylinder must be re-inspected. Compressor operators look for this sticker before filling a cylinder. New cylinders do not require a VIP sticker for the first year of service.

Foreign cylinders will be re-filled provided that they comply with the regulations of their country of origin but the onus is on the cylinder's user to prove that it does comply. Visiting divers should ensure that their cylinders are within specification.

Insurance

Diving by its nature is hazardous and involves some risk, it is recommended that you take out accident insurance. While most dive centre operators would have public liability insurance it is desirable to check with the establishment or with the operator concerned as to the level of cover carried.

Safety

Enquire about local tidal conditions, doctor, hospital and the nearest phone. Know the name of the area in which you are diving and the quickest route to medical facilities.

Marine Rescue

Dial 999 or 112 (both toll free). When the **Emergency Service** answers ask for **Marine Rescue** and state your address or location and what type of assistance is required.

Fire, Ambulance and Garda (Police)

Dial 999 or 112 (both toll free). When the **Emergency Service** answers ask for the **service you require**, when connected state the address or location at which help is required.

Maritime Communications

There are to date 13 VHF radio stations around the Irish coast operating in the range 45–50 nm. These stations operate on different channels depending on where they are located. The nearest station to a particular area is given in each chapter.

Channel 16 VHF should be used **only** if you have failed to make contact on the appropriate working channel. Channel 16 VHF should normally be used for distress, urgency or safety calls. Normal Marine Radio Protocol should be used.

Recompression Chambers

If you require emergency recompression facilities dial 999 or 112 (both toll free) or VHF channel 16. The National Relay Emergency Service will contact the nearest **available** recompression facility for you. Do **not** contact the recompression facility direct. The telephone numbers given below are for non-emergency enquiries only.

Galway City, 091 24222 – ask for the anaesthetist on call.
Craigavon, Co. Armagh, Northern Ireland (08) 0762 334444 – ask for the anaesthetist on call.
Haulbowline, Co. Cork, 021 378777 – ask for the recompression chamber.

Dive Centres

The following information on dive centres has been **supplied by the centres operators themselves** and C.F.T./I.U.C. is not in a position to confirm the accuracy of the information supplied.

Icon Explanation

The dive centre caters only for experienced divers (CMAS, CFT, PADI, BSAC etc.) or groups led by experienced divers

The dive centre is a PADI dive school and caters for divers of all grades. The centre also caters for experienced divers or groups led by experienced divers.

Compressed breathing air supplied to the indicated pressure (Bar)

Enriched air Nitrox available only

Nitrox and Trimix gases available

Diving cylinders (no.) and weights available for hire

Complete diving equipment sets available for hire

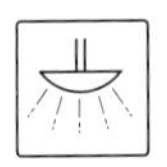

Showers and changing rooms and equipment drying room available

Rigid inflatable boat(s) available of size indicated

Half decked boat(s) available of size indicated

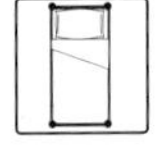

Accommodation available at centre

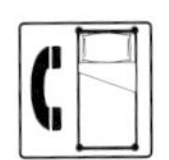

Accommodation can be arranged

Equipment sold and/or serviced

Aquaventures

The Stone House, Baltimore, Co. Cork.
Contact: Rianne and Jerry Smith.
Tel. 028 20511 Fax. 028 20511
E-mail: aquavent@aquaventures.iol.ie

Number of dives logged 1998 season: Not available
Purpose built dive centre and ITB approved B&B in centre of Baltimore. Excellent sheltered sites around Sherkin and Clear Islands. Off-shore reefs for scenic drop-offs, abundant marine life and wrecks including submarine "U260" and "Kowloon Bridge". Courses for all levels PADI, BSAC, TDI, CFT, CMAS. (English, Dutch, German and French spoken).

Ballinskelligs Watersports Ltd

Dungegan, Ballinskelligs, Co. Kerry.
Contact: Sean Feehan.
Tel. 066 79182 Fax. 066 79303
Number of dives logged 1998 season: 4,500

Ballinskelligs cater for the largest number of overseas divers in Ireland. The main diving activity is centred on Ireland's only world renowned dive site, the Skelligs. Since 1994 permits to land boats at the Skelligs have been required and Ballinskelligs Watersports is the only dive centre with these permits and accordingly can guarantee a visit to the Islands. We have six boats ranging from a 22m steel boat to a 5.5m RIB allowing Ballinskelligs to cater for groups from 2 persons to 60 persons. In September of 1997 a 15m trawler sank in Ballinskelligs Bay in 26m we have purchased the wreck from the insurers and have the exclusive rights to dive the wreck.

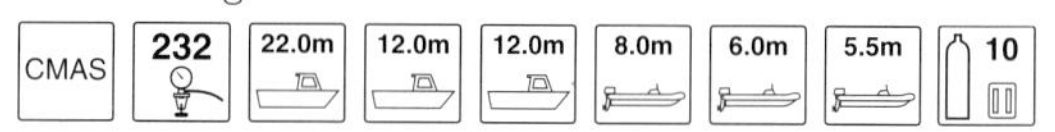

Baltimore Diving and Watersports Centre

Baltimore, Co. Cork.
Contact: John Kearney
Tel. 028 20300 Fax. 028 20300
E-mail: skdiving@iol.ie
Web site: www.foundmark.com/Ireland/
Number of dives logged 1998 season: 1000+

West Cork's most established dive centre offers dive sites from Galley Head to Mizen Head. We have bases in Union Hall, Baltimore and Cape Clear. You will be spoilt for choice of the many reefs, drop offs, caves and wrecks such as the Kowloon Bridge and the WWII Submarine U260. We offer courses from discover diving to instructor with facilities for mixed gas diving. Our shop stocks all top brands and we also have a large service section.

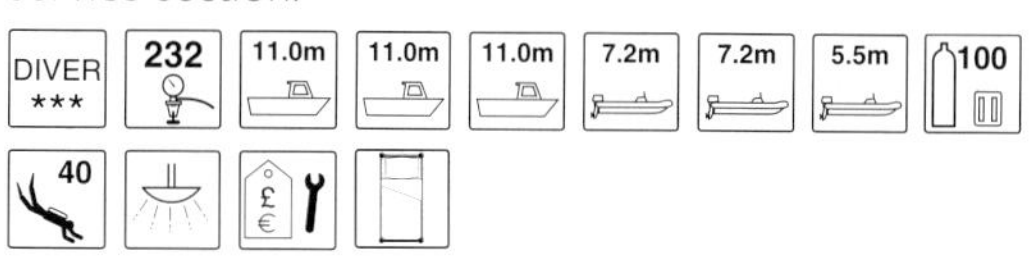

Cape Clear Island Dive Centre

North Harbour, Cape Clear Island, Co. Cork.
Contact: Ciaran O'Driscoll
Tel: 028 39153 Fax. 028 39153
E-mail: ciaranodriscoll@tinet.ie
Number of dives logged 1998 season: 1000+

The Cape Clear centre is a holiday centre with excellent diving facilities in an unique island setting under personal ownership and management. Being an island location, there is always a sheltered site for diving. It is also within easy reach of such famous dive sites as "Kowloon Bridge" and Fastnet Rock. Out of season contact Baltimore Diving and Watersports Centre.

Cuan na Farraige Dive Centre

Aughoose, Pullathomas, Ballina, Co. Mayo.
Contact: Neil and Kathleen McEleney
Tel. 097 87800 Fax. 097 87800
Number of dives logged 1998 season: Not available

"Cuan Na Farraige" is one of Ireland's newest dive centres, which is located on the North West coast of Co. Mayo. The centre itself is situated approximately 30m from the sea. It boasts a 5.8m RIB, 2 hard boats at its disposal, air filling station, 12.5 litre tanks, lecture room, day room, shop, reception area, en-suite accommodation, showers. The centre also has an on-site restaurant (with plenty wholesome Irish food) and ample parking facilities.

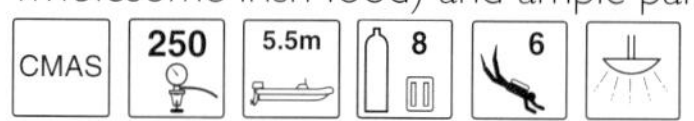

Dol-Fin Divers

Cloughmore Pier, Achill Island, Co. Mayo.
Contact: Jim and Brigit Corrigan.
Tel. 098 45473 Fax. 098 45473
Number of dives logged 1998 season: Not supplied

Dol-Fin Divers a dive school on Achill Island, offering courses from Discover Scuba to Assistant Instructor. Dive groups are catered for all year.

We have two Hard Boats 15m & 12m, a 6.5m. RIB and a 5m Inflatable available.

Changing rooms with hot showers are situated on "Clouglimore Pier". Full gear and air to 230 Bar.

DV Dive Centre

138 Mountstewart Road, Newtonards, Co. Down.
Contact: David Vincent
Tel. (048) 01247 464671
Number of dives logged 1998 season: Not available

DV Diving is a Dive Centre, B.S.A.C. and TDI Premier School based outside Newtownards.

It is run by David and Tony Vincent, both are B S-A C Advanced Instructors and RYA Powerboat Instructors. David is also a B S-A C First Class Diver, Nitrox Course Director, a graduate in Marine Sciences and a qualified teacher. Diving takes place in Belfast and Strangford Loughs and the Irish Sea.

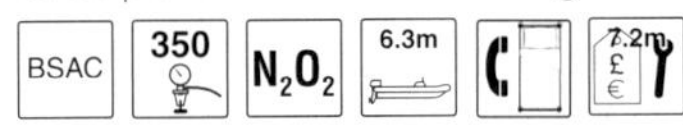

Fastnet Charters

Baltimore, Co. Cork.
Contact: Nick Dent
Tel. 028 36450 Mobile: 086 8240642
Number of dives logged 1998 season: Not available

Wrecks, reefs, drop-offs in Mizen Head, Fastnet Rock, Cape Clear and Stags areas (including the Kowloon Bridge). Offshore 105 with 400 HP engine charter boat, fully equipped and licensed for twelve divers. Owner/skipper with over eighteen years experience. Superb accommodation available. Air and equipment hire available nearby. Pick-up at Baltimore, Schull, Cape Clear or Crookhaven.

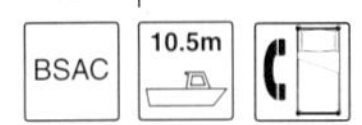

Galway Bay Scubadivers

Coill Rua, Inverin, Co. Galway.
Contact: Nick Pfeiffer
Tel. 091 553065 Fax. 091 553065
Mobile 087 2653024
E-mail: atlanticdiveschool@tinet.ie
Number of dives logged 1998 season: 2,000

In operation since 1994, we offer a full range of diving services to divers wishing to dive the stunning Aran Islands. Package diving holidays can be arranged based on choice of accommodation and including ferry crossing to Ireland.

It is possible to base yourself on the mainland in Connemara or enjoy an island based diving holiday and avail of new first class accommodation and diving facilities opening for the 2000 season at the **Aran Islands Dive Centre** located on Inishmaan. We specialise in Underwater Photography and have full facilities in house for U/W photographic enthusiasts. Contact us for full details and information.

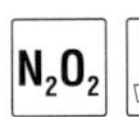
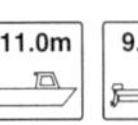
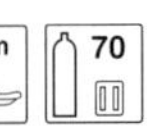

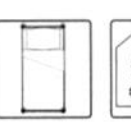

Harbour View Dive Centre

Overlooking Mullaghmore Harbour,
Bunduff, Cliffoney, Co. Sligo.
Contact: Danny or Attracta Boyle.
Tel. 071 66366 Fax. 071 66366
E-mail: danboyle@iol.ie
Number of dives logged 1998 season: New 1998

Harbour View is an unique new diving centre overlooking Mullaghmore Harbour with views of Donegal Bay and Inishmurry Island. Located on the Atlantic coast with some of the clearest waters in Europe excellent for diving. The centre is fully equipped with twin compressors and drying room with showers. Eight self-catering houses plus B+B rooms, outdoor tennis court, pool room, laundry room, pay phone, bicycle hire and children's play area. We cater for diving clubs, divers, their families and friends.

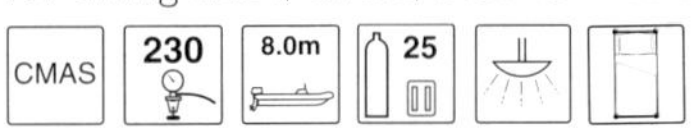

Kilkee Diving and Watersports Centre

Golf Links Road, Kilkee, Co. Clare.
Contact: John Cosgrove
Tel. 065 56707 Fax. 065 56020
Number of dives logged 1998 season: Not available

This fully equipped diving centre is located on the sea front. With depths up to 45m and 20m viability diving is possible all year. The best months are April to October. The dive centre can organise a fully inclusive holiday which would include flight, airport transfer, all types of accommodation, equipment hire and two dives per day.

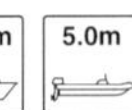

Kinsale Dive Centre

Castlepark, Kinsale, Co. Cork.
Contact: Eddie or Anne McCarthy.
Tel. 021 774959 Fax. 021 774958
E-mail: maritime@indigo.ie
Web page: http://www.indigo.ie/ipress/mt/welcome.htm
Number of dives logged 1998 season: Not available

Kinsale Dive Centre provides all the requirements for a diving holiday based in one of Ireland's most popular Holiday towns. Operating from Castlepark marina, the centre is ideal for groups as it has accommodation, restaurant, pub, full tidal access, compressor and back up facilities. Visiting clubs can berth their RIBs on the marina, store their trailers, and/or hire the centre's 12.5m Aquastar hard boat for off shore dives to the Ling Rocks. Video and lecture space available.

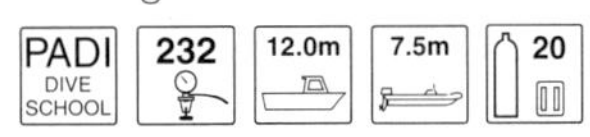

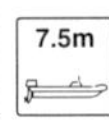
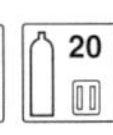

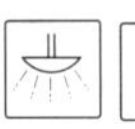

Láthair Muitina An Daingin
On the Waterfront, Dingle, Co. Kerry.
Contact: Micheal Shanahan.
Tel. 066 52422 Fax. 066 52425
E-mail: ifarrell@tinet.ie
Web page: www.oconnor.ie/tourism/diving.html
Number of dives logged 1998 season: Not available

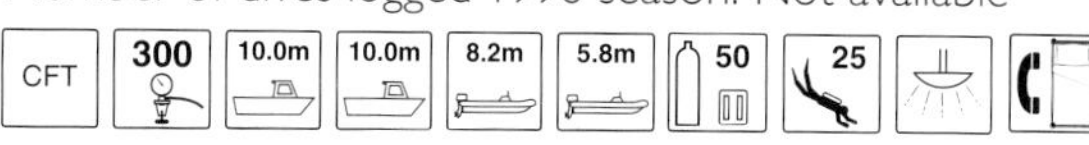

Lavelle's Valentia Diving Centre
Valentia Island, Co. Kerry.
Contact: Des Lavelle
Tel. 066 76124 Fax. 066 76309
Number of dives logged 1998 season: Not available

Lavelles' Valentia Diving Centre was serving sports-divers and exploring the underwater world of the Valentia / Skellig / Puffin Island triangle when diving really was a pioneer sport.

Established before there were any Dive Centre yard sticks to copy, the Lavelles thirty year record that thy got it right.

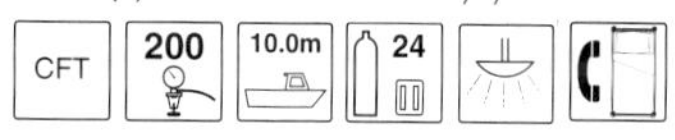

North Irish Lodge Luxury Holiday Cottages and Dive Centre
161 Low Road, Islandmagee, Larne, Co. Antrim BT40 3RF, Northern Ireland.
Contact: Peter and Caroline Steele.
Tel. 01960 382246 Fax. 01960 382246
E-mail: NIL@lagan.net
Website: www.lagan.net/NIL
Number of dives logged 1998 season: Not available

The North Irish Lodge is situated only 15 minutes from Belfast and 30 minutes from the Port of Larne and Carrickfergus Castle with superb sea views overlooking Larne Lough. The accommodation concises of luxury 3 and 4 star cottages.

Over 40 shipwrecks nearby suitable for all grades of diver. The Maidens, a group of rocks 8km off shore provide excellent wreck and scenic diving in crystal clear water. Horse riding, fishing, golf and guided walks can be arranged.

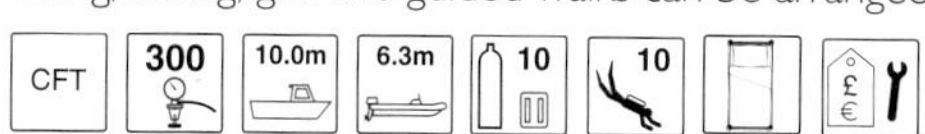

Oceantec Adventures Ltd.
10/11 Marine Terrace, Dun Laoghaire, Co. Dublin.
Contact: Willie Siddall
Tel. 01 2801083 Fax 01 2843885
E-mail: oceantec@indigo.ie
Web site: www.oceantadventures.com
Number of dives logged 1998 season: 2500

Oceantec is the only PADI 5 Star Instructor Development Centre in the country. All levels of diver training are offered from a fully equipped training centre. Rental equipment is changed annually. A comprehensive range of equipment is always in stock and we are also equipped to service regulators, inspect and hydro. test cylinders and deal with repairs to all equipment including drysuits. Dive trips locally from the centre's RIB, regular excursions to the best Irish and International sites.

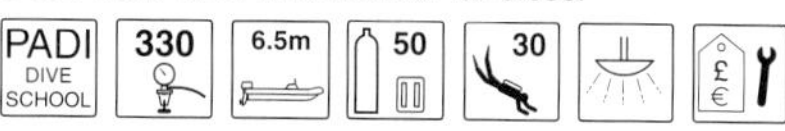

San Miguel Dive Centre
The Harbour, Kilkeel, Co Down.
Contact: Micheal and Eileen McGreevy
Tel. (08) 016937 65885 Fax. (08) 016937 64760

San Miguel operates from Kilkeel, Ireland's largest fishing port five kilometres north of Carlingford Lough where we can arrange wreck, scenic, drift and night dives. Accommodation in the area concises of hotels, camping, caravans, farmhouse, b & b and self-catering cottages. Individual and group bookings welcome.

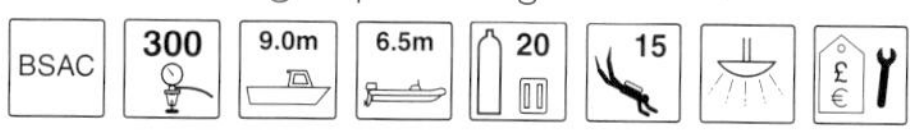

Schull Watersport Centre Ltd.
The Pier, Schull, Co. Cork.
Contact: Simon Nelson
Tel. 028 28554 Fax. 028 28554
Number of dives logged 1998 season: 800

Schull is an ideal base for exploring the wrecks and reefs of the Mizen Head and Fastnet Rock. Boat access is ex excellent and there are many good shore dives. Schull offers a wide range of accommodation and restaurants. The Centre offers air fills, bottle hire and boat charter plus helpful local advice.

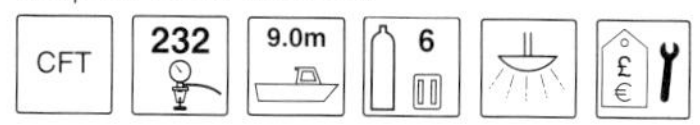

Scubadive West
Renvyle, Co. Galway.
Contact: Shane Gray.
Tel. 095 43922 Fax. 095 43923
E-mail: scuba@anu.ie
Number of dives logged 1998 season: 3,500

Ireland's all-weather dive centre, nestling in an idyllic, sheltered private cove on the shores of Little Killary- the only fjord system in Ireland and Britain. The combination of guaranteed inshore diving and spectacular offshore diving is unique.

The centre offers full and half day dive trips on two hard boats. The "*Offshore Diver*" has a compressor twelve tanks and weight belts permanently on board. The day trips are to Inishbofin, Inishturk or Clare Island with two dives and lunch on the island. The 7.5m "*Dive Taxi*" visits nearer sites morning and afternoon. There are six dive instructors and twenty five full rental sets available at the centre.

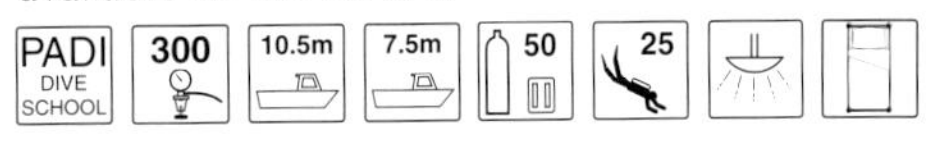

Skellig Aquatics Ltd.

Caherdaniel,
Co. Kerry.
Contact: Traolach Peter and Ena Sweeney
Tel. 066 75277   Fax. 066 75277
E-mail: skelliga@iol.ie
Web page: www.iol.ie/kerry-insight/diving-ireland
Number of dives logged 1998 season: 2,500

Dive with the longest established Dive Centre in Ireland and sample the best dive sites in Western Europe. A qualified marine biologist with 31 years diving experience will guide you to spectacular underwater scenery, teaming with marine life in unpolluted GULF STREAM waters, particularly at the famous "Skellig Islands". Incredible opportunities exist for the photographic diver.

We organise expeditions to nearby uninhabited islands, hill walking expeditions, sea angling and corporate team building activities. We provide all dive facilities including a dive shop. All types of accommodation are available here on the Ring of Kerry. Caherdaniel village has great apres dive life with pubs, trad music, restaurants, fantastic beaches, golf and horse riding etc.

Valentia Island Sea Sports

Knightstown, Valentia Island, Co. Kerry.
Tel. 066 76204   Fax. 066 76367
Contact: Martin and Sandra Moriarty
Website: www.divevalentia.ie
Number of dives logged 1998 season: 1000+

Valentia Is. Sea Sports offers a wide range of dive facilities. We teach the PADI courses from Open Water to Divemaster level. Groups or individuals are catered for. The Lochin hard boat is purpose built for diving with an extended wheelhouse for divers to sit in, dive platform, toilet and galley. The RIB is 8.4 m with an inboard engine and both vessels are licenced to carry twelve divers.

The dive centre is situated right on the sea-front, has showers, toilets, changing and drying room. The guesthouse, which is 200 m from the dive centre, has ten en-suit bedrooms, restaurant and resident lounge. The dive centre and B &B are open from April 1st. until October 31st.

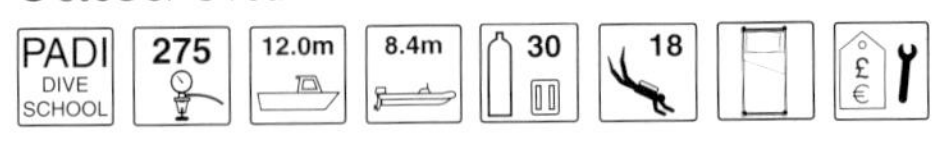

Waterworld

Harbour House, Scraggane Pier, The Maharees,
Castlegregory, Co. Kerry.
Contact: Ronnie Fitzgibbon.
Tel. 066 39292   Fax. 066 39557
E-mail: dive@iol.ie
Web page: http://www.waterworld.ie
Number of dives logged 1998 season: 13,500

Waterworld is a family run PADI 5 STAR, BSAC & TDI dive centre which is based in Castlegregory, thirty kilometres from Tralee. The Maharees Islands which are minutes by boat from the centre are renowned for their safe wreck and scenic diving.

The centre is Ireland's largest. Purpose built with luxury en-suite accommodation, lecture rooms, dive shop, drying, changing, shower rooms and restaurant with panoramic views, offering the complete range of PADI dive courses from beginner to Instructor level including Nitrox.

Complete holiday package, includes dives, equipment, full meals and accommodation together with ferry or fly/drive deals are available. The Blasket Islands and Brandon cliff face dive trips daily. From April to September Waterworld offers a full range of water sports at its Sandy Bay water sports centre.

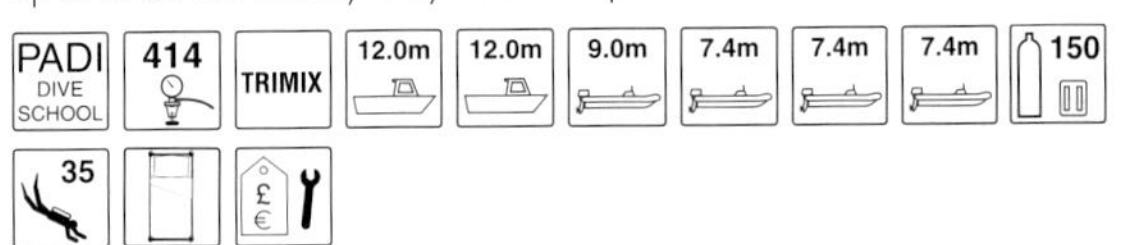

Western Diving Centre

Carraholly, Westport, Co. Mayo.
Contact: Steve Mooney
Tel. 098 28974   Fax. 098 28974

A new centre located beside the sea, with private slip and jetty. Offering 4 star self contained accommodation. Close to the beautiful Georgian town of Westport and local amenities including top class golf course, horse riding and lots of night life. All water sports catered for including water skiing and wake boarding. Dive sites include The Bills, Clare Island, Inishbofin and Inishturk.

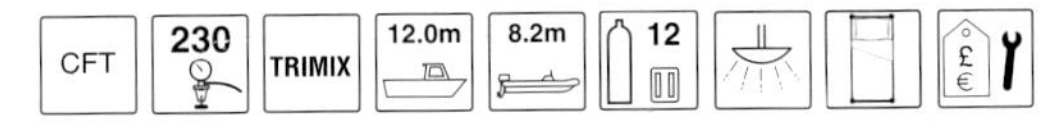

Wexford Diving Holidays

Wexford Diving Centre, Riverstown, Murrington, Co. Wexford.
Contact: Mark and Sandra Robertson
Tel. 053 39373 Fax. 053 39373
E-mail: wexdive@indigo.ie
Number of dives logged 1998 season: Not available

The diving area has the largest concentration of wrecks in Ireland and also has beautiful scenic diving around the Saltee Islands where there is an abundance of seals, dolphins, fish, birds and even whales We have a 9.5m diving vessel, full equipment hire, drying rooms and a 265 l/m 300 bar mobile compressor.

Wexford Diving centre is family run, has bed and breakfast accommodation and also self-catering facilities. There is plenty for non divers to do and Wexford is just 10 minutes down the road

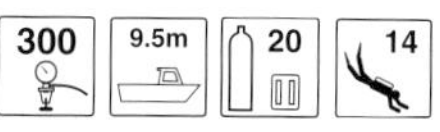

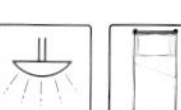

Wine Strand Holiday Centre

Wine Strand, Ballyferriter, Dingle, Co. Kerry.
Contact: Brendan Houlihan
Tel. 061 325125 Fax 061 326450
Number of dives logged 1998 season: 500+

A diving complex in one building on the edge of sea. Having separate changing rooms for men and women. Three phase air compressor with washing and drying room with hangers. Modern self-catering cottages on site. A good area for hill walking, Irish music and language with good craic in the local pubs.

Liveaboards

D. S. V. Melinka

Ex Bantry Bay Divers (see above)
Number dives logged 1998 season: Not available

The Melinka is a 23 m converted trawler with 12 berths in six double cabins for liveaboard diving expeditions which may be chartered by groups of divers who wish to reach dive sites out of the range of RIBs or small hard bottles. The liveaboard, operating between Kinsale and Dingle, will make for a new port each night so you wilt not miss out on any of the shore side enjoyments connected with the sport!! This vessel, with an experienced skipper, full electronics, equipped with a compressor and facilities to mix Nitrox and Trimix. would make an excellent TEK mission support vessel.

MV Kerry Breeze

Ex Ballinskelligs Watersports (see above)
Number dives logged 1998 season: Not available

New in 1996, the liveaboard the MV Kerry Breeze offers accommodation for 6 guests and 3 crew. The craft is thoroughly equipped with galley, 2 toilets and showers. VHF, radar, weatherfax and GPS ensuring accuracy on dive sites and up to the minute meteorological reports and high safety standards. The MV Kerry Breeze will operate between Baltimore and Dingle from mid March to mid September. Sites include the underwater gardens of the Skelligs, Mizen Head, drift diving the Fastnet, diving the Kowloon Bridge, Europe's largest wreck and not forgetting the German U-boat, the U-260.

MV Salutay

Norsemaid Sea Enterprises Ltd.
152 Portaferry Road, Newtownards, Co. Down BT22 2AJ, Northern Ireland.
Tel. 01247 812081 Fax. 01247 820194
E-mail: salutay@btinternet.com
Approx. number dives logged 1998 season: 2000+

Boat length:
18 m

Engines:
2 x 90 HP

Equipment:
2 x DGPS
2 colour sounders
DECCA
2 x RADAR sets

Accommodation:
1 x double cabin; 2 x 4 birth cabins.

Diving equipment:
Air 400 l/min @ 300 bar. Nitrox. Trimix.

Norsemaid Sea Enterprises Ltd have over 20 years experience in organising diving expeditions and our liveaboard dive vessel Salutay is one of the foremost in the British Isles. We are renowned for our excellent hospitality and providing the very best diving in Irish waters and beyond. We are fully equipped for technical and air diving.

Advertisers in SubSea

The following Dive Centres, suppliers etc. have recently advertised in "SubSea" the official publication of The Irish Underwater Council.

Diving Centres and Operators

Aquaventures
The Stone House, Lifeboat Road, Baltimore, Co. Cork.
Tel. / Fax. 028 29511
E-mail aquaventures@aquaventures.iol.ie
New dive centre for 1998 diving the West Cork area.

Bantry Bay Divers
Main Street, Glengarriff, Co. Cork.
Tel. 027 51310 Fax. 027 52175
E-mail: divebantry@aol.ie
Diving expeditions in the West Cork area, nitrox, trimix and equipment sales.

Baltimore Diving & Watersports Centre
Baltimore, West Cork.
Tel. / Fax. 028 20300
E-mail: jkdiving@iol.ie
Diving expeditions in the West Cork area, nitrox and equipment sales.

Castlepark Dive Centre
Kinsale, Co. Cork.
Tel. 021 774959 Fax. 021 774958
E-mail maritime@indigo.ie
This dive centre at Castlepark has everything you need.

Clew Bay Adventures
Quay Cottage, Westport Harbour, Westport, Co. Mayo.
Tel. 089 41236 Fax. 098 28120.
Skippered dive charter based in Westport.

Cnoc ard Yard
Oysterhaven, Co. Cork.
Tel. 021 770748 Fax. 021 294808 / 770748
Wonderful accommodation, air, gear hire, boats group rates.

D. V. Diving,
138 Mountstewart Road, Newtownards, Co. Down, Northern Ireland. BT22 2ES
Tel. / Fax. (08) 01247 464671
Diving in Northern Ireland, Technical diving and diving holidays.

Dingle Marina Dive Centre
On the Waterfront, Dingle, Co. Kerry.
Tel. 06652422 Fax. 06652425
E-mail: lfarrell@tinet.ie

Dol-fin Divers
Achill, Co. Mayo.
Tel. / Fax. 098 45473
Instructor with skippers ticket, gear hire and air to 240 bar.

Galway Bay Scubadivers
Inverin, Connemara, Co. Galway.
Tel. 091 553065 Mobile: 088 653024
PADI dive centre diving South Connemara and the Aran Islands.

Kilkee Diving Centre
The Harbour, East End, Kilkee, Co. Clare.
Tel. 065 56707 Fax. 065 56020
E-mail: Kilkee@iol.ie
Diving centre and watersports equipment sales.

Malinmore Adventure Centre
Glencolmcille, Co. Donegal.
Tel. 073 30123 / 30311
E-mail: megannwv@tinet.ie

Moorings Marine,
Tel. / Fax. 01 2840269 Mobile 086 2683635
E-mail macallister@tinet.ie
Diving charters with Lochin 33 "Mohawk".

National Diving School Ireland
8 St. James' Terrace, Malihide, Co. Dublin.
Tel. 01 8452000 Fax. 01 8452920
E-mail: national-diving@hotmail.com
Diving school & holiday arranged, equipment sales.

Oceantec Adventures
10 / 11 Marine Terrace, Dun Laoghaire, Co. Dublin.
Tel. 01 2801083 Fax. 01 2843885
E-mail: oceantec@indigo.ie
PADI 5 star dive centre with equipment rental and equipment sales.

San Miguel
The Slipways, The Harbour, Kilkeel, Co. Down. Northern Ireland BT34 4AX.
Tel. (08) 016937 65885 Fax. (08) 016937 64760
New diving operating out of Kilkeel, Co. Down.

Scubadive West
Renvyle, Co. Galway.
Tel. 095 43922 Fax. 095 43923
E-mail: scuba@anu.ie
PADI dive centre operating out of Little Killary harbour. Scubadive West also organise foreign diving holidays.

The Anserina
Tel. 096 43044 / 32439 Fax. 096 43044.
A Cygnus 32 foot boat works the North Mayo Downpatrick head area.

Valentia Island Sea Sports
Knightstown, Valentia Island, Co. Kerry.
Tel. 066 76204 Fax. 066 76367
A PADI dive centre operating out of Valentia.

Holiday Accommodation and Operators

Blue Moon Hostel
Dunkineely, Co. Donegal.
Tel. 073 37264.
Self catering with 23 bunks and compressed air and bottle hire.

Ceide House
Ballycastle, Co. Mayo.
Tel. 096 43105 / 43459
Bar, restaurant and Bed and Breakfast.

Divers World
125 East Barnet Road, New Barnet, Hertfordshire EN4 8RF, England.
Tel 0181 275 0101 Fax. 0181 440 8430
Diving holidays worldwide.
Irish agent: Flagship Scubadiving Ltd.

Harbour Lights
Saint John's Point, Dunkineely, Co. Donegal.
Tel. 073 37291
Close to the dive sites at St. John's Point.

Michael Stein Travel
77 Lower Camden Street, Dublin 2.
Tel. 01 4755401 Fax. 01 4781809.
International travel agents will organise your dive holiday.

Oonas Dive Club
Tel. 01323 648924
E-mail: info@oonasdivers.com
The Oonas Dive Club invites you to party with them in Sharm.

Renvyle Inn
Tully Village, Renvyle, Connemara, Co. Galway.
Tel. 095 43954
Compressed air free to resident divers.

Hotel Saltees
Kilmore Quay, Co. Wexford.
Tel. 053 29601 Fax. 053 29602.
Fabulous base for diving the Saltees Islands with new marina nearby.

Valentia Island Sea Sports
Knightstown, Valentia Island, Co. Kerry.
Tel. 066 76204 Fax. 066 76367
A pier front guest house and restaurant which caters for divers.

Diving Supplies and Equipment

Atlantis Diving
42 Carleton Street, Portadown,
Co. Armagh BT62 3EP, Northern Ireland.
Tel. (08) 01762 333332 Fax. (08) 01762 352374
Courses on Nitrox and Technical diving.

Blandford Sub-Aqua
Blandford House, Holly Industrial Park,
Imperial Way, Herts. Wd2 4TP, England.
Tel. 01923 801572 Fax. 01923 801573
Mares diving equipment.

Dry Suit Repairs
199 Newvale Cottages, Library Road, Shankill, Co. Dublin.
Tel. 01 2721255
Dry suit repairs.

Festina Ireland
Tel. 01 2841067 Fax. 01 2804481
Analog depth metre watches.

Flagship Scubadiving Ltd.
"Naomh Eanna", Charlotte Quay, Grand Canal Basin, Ringsend, Dublin 4
Tel. 01 6670988 Fax. 016675824
Main agents for Northern Diver suits products and accessories. Digitally controlled Nitrox blending.

Great Outdoors,
Chatham Street, Dublin 2.
Tel. 01 6794293 Fax 01 6794554
Full equipment for the diver.

IANTD Ireland Ltd.
54/55 Great Strand Street, Dublin 1.
Tel. 01 8733044/8435643 Fax. 01 8733969
E-mail: IANTDIRL@aol.com
Nitrox & technical diving training.

Industrial Pressure Testing Ltd.
Unit H5, Marina Commercial Park, Cork.
Cylinder VIP's, Nitrox and oxygen service.

Jackson Sports
70 High Street, Belfast BT1 2BE, Northern Ireland.
Tel. / Fax. (08) 01232238572
Full equipment for the diver.

Lambay Diving & Watersports Ltd.
Kilmessan, Navan, Co. Meath.
Tel. 046 25164 Fax. 046 26085
E-mail: Walshe@indigo.ie
Cylinder testing to BS 5430.

Midland Diving Centre
Sruthan, Marlinstown, Mullingar, Co. Westmeath.
Tel. / Fax. 044 42134
Full equipment for the diver.

Modern Tool (Ireland) Ltd.
J.F. Kennedy Ave., Naas Road, Dublin 12.
Tel. 01 4509488 Fax. 01 4509750
Portable Clotri-Sub diving compressors.

O.M.E. Drysuits
Killmascally Road, Ardboe, Dungannon,
Co. Tyrone BT71 5BH, Northern Ireland.
Tel. (08) 016487 36795 Fax. (08) 016487 36796.
Suppliers of compressed neoprene drysuits.

Simpson-Lawrence Ltd.
218-228 Edmiston Drive,
Glasgow G51 2YT, Scotland.
Fax. 0141 426 5419 E-mail: info@simpson-lawrence.co.uk
Distributors for Beuchat diving equipment.

South Coast Marine Ltd.
Cork.
Tel. 087 597855 Fax. 021 274093
Manufacturers of offshore commercial boats. Agents for Ribcraft RIBs.

Uwatec UK Ltd.
172 Winchester Road, Four Marks Alton,
Hampshire GU34 5HZ, England.
Tel. 01420 561412 Fax. 01420 561424
Aladin dive computers.

Viking Marine
115 Lower Georges Street, Dun Laoghaire, Co. Dublin.
Tel. 10 2806654 Fax. 01 2803712.
Full equipment for the diver.

Clubs and Societies

The Basking Shark Society
Cronk Mooar, Curragh Road, St. Johns, Isle of Man IM4 3LN
Tel. 01624 801207 E-mail bskshark@enterprise.net
A registered charity researches into and endeavours to protect the basking shark..

Irish laws which affect diving

This summary of the legislation relevant to scuba diving in Ireland was prepared to make divers aware of the various laws which apply to their activities. It does not purport to be a legal interpretation. It is intended to be a layman's guide to the restrictions on divers.

Penalties for illegal activity can be severe and include seizure of equipment and vehicles, fines and custodial sentences. Prosecutions can be taken by gardai, customs officers, wildlife wardens or other warranted officials.

Shellfish

The taking of any shellfish, lobsters, crawfish, crabs, etc., by divers using scuba is prohibited (Shellfish by-law 533 made on 14-3-1966). Snorkelling for shellfish does not seem to be forbidden. However, this law does not apply to Northern Ireland where the taking of shellfish is still allowed.

The taking of oysters is prohibited other than by dredging in specified areas. Pollution of or interference with an oyster bed is forbidden, (Fisheries Consolidation Act no. 14, 1959).

Spearfishing in Ireland

There are no regulations in force governing spearfishing in the sea, apart from certain bays and estuaries where aquaculture is practised. Salmon in most estuaries may not be spearfished. Many rivers, lakes and some canals also have fishery restrictions, and if in doubt, enquire locally.

The IUC/CFT has a "no spearfishing while using aqualung" rule, but again this is a voluntary restriction. Spearfishing competitions are no longer held in Ireland, again as a voluntary contribution to the environment.

Lough Hyne Co. Cork

Diving and boating in the Lough Hyne nature reserve is prohibited except with a permit (Statutory Instrument no. 207, 1981). Permits may be obtained from Mr Declan O'Donnell, Wildlife Warden, Direenlomane, Ballydehob, Co. Cork. (Tel. 028-37347).

Noise

The Environmental Protection Agency (EPA) Act (noise) Regulations, Statutory Instrument no. 179, 1994 allows any member of the public to formally complain about noise pollution. Prior to this regulation noise nuisance was a general nuisance offence. Divers should be conscious of the need to minimise or eliminate compressor noise at dive sites.

Wild Birds

The Wildlife Act 1976 empowers the Minister with responsibility for the Office of Public Works (OPW) to make orders designating special protection areas under article 4 of the EU Directive 79/409/EEC. The orders forbid wilful disturbance of birds. Some, but not all of the orders, forbid operation of a motor which causes disturbance to any designated bird. The orders also prohibit climbing on the cliffs, shooting and drift netting.

The sites of diving interest which are protected are: Saltees, Co. Wexford; Puffin Island, Co. Kerry; Iniskea, Cliffs of Moher, Co. Clare; Skelligs, Co. Kerry; Blaskets, Co. Kerry; Horn Head, Rockabill, Co. Dublin; Tralee Bay, Old Head of Kinsale and Ballycotton Bay Co. Cork.

Speedboats

A local authority may apply to have an order made under the Merchant Shipping Act 1992, jet skis and fast power boats regulations (Statutory Instrument no. 387, 1992). A fast power boat means a pleasure craft capable of speeds which may constitute a danger to persons on or in the water.

About 60 such proposals are before the Department of the Marine including Ballybunion, Smerwick, Ventry, Derrynane, Rosses Point, Baltimore, Carlingford, Seapoint and Sandycove. The legislation could be applied to dive RIBs and the operative word **capable** (speed) is not defined.

Verbally it has been indicated that dive boats are not targeted, but authorised officers can be from the Commissioners of Public Works, local authorities, Regional Fisheries Boards, etc. Local interpretation can vary. Already there has been comment at the Forty Foot Bathing Place, Sandycove, Co Dublin.

Carriage of Passengers

The carriage of passengers for reward is forbidden except in boats licensed by the Department of the Marine. These boats are inspected before a licence is issued. Cox'ns need to be aware that passengers should not be carried on a fee paying basis from islands, etc. The payment of a boat fee for a dive may need consideration.

Licensing of Boats

While trawlers need to have a registration number displayed, small pleasure boats are exempt from this requirement. This differs from the situation in Europe where all such craft are registered and the operator requires certification of competence. Proposals for such regulation in the UK were recently rejected.

Salvage

All wrecks are owned by somebody. All material recovered from any wreck should be declared to the receiver of wreck. This is the local customs officer or the local gardai. The receiver will make enquiries as to the legitimate owner. Usually no value is attributed to small souvenirs and the material is left with the finder.

However undeclared salvage is stolen goods and the perpetrator can be charged with larceny. The Merchant Shipping Salvage and Wreck Act 1994, forbids the boarding of any wreck without the permission of the owner or master. There is no reference to the age of the wreck. Wreck is defined as on shore or under water. This Act appointed the gardai as Receivers of Wreck.

Wrecks over 100 years old

The National Monuments Amendment Act (no. 17 of 1984) forbids diving directed at the exploration of a shipwreck more than 100 years old without a permit. Use of a metal detector is also forbidden. The onus is on the diver to prove his innocence under this legislation. Permits to dive on 100 year old wrecks may be obtained from National Monuments Branch, Office of Public Works, 51 St Stephen's Green, Dublin 2.

Heritage Orders

Some significant underwater sites may be made the subject of Heritage Orders. If a garda suspects that a such a site is being interfered with and that an offence has been committed under the National Monuments Acts he may seize without warrant, equipment capable of interfering with such a wreck or site (National Monuments amendment Act no.17 of 1994).

Marine Radio

Marine radio communications should be used by qualified operators. The minimum qualification is a Restricted Certificate of Competence (VHF only) licence. This is awarded following an exam run by Department of the Marine. The radio itself and the craft in which it is used should be licensed. Licences are available for a fee of £5 from Department of the Marine, Leeson Lane, Dublin 2.

Foreshore

The foreshore belongs to the State except in a few rare cases. Access to the foreshore however could be in private ownership. The Minister for the Marine may give leases to individuals to build structures. A licence may be given for a trivial matter. The 1992 amendment forbids removal of material from the foreshore except with a licence. The tenure of bathing places like the "Forty Foot", Sandycove, Co. Dublin would typically be under the Foreshore Acts (no. 12, 1933 and no. 17, 1992).

Weather and Tide Times

Weather forecasts

The Irish Meterological Service issue regular marine weather forecasts on RTE Radio 1 at the following times:-

06.02	12.47	19.02*	23.55

*Monday to Friday only

The coast radio stations also broadcast these forecasts on Channel 16 every three hours beginning at 0000 GMT. Gale warnings are broadcast when issued and every hour thereafter.

A forecast may also be obtained from the telephone Weather Dial service where recorder sea area forecasts and gale warnings are available for your area. The Dublin area forecast also gives the times of high water in Dublin Bay.

Weather Dial 1550 123 **+**

855	Sea Area
854	Dublin (also tide times)
850	Munster
851	Leinster
852	Connaught
853	Ulster

There is a charge of 58 pence per min. for this service.

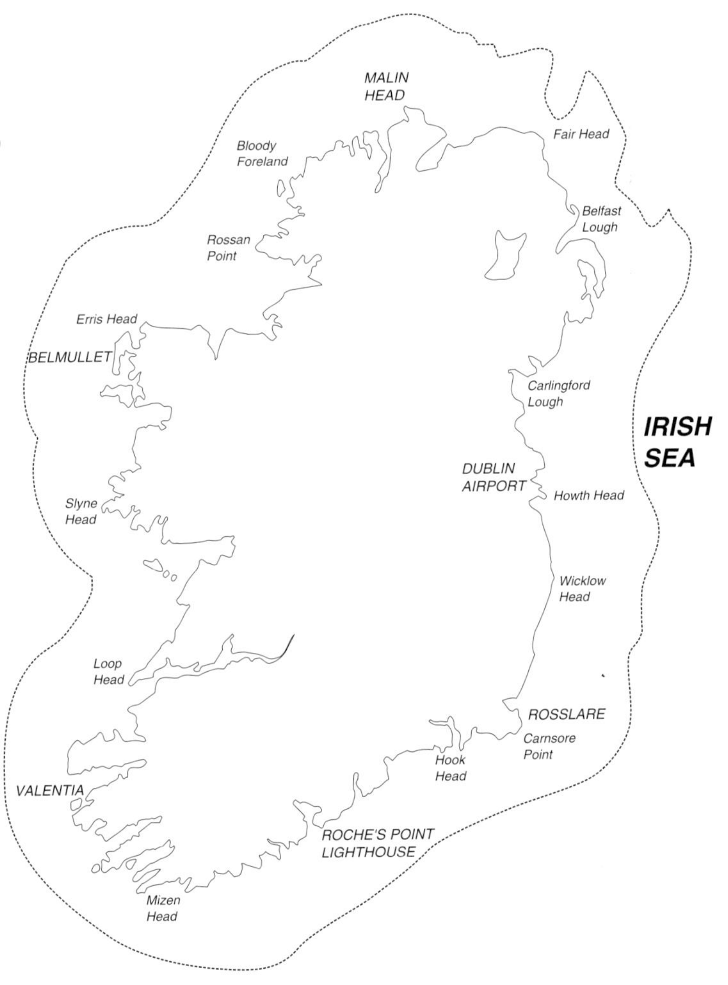

Tide Times

Particular care must be taken of the tidal current in each area. This can vary greatly from site to site. Headlands, islands, shallows etc. will all have an effect on the current flow. Which in some places can achieve speeds of 2–3m/sec.

There are many sources from which tidal time information may be obtained, for instance, Irish Nautical Almanac. But the most available source is the daily newspapers. The insert shows a typical tidal information from the Irish Times newspaper of the 9th July 1998.

Each site guide gives a Tidal Constant for the locality, which must be added to (or subtracted from) the tide time given for the Dublin Bay or Belfast Lough,. These are the easiest tide times to obtain. As well as the sources above, Weather Dial for Dublin (1550 123 854) also gives the tide time for Dublin Bay.

Tide times are given in GMT (Greenwich Mean Time) adjust, if necessary, for BST (British Summer Time) by adding one hour.

The times given are for high water usually the best time to dive when the flow is at its slackest and the water is at its maximum depth and therefore maximum visibility. Low water (also slack, but less depth and generally poorer visibility) is approximately six hours later.
Between these times the flow rate increases to a maximum about three hours after full tide. Decreasing thereafter to a minimum again at low tide.

WEATHER FORECAST

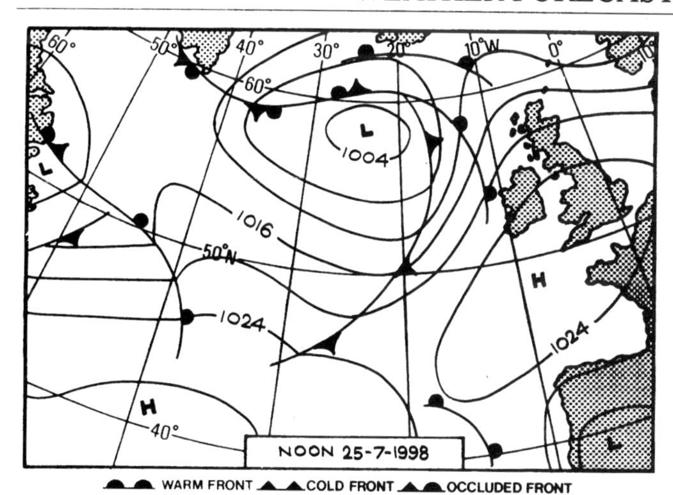

A ridge over Ireland is weakening as a warm front approaches from the Atlantic.

FORECAST for the period 6 am to midnight:

Connacht, west Ulster and west Munster: Mostly dry at first with some hazy sunshine. Increasing cloud will bring rain, drizzle and fog to many coastal areas by around noon. The rain, drizzle and fog will gradually extend inland to other parts later in the day with rain turning heavy in places. Very mild with top temperatures of 17 to 20 Celsius. Winds increasing fresh to strong southerly.

Leinster, east Munster and east Ulster: Dry for much of the day with sunny spells, but cloud increasing later. Rather warm with top temperatures of 18 to 22 Celsius. Outbreaks of rain extending eastwards this evening or tonight with some fog on hills and coasts. Winds becoming moderate to fresh southerly later.

TODAY'S TIDES

	Morning	Evening
Dublin	0123	1347
Arklow	1112	2325
Warrenpoint	0108	1332
Drogheda	0103	1327
Dundalk	0113	1337
Dun Laoghaire	0118	1342
Greystones	0113	1337
Howth	0113	1337
Skerries	0103	1327
Wexford	0812	2025
Wicklow	0042	1306
Cobh	0720	1944
Bantry	0650	1914
Cahirciveen	0605	1829
Castletownbere	0635	1859
Dingle	0630	1854
Dungarvan	0728	1952
Kinsale	0638	1902
Schull	0653	1917
Tralee	0643	1907

	Morning	Evening
Waterford Bridge	0816	2029
Youghal	0733	1957
Galway	0709	1933
Killybegs	0754	2018
Limerick Docks	0838	2051
Rathmullen	0816	2040
Sligo	0713	1937
Westport	0730	1954
Belfast	0044	1308
Annalong	0108	1332
Kilkeel	0054	1318
Larne	0049	1313
Derry	1015	2228
Ballycastle	0830	2043
Portrush	0835	2048
Moville	0925	2138

SUN

Rises	0530
Sets	2132
Lighting-up time	2202

Outlook

Windy with widespread rain, heavy in places. Fog on hills and coasts. A clearance to sunshine and showers following from the west tomorrow with winds moderating.

Sunburn index: High in sunshine.

Tourist Offices

Republic of Ireland

The Tourist Offices listed below operate throughout the year, except for those marked thus (*) which are open during the summer months. A full list is available from any Bord Fáilte – Irish Tourist Board Office

***Aran Islands** (Kironan)	099 61263
***Athlone**, Co. Westmeath	0902 94630
Baggot St. Bridge (Head Office)	01 602 4000
Bundoran, Co. Donegal	072 41350
Carlow, College Street, Co. Carlow	0503 31554
***Cliffs of Moher**, Liscannor	065 81171
Cork, Tourist House, Grand Parade	021 273251
***Dingle**, Co. Kerry	066 51188
Donegal Town, The Quay	073 21148
***Drogheda**, Co. Louth	041 37070
Dublin, Suffolk Street, Dublin 2	01 605 7799
	1550 112 233
***Dungarvan,** Co. Waterford	058 41741
Dunglow, Co. Donegal	075 21297
Ennis, Clare Road, Co Clare	065 28366
Galway, Victoria Place, Eyre Square	091 563081
Killarney, Town Hall, Co. Kerry	064 31 633
***Kinsale**, Co. Cork	021 772234
***Knock Airport**, Co. Mayo	094 67247
Letterkenny, Derry Road	074 211 60
Limerick City, Arthurs Quay	061 317522
***New Ross**, Co. Wexford	051 21857
***Rosslare Ferry Terminal**	053 33622
Shannon Airport	061 471664
Skibbereen, Town Hall, Co. Cork	028 21766
Sligo, Temple Street, Co. Sligo	071 61201
***Tramore**, Co. Waterford	051 381572
Tralee, Co. Kerry	066 21 288
Waterford, 41 The Quay	051 875788
Westport, The Mall, Co. Mayo	098 25711
Wexford, Crescent Quay	053 23111
Wicklow, Fitzwilliam Square	0404 69117

International Offices

Belfast, 53 Castle Street	01232 327888
Derry, 8 Bishop Street	01504 369501
London, 150 New Bond Street	0171 493 3201
London, 12 Regent Street	0171 839 8416
Paris, 33 Rue de Miromesnil	0153 43 1212
Madrid, Claudio Coello 73	91 577 1787
Milan, via S Maria Segreta 6	02 869 0541
Frankfurt, Untermainanlage 7	069 236492
Amsterdam, Spuistraat 106-108	020 622 3101
Brussels, Avenue de Beaulieu 25	02 673 9940
Stockholm, Sipyllegatan 49	08 662 8510
Copenhagan, Klostergarden, Amagertory 293	33 15 8045
New York, 345 Park Avenue	212 418 0800
Sydney, 36 Carrington Street	02 9299 6177
Tokyo, 2-10-7 Kojimachi, Chiyoda-ku	03 5275 1611

Northern Ireland Tourist Board

Head Office 59 North Street, Belfast. BT1 1NB	 Fax.	01 232 23 1221 01 232 24 0960
Dublin 16 Nassau Street, Dublin 2	 Fax.	01 679 1977 01 679 1863
London 11 Berkley Street, London W1X 5AD	 Fax.	0171 3555040 0171 409 0487
Glasgow 135 Buchanon Street, Glasgow CL 2JA	 Fax.	0141 204 4454 0141 204 4033
USA 551 Fifth Avenue, Suite 701, New York NY 10176	 Fax.	212 922 0101 212 922 0099
Canada 111 Avenue Road, Suite 450, Toronto M5R 3J8	 fax	416 925 6368 416 961 2175
France 3 Rue de Pontoise, 78100 St, Germain-en-Laye	 fax	139 21 93 80 139 21 93 90
Germany Taunusstrasse 52-60, 60329 Frankfurt/Main	 fax	069 23 4504 069 23 3480

Networked Tourist Information Centres

The Tourist Information Centre Network provides a first-class information service for visitors to Northern Ireland and for local residents. Services available at these offices include free information on the local area – tourist attractions, accommodations, where to eat, events; free in formation on holidays throughout Northern Ireland, accommodation booking for Ireland and the U K. when phoning from the RoI use the prefix 08 with the numbers below, When phoning from outside the UK use normal access codes.

Belfast, St. Anne's Court, 59 North Street – Head Office	01232 246609
Antrim, Pogues Entry, Church Street	01849 428331
Armagh,. Old Bank Building, 40 English Street	01861 521800
Ballycastle, Sheskburn House, 7 Mary Street	012657 62024
Bangor, 34 Quay Street	01247 270069
Belfast City Airport, Sydenham Bypass	01232 457745
Belfast International Airport	01849 422888
Carrickfergus, Heritage Plaza, Antrim Street	01960 366455
Coleraine, Railway Road	01265 44723
Downpatrick, 74 Market Street	01396 612233
Enniskillen, Wellington Road	01365 323110
Giant's Causeway, 44 Causeway Road, Bushmills	012657 31855
Kilkeel, 6 Newcastle Street	016937 62525
Killymaddy, Ballygawley Road, Dungannon	01868 767259
Larne, Narrow Gauge Road	01574 260088
Limavady, Council Offices, 7 Connell Street	015047 22226
Lisburn, Linen Centre & Lisburn Museum, Market Square	01846 660038
Londonderry, 8 Bishop Street	01504 267284
Newcastle, 10–14 Central Promenade	013967 22222
Newtownards, 31 Regent Street	01247 826846
Portrush, Dunluce Centre, Sandhill Drive	01265 823333

Irish Place Names Explained

The present anglicised forms of Irish place names are derived from the ancient Irish. When they were first written down, by cartographers in the eighteenth and nineteenth centuries, the original pronunciation was represented using English letters sounding as close to the original pronunciation as possible. Irish names tended to be descriptive, i.e. Drumroe; *Druim-ruadh*, Red ridge or Drumfad, *Druim-fada*, Long ridge. Listed below are some of the more common names used of which a place name may contain two or more Irish words.

Aw, ow	*Abh* [aw,ow]	a river
Agha	*Achadh* [Aha]	a field
Aille	*Aill* [ail]	a cliff
An		the definite article "the"
Annagh	*Eanach* [annagh]	a marsh
Are, aur, air	*Ar* [awr]	a place of slaughter
Ard	*Ard* [Ard]	a height
Ass, assan, assaun	*Eas* [ass]	a waterfall
Ath	*Atha* [Aha]	a ford of a river
Bad	*Bád* [baud]	a boat
Ballagh	*Bealach*	a road or pass
Bella, bell	*Bél* [bale]	the mouth, an entrance
Ball, balli, bally	*Baile*, [bally]	a town
Barna	*Bearna*	a gap
Behy,beha, beagh, veha	*Beith* [beh]	the birch tree
Ben	*Beann* [ben]	a peak, a pointed hill
Billa, billy, villa,villy	*Bile* [billa]	a ancient venerated tree
Boher, batter, booter	*Bothar*	a road
Bo	*Bo*	a cow
Boley, boole, booley	*Buaile*	a milking place for cattle
Bree, bray	*Bri* [bree]	a hill
Brookagh, brocky	*Brocach* [bruckagh]	a badger warren
Bun	*Bun*	the mouth of a river
Burren, burris:	*Boireann* [burren]	a rock, a rocky area
Cabragh		bad land
Caher	*Cathair*	a circular stone fort
Clan, clann	*Clann*	children, a tribe
Cloghan, cloghane	*Clochan*, [clohan]	stepping stones across a river
Car, carra, carha	*Cairthe* [carha]	a stone pillar
Cappa, cappagh	*Ceapach*	a plot of tilled land
Carhoo, carrow	*Ceathramhadh* [Carhoo]	a quarter of land
Carn		a monumental heap of stones
Carrick, carrig, craig	*Carrig*	a rock
Cavan	*Cabhan*	a hollow place
Clara, claragh, clare	*Clar*	a level place
Claggan, cleggen	*Claigeann*	the skull, a round hill
Clash	*Clais*	a trench or furrow
Clogh, clough	*Cloch*	a stone, sometimes a stone castle
Clon, cloon	*Cluain*	a meadow

Cor, corra, curra, cur	*Cora* [cora]	a weir
Cool, coole	*Cuil*	a corner or dead end
Cowly, howly, coltig	*Cobhlach* [cowlagh]	a fleet
Coom, coum,coombe	*Cúm* [coom]	a hollow, a dell, an enclosed valley
Coos, coose	*Cuas*	a cave
Cork	*Corcach*	a march
Cran	*Crann*	a tree
Croagh, crock	*Cruach*	a rick or stacked up hill
Curra, curragh	*Currach*	a march or sometimes a race course
Da, daw	*Da* [daw]	two (number)
Dandan	*Daingean* [dangan]	a fortress
Darragh, derry	*Doire* [derry]	an oak grove or wood
Derk, dirk, dark	*Dearc* [derk]	a cave
Desert, disert	*Disert*	a desert or hermitage
Donagh	*Domhnach* [downagh]	a church
Dooey, dooa, doo, doe	*Dumha* [dooa]	a burial mound
Doon, dun	*Dun*	a fortress
Drim, drom, drum	*Druim* [drum]	a ridge or long hill
Eden	*Euden* [adan]	the brow, a hill brow
Ellagh, elly	*Aileach* [ellagh]	a circular stone fort
Ennis	*Inis* [inish]	an island, a meadow along a river
Esker	*Eiscir* [esker]	a sand hill
Faddan, fadden	*Feadán* [faddaun]	a small brook
Faddock, feddock, viddoge	*Feadog* [faddoge]	a plover
Feenagh, fenagh	*Fiodhnach* [feenagh]	a woody place
Fer, fir	*Fear* [far]	a man
Foil, foyle	*Faill* [foyle]	a cliff
Freagh, freugh	*Fraech* [freagh]	heath, a heathy place
Gall, gal	*Gall* [gaul]	a foreigner, Englishman
Garriff, garve, garra	*Gaarbh* [garriv]	rough, rugged
Garran, garraun	*Garran* [garraun]	a shrubbery
Garry	*Garrdha* [gaura]	a garden
Gee, geeha,geeth	*Gaeth* [gwee]	the wind
Glasha, glash, glas	*Glaise* [glash]	a streamlet
Glen	*Gleann*	a glen
Goelan, golden	*Guala* [goola]	the shoulder, a hill
Gort	*Gort*	a tilled field
Goul, gole, gowle	*Gabhal* [goul]	a fork, a river fork
Gow, goe, go, gowan	*Gobha* [gow]	a smith
Gower, gour, gore	*Gabhar* [gour]	a goat
Graigue, grag, greg	*Graige*	a village
Illan, illane, illaun	*Oilean* [oilaun]	an island
Inch, inis	*Inis*	an island, a low meadow along a river
Inver	*Inbhear* [inver]	the mouth of a river
Keale, keel	*Caol*	narrow, a narrow place
Keagh, kee	*Caech* [kay]	blind, purblind, one-eyed
Kil, kill, kyle	*Cill*	a church

Kish, kesh	*Ceis* [Kesh]	a wickerwork causeway
Kin	*Ceann*	a head
Knock	*Cnoc*	a hill
Labba, labby	*Leaba* [labba]	a bed, a grave
Lack, leck, lick	*Leac* [lack]	a stone, flag stone
Lacka, leckan, leckaun	*Leac* [lack]	the side of a hill
Law, la	*Lágh* [law]	a hill
Leam, lem, lim	*Léim* [lame]	a leap
Letter, letteragh	*Leitir*	a wet hill side
Lis, liss	*Lios* [lis]	a circular earthen fort
Lough	*Lough*	a lake, an inlet of the sea
Maddy, maddra, vaddy	*Madradh [Maddra]*	a dog
Mace	*Mas* [mauce]	the thigh, a long low hill
Maghera	*Machaire*	a plain
Maul	*Meall*	a lump, a hillock
Maum	*Madhm* [maum]	a high mountain pass
Maw	*Magh* [maw]	a plain
Meelick	*Miliuc* [meeluck]	low marshy ground
Moan, mon	*Moin* [mone]	a bog
Mohill, mothel	*Maethail* [mwayhill]	soft or spongy land
Moy, muff	*Magh* [mah]	a plain
Moyle	*Mael* [mwail]	a bald or bear hill
Mullagh	*Mullach*	a summit
Mullen, mullin	*Muileann* [mullen]	a mill
Na		preposition, "of" or "of the"
Naas, nash	*Nás* [nauce]	an assembly place
Ned, nid, neth	*Nead* [ned]	a bird's nest
Oran	*Uaran* [uran]	a cold spring
Park	*Pairc*	a field
Poll, pull	*Poll*	a hole, pit or pool
Port	*Port*	the bank or landing place
Preban, prebaun, pribbaun	*Preaban*	a patch
Pubble, pobble, pobul	*Pobul* [pubble]	people
Quilly	*Coillidh* [cuilly]	woodland
Rath, raigh	*Rath*	a circular or ring fort
Rink, rinka, rinky	*Rince* [rinka]	dance
Rin, rine, rinn	*Rinn*	a point of land
Ross	*Ros*	in the south a wood, in the north a peninsula
Scalp	*Scealp* [scalp]	a cleft or chasm
Scarriff	*Scairbh* [scarriv]	a rugged shallow ford
Scart	*Scairt* [scart]	a thicket or cluster
See	*Suidhe*, [see]	a seat or sitting place
Seer, teer	*Saer* [sair]	a carpenter

Shan	*Sean* [shan]	old
Shee	*Sidh* [shee]	a fairy, a fairy hill
Skellig	*Sceilig* [skellig]	a rock
Skreen, skryne,skreena	*Serin* [skreen	a shrine
Slee	*Slighe* [slee]	a road
Slieve	*Slighe* [sleeve]	a mountain
Srough	*Sruth* [sruh]	a stream
Stook	*Stuaic* [stook]	a pointed pinnacle
Straid, Strade, Sraud	*Sraid* [sraud]	a street
Tagh, tin	*Teach* [Tagh]	a house
Tarriv, tarriff, tarf	*Tarbh* [tarriv]	a bull
Teev, teeve, tieve	*Taebh* [teeve]	a side, a hillside
Temple	*Teampull*	a church
Tober, tubbrid	*Tobar*	a well
Tonagh, Ton	*Tamhnach* [townagh]	a field
Toor, tore, tour	*Tuar*	a bleach green or drying place
tor	*tor*	a tower,a tower-like rock
Tra	*Tra*	a beach or strand
Tulla, tullagh, tullow	*Tulach*	a little hill
Uragh	*Iubhrach* [yuragh]	yew land
Urney, urny	*Urnaidhe* [urny]	an oratory
Wheelion, weelaun	*Facilean* [fweelaun]	a seagull

Adjective suffix

Many place names end with the following adjectives

-afad, ada, fhada, fadda		long
-allen	*Aliunn* [aulin]	beautiful
-amon	*na-mban* [na-maan]	of the women
-ard	*ard*	high
-beg	*bheag*	small, little
-bawn, bane	*bán* [bawn]	white
-boy	*buidhe*	yellow
-	*dubh*[duv]	black
-een	*in*	also small
-fin, finn	*fin*	white
-glass	*glas*	green
-gorm	*gorm*	blue
-keen	*caein*	beautiful
-kil	*coill* [kil]	of the wood, forest
-lee	*liath* [lee]	grey
-manach		of the monks
-maun		little
-meen	*min* [meen]	smooth
-mor, more	*mor*	great, large,
-muck, muc	*muic* [muck]	pig
-roe	*ruadh* [roo]	red
-turk	*torcs*	wild boar

Books of Interest

Flora and Fauna

Ireland's Marine Life – A World of Beauty
Matt and Susan Murphy.
Sherkin Island Marine Station Publications.

The Sea Shore, Collins Pocket Guide to
John Barrett & C.M. Young

Fresh and Saltwater Fish, Collins Gem Guide to
Keith Linsell & Michael Prichard

A Handguide to the Irish Coast
John Barrett & Denys Ovenden,
Treasure Press, London.

The Fish of Ireland
Ian Hill,
Appletree Press,
Belfast BT2 8DL.

Seabirds, an identification guide
Peter Harrison,
Croom Helm, London.

Where to Watch Birds in Ireland
Clive Huchinson,
A & C Black, London.

The Birds of Ireland, Pocket guide to
Gordon D'Arcy,
Appletree Press,
Belfast BT2 8DL.

Irish Wild Flowers, Pocket guide to
Ruth Isobel Ross,
Appletree Press,
Belfast BT2 8DL

Historical Interest

Death in the Irish Sea – the sinking of the RMS Leinster
Roy Stokes
Collins Press, Cork.

Donegal Shiprwecks
Ian Wilson
Impact, Coleraine

The Lusitania – Unravelling the Mysteries
Patrick O'Sullivan
Collins Press, Cork.

Ireland's Armada Legacy
Laurence Flanagan,
Gill and Macmillan, Dublin 8.

The Harsh Winds of Rathlin
Tommy Cecil

Shipwrecks of the Irish Coast, 1105-1993 (Parts I and II)
Edward J. Bourke,
Power Press, Rush, Co. Dublin.

Shipwrecks of Great Britain & Ireland
Richard Larn,
Newton Abbot, London.

The Brendan Voyage
Tim Severin,
Hutchinson, London.

The Skellig Story
Des Lavelle,
The O'Brien Press, Dublin 6.

Historic Hook Head, Co. Wexford.
Billy Colfer,
Slade Heritage Services, Co. Wexford.

General

Ireland Guide
Bord Failte (Irish Tourest Board)
Baggot St. Bridge, Dublin 2.

Sailing Around Ireland
Wallace Clark,
B.T. Batsford Ltd., London.

Irish Nautical Almanac '99
Vincent Macdowell,
Annamount Press,
Annamount House, Mulgrave St.,
Dun Laoghaire, Co. Dublin.

The Shell Guide To Ireland
Lord Killanin & M.V. Duignan,
Ebury Press, London.

The Shell Guide to Reading the Irish Landscape
Frank Mitchell,
Country House,
2 Cambridge Villas, Dublin 6.

Sherkin Island. A Walk in West Cork.
Anthony Beese,
Carraigex Press, Cork.

The Visitor's Guide to Northern Ireland
Rosemary Evans,
M P C Hunter Publishing Inc.,
Edison, NJ 08818, U.S.A.

Valentia, Portrait of an Island
Daphne D.C. Pochin Mould,
Blackwater Press, Dublin.

The Coast of West Cork
Peter Somerville Large,
Victor Gollancy Ltd., London.

West of West, West Cork
Brian Lalor,
Brandon Book Publishers Ltd.,
Cooleen, Dingle, Co. Kerry.

Saltees, Islands of Birds & Legends
Richard Roche & Oscar Merne,
The O'Brien Press, Dublin 2.

The Aran Reader
Breandan & Ruairi hEithir,
Lilliput Press Ltd., Dublin 7.

The Blasket Islands, next parish America
Joan & Ray Stagles,
The O'Brien Press, Dublin 2.

Accommodation

Accommodation Guide
Bord Failte (Irish Tourist Board)
Baggot St. Bridge, Dublin 2.

Ireland '99, Self catering guide
Bord Failte.
Baggot St. Bridge, Dublin 2.

Ireland '94-'95 on $45 per day
Susan Poole,
Prentice Hall Travel, London.

Map of Dive Site Locations

Divisions are Regions of the Irish Underwater Council

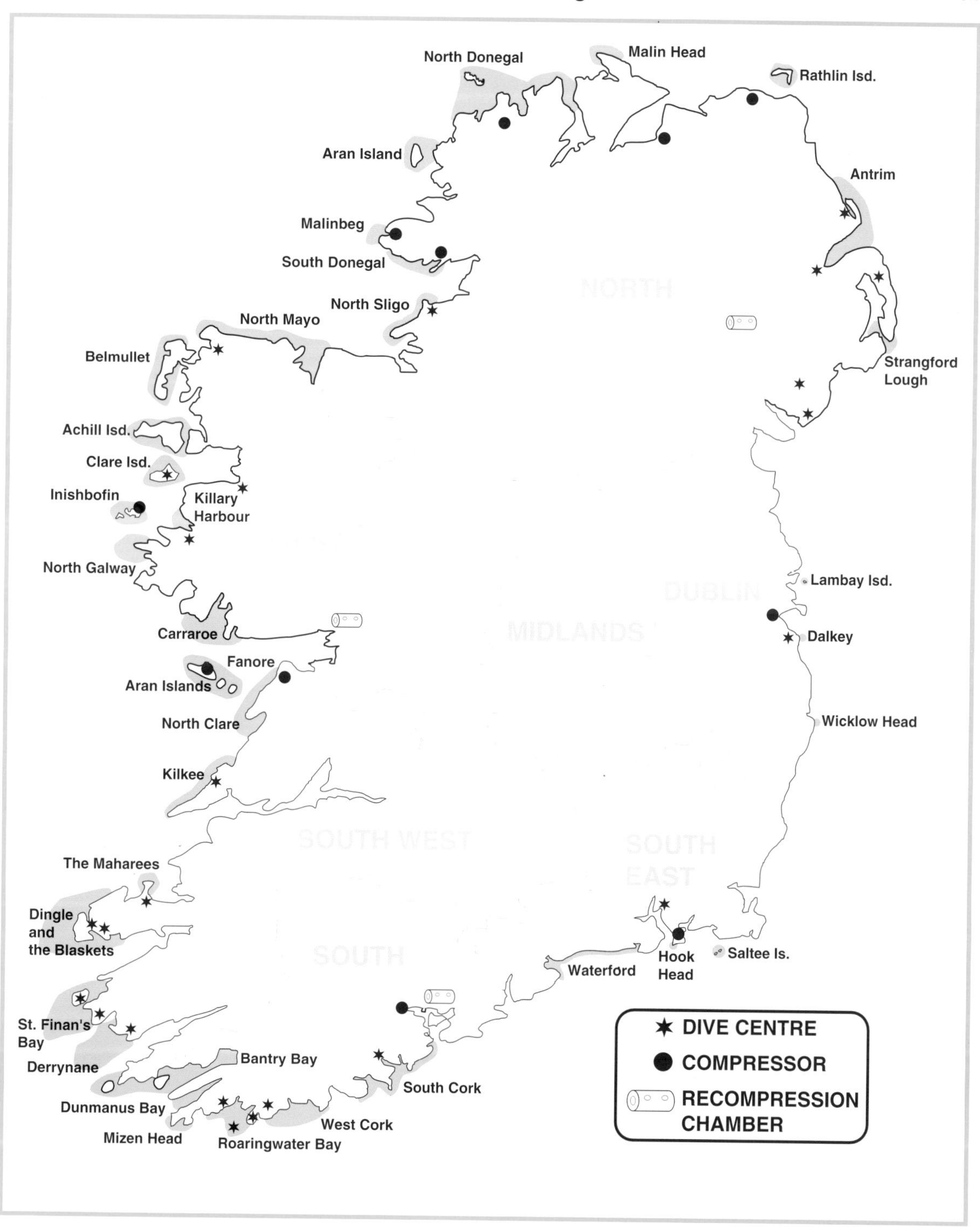

John Dory in Dublin Bay *Photo: Nigel Motyer*

Diver at the Muglins *Photo: Nigel Motyer*

Hook Head *Photo: Nigel Motyer*

Diver with camera at Hook Head *Photo: Nigel Motyer*

Leaping at Hook Head *Photo: Nigel Motyer*

U-260 West Cork *Photo: John Collins*

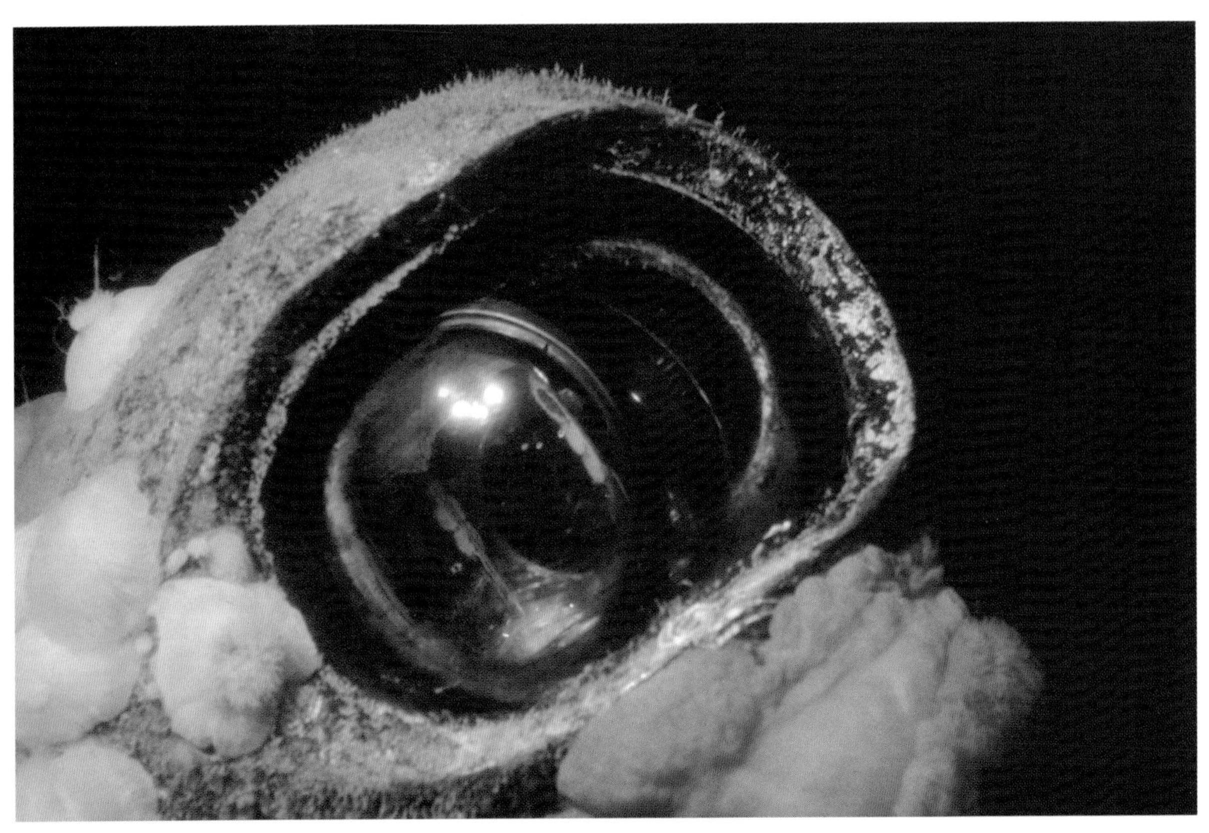

Periscope lens of U-260 – West Cork *Photo: John Collins*

Common seal ***Photo: Nigel Motyer***

Crawfish – Scarriff Island *Photo: Nigel Motyer*

Squat Lobster – Dublin Bay *Photo: Nigel Motyer*

Dalkey Island and The Muglins

At the southern end of Dublin Bay lie two islands about 1km from the shore. These islands are probably two of the most dived-on places in Ireland. The largest is Dalkey Island and the smaller, not much bigger than a large rock, is The Muglins. When the conditions are good diving here can rival many of the best sites in the West of Ireland. Normal visibility is about 2–3m, but in summer this can increase up to 6–10m.

There is a wealth of sea life supported by the nutrient rich waters. Anemones, starfish, sponges, mussels and seaweeds adorn the rocks while pollack, wrasse, conger, ling etc. swim in the immediate vicinity. Crabs, lobsters and octopus hide in the rocky crevices.

Diving these islands is not as easy as it appears. Even on a calm day there is considerable turbulence from the strong currents that flow around them, but provided one knows these currents the islands are a pleasure to dive. A SMB, a compass and a torch are almost mandatory items of equipment for safe diving. Needless to say, it is an area for experienced divers only. The best diving areas are affected by easterly winds.

Dalkey Island is separated from the mainland by Dalkey Sound which is about 500m wide and 12m deep. As there is nearly always a strong tidal current flowing it is a good site for a drift dive provided adequate precautions are taken and there is not too much boat traffic around. However, there is at least one shore dive site.

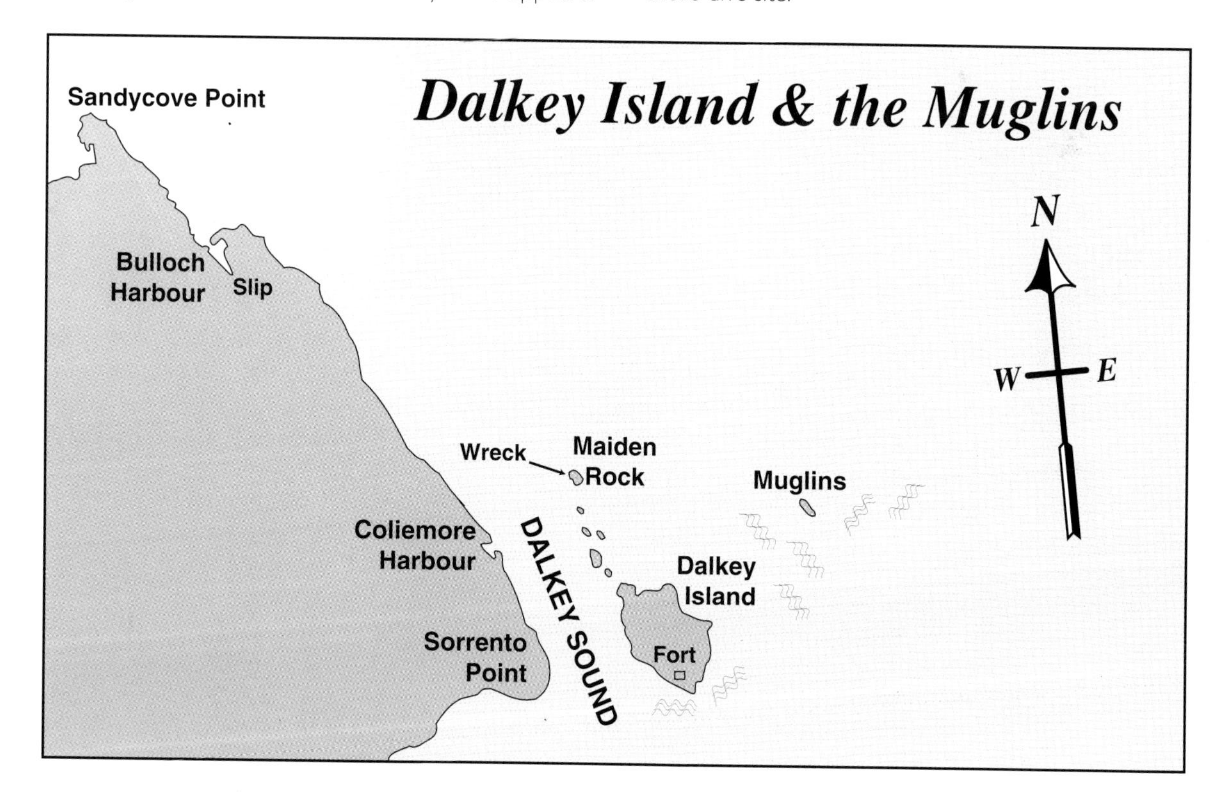

Dive Sites

1. Dalkey Sound

The sound may be accessed through the People's Park south of Dalkey village. Pass through the village, veer left past the Loreto Convent and about 200m after Collimore Harbour, up the hill there is a park on the left. Park on the road. Descend 60m towards the sea passing the statue of a goat, at the corner of the small field there is a small path through some bushes leading to the steps beside a large rock.

The bottom is at 10–12m on sand at the edge of the boulder shoreline. Visibility is usually 5–7m as the area is kept clear by strong currents. Keep close to the shore as the sound can sweep a diver along at 4 knots. Access is easy at high tide but the steps dry out at 2 hours below low tide. A southeasterly swell can make landing difficult.

This is a good spot for a quick shore dive on a summer evening, the fish life rarely disappoints and lobster, crab (don't touch) and wrasse are common with dogfish and even squid appearing occasionally. This is also a favourite sea angling site so beware of lines tangled on the bottom. The park provides a suitable amusement area for any non-diving companions.

2. Dalkey Island

Apart from the south eastern end of the island the diving is shallow, 8–10m, with rocks covered with thick kelp on a sandy bottom. This makes for interesting pottering about type diving, if you are into that sort of thing or an excellent place for a novice diver.

The southeastern end, under the old fort, starts in a similar manner but slopes away to 30m. The bottom consists of large boulders, rock ledges and patches of mud and sand. Below 20m it becomes very dark and a good torch is an absolute necessity. At 30m it is dark!. The sea life is not as good here as on the Muglins but it may be dived in strong N/NW winds and it is also suitable for the less experienced.

The strong currents of the area do not adversely affect diving provided one keeps away from Dalkey Sound where current speeds of up to 4 knots can occur at mid tide. The best dive plan is to submerge near, or to the east of the fort, swim out southeasterly underwater to your required depth and return on a reciprocal bearing to your starting point.

Do not continue into the current should you stumble across it. On ebb tides a strong rip current sweeps out of Dalkey Sound around the fort point. On the flood tide there is a strong to the East of the island.

Dalkey Island, which has a long history dating back to the Stone Age, gets its name from the Irish *Delginis* meaning Thorn Island. It was fortified by the Danes and later by the English in Napoleonic times. There is also a small medieval oratory. The island is unusual in having a herd of wild goats. A landing stage opposite Collimore Harbour facilitates exploration.

3. The Muglins

The island is oval in shape and about 100m long, and 17m at its widest, high at the northern end tapering off southwards. The rock is granite and has a cigar shaped, red and white navigation beacon on top. There is a small quay on the western side facing Dalkey Island.

The Muglins is populated by seagulls, shags, cormorants and other sea birds above water with a great variety of fish and seals in the water. They are well used to human activity and the seals may even give your fins a playful nip.

The backbone of the island runs in a southwest direction, the flood tide sweeps out of Killiney Bay and around the Muglins to the northeast, on the ebb tide the current flows north to south resulting in slack areas around the rock no matter how strong the tide is flowing. On the flood tide the east and north sides are diveable and on the ebb tide the southwestern side is diveable.

There is a tidal rip visible at each end of the island, on the flood the south end and on the ebb the north end, which should be avoided. It is inside these rip tides that diving is possible if you are unable to dive at slack water.

The best diving is on the eastern side, sea side, of the rock. The slope of the rock visible above the water continues underwater to about 30m. Tumbling down in a series of cliffs, ledges and boulders. The slope is steepest at the northern end but at the

southern there is evidence of at least one wreck.
At depth it is possible to "see" where slack water ends and the current starts by observing the tumbling shells and weed a metre off while remaining in calm water. Do not enter the current unless it is part of your dive plan!

The western side of the island is shallower and less precipitous. If the tide is flowing it is only possible to dive between the landing stage and the southern point. The bottom slopes more gently out towards the sound in series of ledges, boulders and sand. Again beware of swimming out into the current, unless planned.
The nearest place where one can launch a boat is from the slip in Bulloch Harbour, about 4km from the Muglins. Unfortunately this slip is tidal, and is only useable within 3 hours of high water. Dun Laoghaire Harbour, about 6km from the Muglins, has a public slip in the inner harbour but this too is tidal.

Boats may be hired in Bullock Harbour. These boats are mostly used by fishermen and are wooden clinker built or fibreglass hulled with low powered engines.

Dublin Bay Wrecks

4. RMS Leinster (GPS 053.18.88N 005.47.51W)
The RMS Leinster, a mail and passenger boat was sunk in October 1918, one month before Armistice. Over 600 people were lost after being torpedoed by the German sub UB-123. Regularly visited by divers, the hull is intact her but its condition is poor and badly silted. As currents are in the area are strong she is best dived at slack water. As she lies in the path of the Dun Laoghaire-Hollyhead car ferry good visibility is essential.

5. HMS Guide Me (GPS 50.16.58N 06.02.94W)
The Guide Me is a small armed steam trawler of WW1 vintage second sunk some years previously. She is lying a several hundred metres southeast of the Muglins in about 35m, As visibility is usually poor good lighting is essential. Unfortunately the gun was removed a few years ago.

Expeditions are arranged periodically by Oceantec Adventures Ltd., a PADI dive school.

Local Facilities and Information

Compressor:	Oceantec Adventures Ltd., Marine Terrace, Dun Laoghaire Tel. 01 2801083	 Fax. 01 2843885
Small Hardboat Hire:	Bulloch Harbour Monica or Dolores Chris	 Tel. 01 2806517 Tel. 01 2800915
Tidal Constant:	Dublin -00 45	
Local VHF station:	Dublin Radio Ch. 16, 87	
Chart:	1415, 1468	
Maps:	½":1 mile No. 16	1:50,000 No. 50

Wicklow Head
Co. Wicklow

Wicklow Head is located 2.5km south of Wicklow Harbour. It can be easily identified by its three light-houses, two of which are disused. The headland itself is home for many species of birds including gulls, gannets and puffins and also boasts a large seal colony. The head is approximately 400m and is 80m at its highest point. For its entire length the head presents a sheer cliff face to the sea, making a boat dive the only possibility.

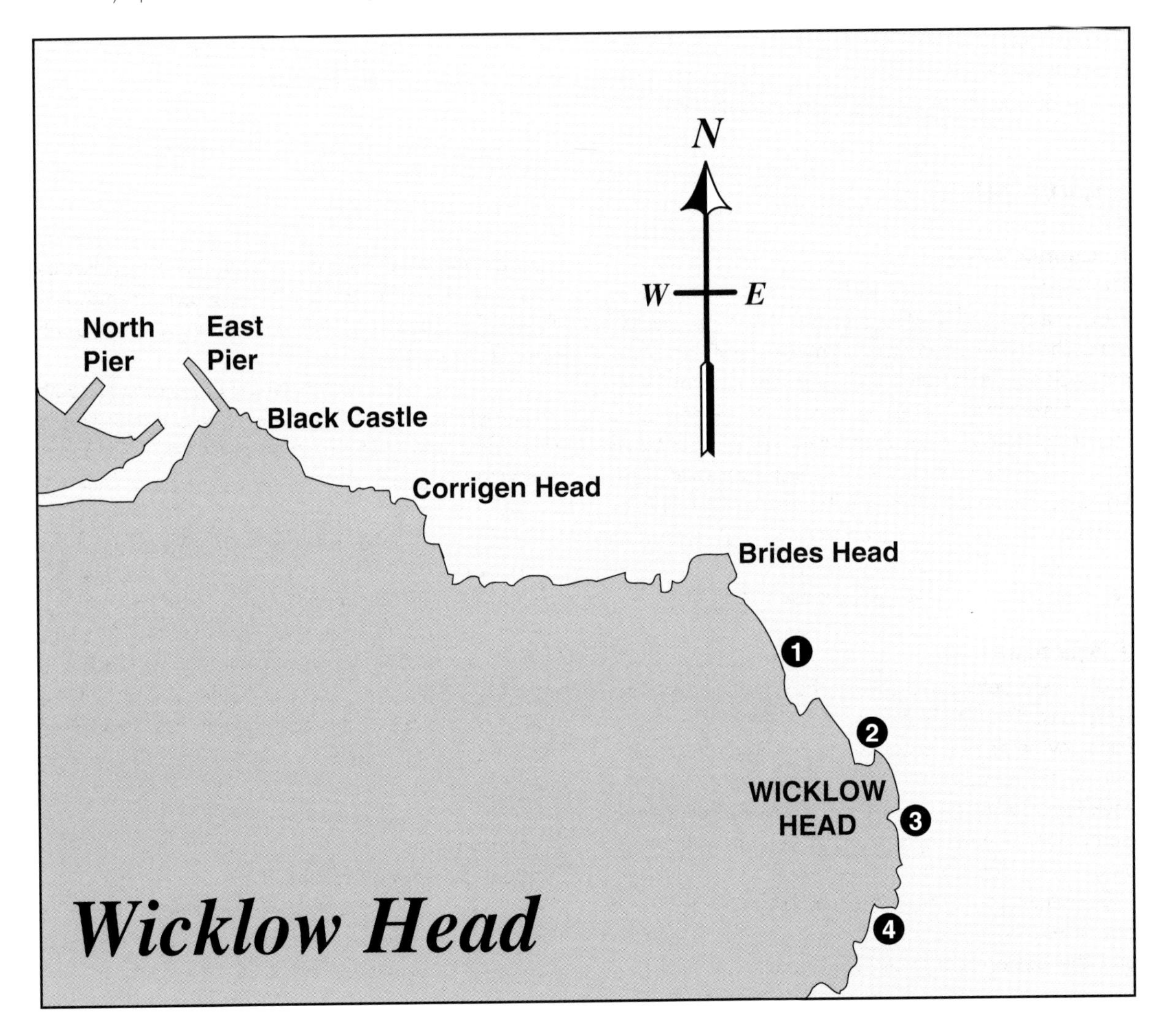

Boats may be launched in Wicklow Harbour where there are two slips, on the north and on the east side of the Hharbour. The north side is probably the most useful because a launch can be made at any stage of the tide. On the East side (near the Lifeboat Station) the slip is difficult to use at low tide and can be very congested on Sundays. Do not leave trailers or cars close to the slip.

On leaving the harbour keep well clear of the "Black Castle", because of the rocks close to the surface, and steer for Brides Head, which is the first headland which will be seen. Keep at least 50m off Brides Head while rounding it. Wicklow Head is the next point, with its distinctive lighthouses. Also keep a good watch for marker buoys on fishing nets and lobster pots. There is a 5 knot speed limit within the harbour.

When diving Wicklow Head the most important factor to be considered is the tide. Locally it can reach speeds of 6 knots, on spring flood and ebb tides. This combined with wind can generate quite rough sea conditions. The cardinal rule when diving in this area is: "always dive in the lee of the tide". If the tide is running south, dive on the south side, etc.. The coxswain must be vigilant at all times because of the danger of someone getting swept away. SMBs should be used.

Because the head is so large it provides good shelter in southerly winds. The head is also very exposed to wind from the northeast and because of its proximity to Brittas Bay the visibility can be poor for a time after windy conditions. These points are worth noting when planning a dive in the area. If in doubt, before putting the boats into the water drive along the coast road to the lighthouse and check local conditions.

These locations are, arguably, the best dive sites on the head. But diving can take place at any point along the headland, if the tide and weather conditions are suitable.

Dive Sites

1. Captain's Planet

This area is not actually part of the head but does warrant a mention. A dive is possible here on any tidal state. The maximum depth is 12m. Descending close to the rock face it is quite shallow, with a lot of gullies which make for an interesting dive. There are normally a number of seals around which keep a cautious distance. The rock formations give way, at 10m, to a flat sandy bottom. Numerous fish are to be found including wrasse, dogfish, pollack and flatfish, with the usual assortment of crabs, lobsters and other shellfish. Diving here is interesting and very safe, ideal for the novice.

2. The Pond

A dive here before mid-day can be as spectacular as a west coast dive. The high cliffs around the site are home for many nesting birds, which makes an interesting day out for the non-divers. A cave which runs through the rock for 15m normally has a few seals in residence. Remember if entering a cave, never block the exit, always swim close to the wall, and in single file.

Enter the water close to the "Landing Steps" and head out to sea along the reef. The kelp bed ends at 10m and the bottom continues to 15m. Alternatively, go through the cave and return back into the pond by rounding the point. There is an abundance of fish and fauna. The Pond is noted for the number of shellfish which can be seen.

Never dive at this spot when the tide is running south because the cave acts like a funnel with everything being sucked in and spat out the other side with quite spectacular results. When dived in the right condition it is highly recommended.

3. Gull Rock

Known as the Gull Rock because of the number of nesting seagulls, it's maximum depth is 10m. It opens into a sheltered bay area with a flat sandy bottom, a good area for a first dive. The further out to sea the greater the effect of the tidal current. Normally there are a lot of dogfish and sand dabs. This is also a good area for snorkel diving.

4. Carraigwee

Named Carraigwee because of the lichens which give the rocks a yellow colour, this is the deepest point at the head, with 20m at high tide. Descend at the rock face and proceed along the bottom keeping the reef on your left-hand side. Underwater, the reef heads almost due south, the further out the greater the tidal effect.

This is a very good dive with the reef being home for many creatures including large conger eels. It is again important to note diving in Carraigwee should only be undertaken when the tide is running south.

One possibility which is not discussed above is a drift dive around the head. This should only be attempted 2 hours either side of slack water and when weather conditions are ideal. It is also not suitable for novice divers. SMBs will be invaluable help to the coxswain. The drift dive can be an exhilarating experience and requires little effort. The bottom rises and falls as you're being swept along with each glance revealing something new. The bottom has been swept clean of weed but does have an array of shellfish including mussels, whelk and winkles.

Local Facilities and Information

Compressor:	Oceantec Adventures Ltd. Marine Tce., Dun Laoghaire. Tel 01 2801083 Fax 01 2843885
Tidal Constant:	Dublin -00 40
Local VHF station:	Wicklow Head Ch. 87
Chart:	1468
Maps:	½":1 mile No.16 1:50,000 No. 56

Short spined sea scorpion ***Photo: Nigel Motyer***

Hook Head
Co. Wexford

Hook Head peninsula is situated on the southeast coast of Ireland and is accessed from the Wexford/Duncannon Road. Follow the L159 A road to Fethard-on-Sea and turn right in the village for Hook Head. This road ends at a T-junction, turn left for Slade Harbour or turn right for Churchtown and the Hook Lighthouse.

Boats may be launched from the slipway in the harbour, but this dries out two hours before low water. All the dives mentioned below, and more may be reached by boat. The coastline between the Black Chan (see below) and the lighthouse, which may only be accessed by boat, is interesting, colourful and about 20m max.

There are three main diving areas on the "Hook", the coast to the south of the harbour, Doornoge Point near Churchtown and under the lighthouse. The visibility on the Churchtown/ Hook side of the peninsula can sometimes be affected by silt from the confluence of three rivers in Waterford Harbour.

All the dives may be accessed, weather permitting, from the shore. Care must be taken in selecting exit points to allow for any change in the tide.

Slade Harbour

The shoreline may be reached through an arch in the harbour wall, taking care to walk on the headlands, there are at least three shore dives. All of which offer interesting, safe and shallow dives ideal for the inexperienced or early season divers.

The sea bottom consists of kelp, rocky gullies and sand with a plentiful sea life. These gullies continue as ridges, about 2–3m high, for several hundred metres out to sea. It is possible to fin out in under one ridge and return in a different one almost without the use of a compass. Near the shore the tidal current is always fairly slack.

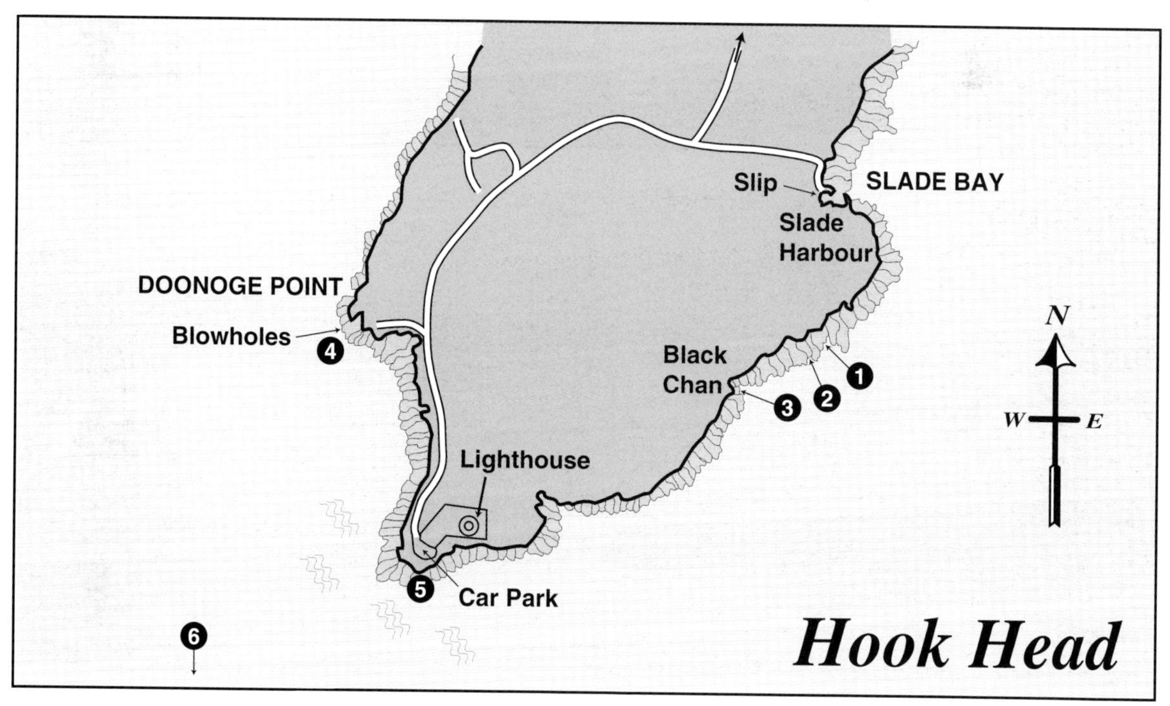

Dive Sites

1. Solomon's hole

About 250m from the harbour there is a natural rock arch, under which there is a flat ledge. This ledge is one side of a gully which runs east for about 20m from the shore to a max. depth of 12m before opening out onto sand and rock. The ledge is covered by about 1m at high tide.

2. Carragahoy

Continuing a further 150m along the coastline there is a promontory one side of which is straight and stepped. These steps make dive entry and exit easy in all tidal stages.

3. Black Chan

South 200m from Carraigahoy there is a natural slope in the cliff face. A steel hulled trawler was wrecked here in the late 1960s, the remains of which may still be seen. The slope facilitates entries and exits and shows the general layout of the underwater ridges.

4. Doonoge Point

Having turned right at the T-junction continue through Churchtown to a point where the sea nearly bisects the road. Park wherever possible. The dive site, to the right of the inlet, is accessed through a gate and a rough track across the fields.

The area has several gullies some of which terminate in caves/ blow holes. These make a interesting night dive. The gullies, in one of which there are the remains of a wreck of a German lugger, the "Slazine", continue for about 50m before opening out. The bottom again consists of kelp, rock and some sand patches near the shore but further out the bottom is affected by river silt. To the left of the inlet, about 100m out, there is another trawler wreck. Tides in this area are stronger than in the Slade area.

5. Hook Head

Continue along the road until reaching the car park. There are several entry/exit points in the area below the car park. In 1850 the "Royal Arthur" was wrecked here with a cargo of walrus tusks, none have been found recently but you might be lucky. The sea floor is similar to the previously mentioned dive sites with the added attraction of "tame" seals.

Warning!, there is a tidal race off the point so it is advisable to dive this area only at slack water.

6. Three Mile Rock and Western Rock

These are two boat dives which can be accessed from the Hook area. Their positions and details may be found in the chapter on Dunmore East.

Local Facilities and Information

Compressor:	Hotel Naomh Seosaimh, Fethard on Sea Tel. 051 397129 WEXFORD DIVING CENTRE, Riverstown, Murrintown, Co. Wexford Tel./Fax. 053 39373	
Tidal constant:	Dublin +06 10	
Local VHF Station:	Rosslare Radio Ch. 16, 23	
Chart:	2046, 2049	
Maps:	½":1 mile No. 23	1:50,000 No. 76

The Saltee Islands
Co. Wexford

The Saltee Islands lie 5km out to sea from Kilmore Quay, which is approximately 25km from Wexford town. When approaching Wexford, follow the ring road system toward the Rosslare ferry port (N25) and turn right at the signpost for Kilmore. The two islands are notable for their abundant bird life that can exceed 150,000 with over 200 different species. Both the islands and offshore rocks are home to the Atlantic grey seal and while not common, basking sharks and dolphins can be sometimes seen. If you're lucky you may come across minke whales.

The history of the islands is very interesting as the caves once acted as a hiding place not only for pirates and their plunder, but for escaping leaders of the 1798 rebellion. In later years the islands were owned by a self declared "Prince" Michael Neale, who contemplated building a casino on it and bringing in gamblers by plane.

Due to the Saltees being a wildlife sanctuary it's important to keep noise to a minimum. When motoring around and between the islands be careful of hidden rocks and shallows. Keep to deep water. Tides around the area can be very strong, especially during spring tides and as such special precautions should be taken to ensure being spotted on the surface. Slack water is often unpredictable and short, but is generally around two and a half hours before high water. All sites can be reached in less than 20 min. in a good boat.

The exposed coastline gives no shelter from strong winds, the exception being northerly winds. It would be advisable to ring the Diving Officer of the Wexford Club (number available from CFT head office) to see if the trip is worthwhile. Kilmore Quay is a busy fishing port and holiday area with good all-weather launching slips, toilet facilities and parking. Boats may be chartered but the islands may be dived by an independent, well equipped and organised group. Two boats with radios are the bare minimum.

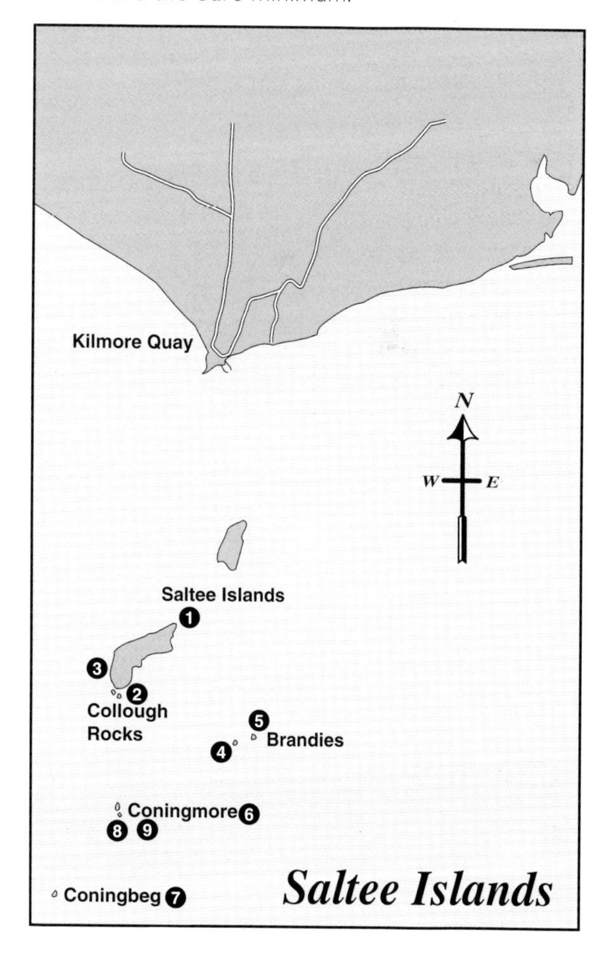

Dive Sites

1. Makestone Rock

This dive site lies on the east end of the Great Saltee. It is a submerged rock which comes within a few metres of the surface. The general depth around it is 10–15m, it can be prone to a silt current. On each side of the rock there is a flat sandy bottom. The area is suitable for trainees and makes a pleasant second dive.

2. SS Lennox (GPS 52.06.789 N 6.36.757 W)

At the back of the large island is the wreck of the SS Lennox. While trying to avoid the unwanted attentions of a German U-boat in 1917, she hit one of the rocks behind the island and sank. Her Chinese crew made the short swim to the island and onward to Kilmore. You too should pay attention when motoring around here as there is a sunken rock (which can be dived when it shows) to the right of the bay as you approach from seaward. The GPS co-ordinates are an idea of the location of the wreck but you should confirm it by searching for the large sonar readings of the bow or boilers on your sounder. The wreck lies parallel to the Collough Rocks with its bow pointing out to sea.

Two large boilers are on the bottom and come to within 5m of the surface. To head toward the island from here (north) brings you to the stern of the ship and a projecting davit arm is on your left. The best plan is to swim directly out to sea where the bow lies upright on the bottom. Keep an eye out for the anchor on your left and its winch. This site can be dived at any time and is affected by only the slightest of currents. If visibility is good you may get the chance to see razorbills dive underwater and swim around you.

3. West End

This area is prone to strong currents but is worth a drift dive for the more qualified diver with good boat cover. The general depth is around 15–20m. It has a rocky sandy bottom and a wide variety of fish life.

4. West Brandy (GPS 52.05.847N 06.35.034W)

This is a spectacular dive site. The rocks are covered with anemones. The seaward side has a very dramatic drop off to a depth of 35m. It is advisable to seek local knowledge on slack tide times due to strong currents in this area.

5. East Brandy

Lying to the east of West Brandy this is another good dive site, but again prone to strong currents. The rock shape is not as sharp as the West's but it does go down to 33m. The wreck of the "Verfradio" lies at it's centre at a comfortable 20m.

6. Coningmore Rock (GPS 52.08.152 N 06.37.465 W)

The Coningmore rock is easily seen at all times, as it stands up large from the water. It is situated due south from the larger island. It is possible to get shelter here from a strong running tide. When diving, keep in the shelter of the rock so as not to be carried away during your safety stop. As scenic dives go it is brilliant, but the thing that makes this dive is the large colony of grey seals that will immediately enter the water when a dive boat appears. On the dive they will circle you, come up to your mask looking at you with their huge black eyes and chew at your fins. The majority of the time the seals are very placid, but during the mating season the big males can become more aggressive. Do not panic and avoid being isolated in mid water where the seals can become a real nuisance. Keep close to the rock. As wonderful as these creature are, they are wild, so if you like your fingers intact don't pet them. It is unusual for the seals to follow you below depths of 15m. The shallow safety stop can often go on longer as you watch these wonderful creatures swimming around you with incredible speed and agility. This is the one dive guaranteed to make everyone surface with a smile. Maximum depth here is around 25m.

7. Coningbeg Rock (GPS 52.04.16N 6.38.517W)

Further to the west of the Coningmore lies the washed rock of the Coningbeg. Underwater you may come across metal pylons which were the main supports for an aborted lighthouse. From your entry point on the surface you can dive quickly down the rock wall to 45m. The Coningbeg is a site that even hardened wreck divers rave about, as it has profuse fish life and fantastic colours. Again, beware your approach, like its larger namesake the Coningbeg is prone to strong currents.

8. The Invercauld (1917)

The Invercauld was a large iron barque which was attacked and sunk by the German U-boat U84 off Mine Head. It apparently drifted and sank just south of the Coningmore Rocks. The wreck is sitting upright and is discernable throughout its length, its ornate bow is worth inspection. The wreck lies in 45m and as the vessel was quite large it is difficult to see the whole ship on one dive. As with all diving in this area it must be dived in slack tide otherwise the currents are treacherous.

9. The Idaho (1878)

An other shipwreck worth a mention is that of the 3500 ton sailing steamer Idaho. Wrecked during a fog on the Coningmore Rocks in 1878, thankfully without loss of human life. The Idaho's remains are extensive but far less intact than the Invercauld. Although collapsed and silted there are many wreck-holes to explore with the bright surrounding sand contributing to the visibility. The bell and an excellent model of the Idaho may be seen in Kehoe's Pub and Parlour bar, Kilmore Quay.

10. U-Boat 104 (GPS 51.59N, 06.26W)

U-104 was damaged on 23 April 1918 by the USS Cushing and sunk two days later when HMS Jessamine found her surfaced. Captain Bernis dived but was blown to the surface by three depth charges. Ten men tried to escape but only one was picked up. He was the sole survivor of a crew of 41. The U104 was launched on 3-7-1917 and the deck gun at the Wooden House, Kilmore Quay.

Local Facilities and Information

Compressor:	Wexford Diving Centre, Riverstown, Murrintown, Co.Wexford Tel. 053 39373	
Tidal Constant:	Dublin +06 11	
Local VHF station:	Rosslare Radio Ch.16, 67, 23	
Chart:	2740, 1410	
Maps:	½":1 mile No.23	1:50,000 No.77.

Waterford

Dunmore East

In Waterford at the traffic lights at Reginalds Tower on the Quay, take the R684 to Dunmore East (about 16km). It is a small seaside town with plenty of holiday accommodation much frequented by the national and international sailing community. There are three small beaches and plenty of small rock coves where families can swim. Most can be seen from the lighthouse on the pier; chose your site and ask directions how to get there.

There is an easily accessible public slipway in the harbour behind the sailing club building. This slip, which is accessible at all stages of the tide, is very busy, please do not obstruct it. There is ample parking in and around the harbour area beside of the Sailing Club building.

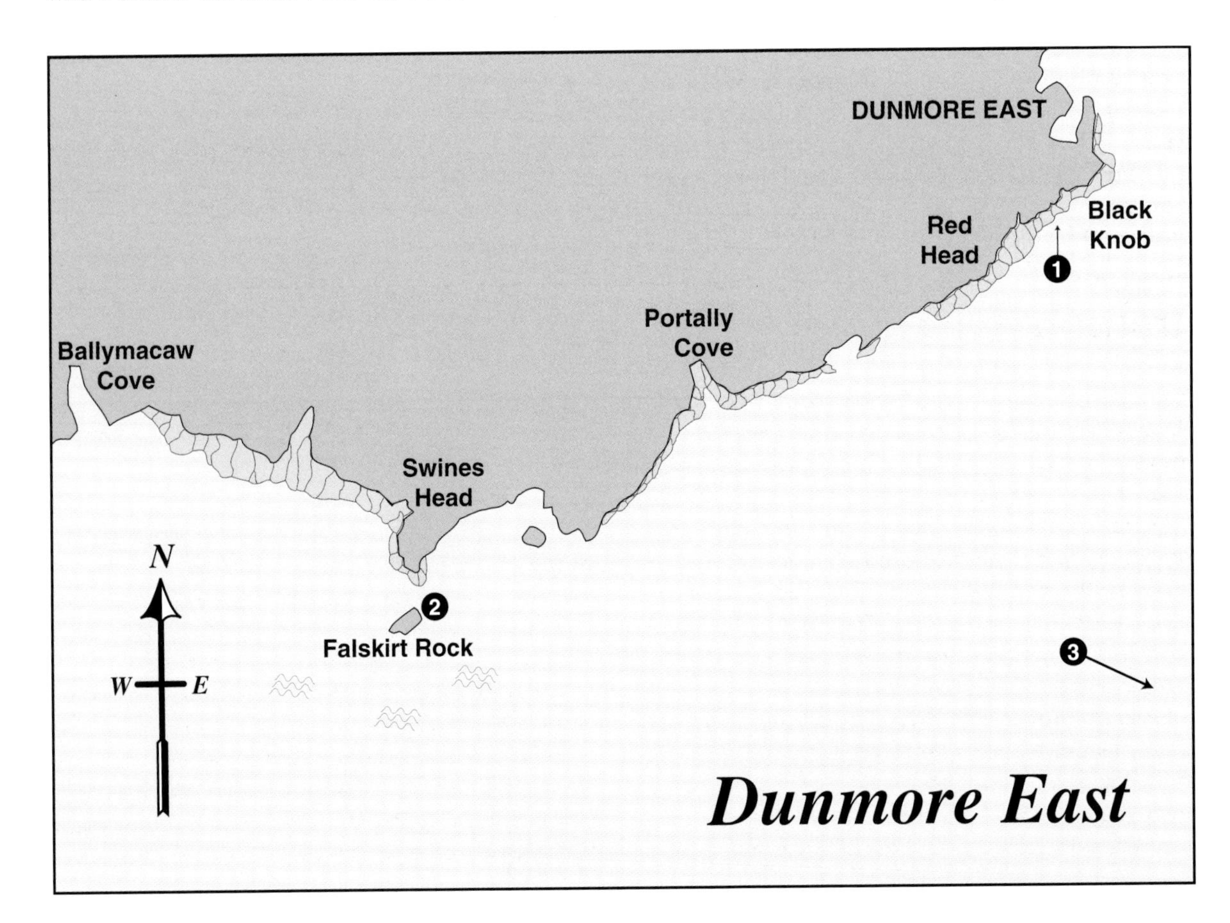

Dunmore East Dive Sites

1. The Flat Rocks

Between black knob and red head going through the village on the way to the harbour you will see a large building (once a Convent now a restaurant) immediately in front of you just before you descend into the harbour. Take the right turn here. Just at the back of the restaurant there is a dirt track on your left, follow this down to a flat area of limited parking, the flat rocks are now below you. This dive is not to be attempted in rough weather as there is a wash up and down the rocks, but on a good day it is a lovely dive (depth 10–12m) with plenty of sea life, big rocks, sea weed – a nice dive for beginners.

2. Falskirt Rock (off Swines head)

A boat dive, exit the harbour, around the lighthouse and head west along the coast for about Ikm you will see the water breaking on the top of the rock on a full tide and the rock on a low tide. This is an excellent dive, depth 10m to possibly 20m, on the seaward side of the rock. Long gullies run parallel to the coastline and there is abundant sea life, a very enjoyable dive.

During the half tides there is a bit of a current running west (1–1.5 knots) up as far as Brownstown Head, particularly from mid water to the surface. Go down one gully, cross over the top and back the next gully to the rock to do your decom. stops, for beginners and experienced.

3. Three Mile Rock

(Location SE of Hook Head GPS: 52.54.65N 6.51.47W) This is definitely a boat dive. It is about 20 min. out of Dunmore in a RIB. Some of the local clubs have marker buoys on the rock. Contact a local club if you want to dive this site, if the marker is not there you need sonar to locate the rock as there is no surface evidence of it. Depth 20–35m – an excellent dive, plenty of sea life and not much weed. It is a large plateau of rock approx. 15m off the bottom, you have a very enjoyable dive at 20m all around the top of the rock. Experienced divers only.

4. Western Rock

(Location SE of Hook Head GPS: 52.49.38N 6.51.14W) Definitely a boat dive. Again another plateau of rock west of Three Mile Rock and to the seaward. It is about 30 min. out of Dunmore East with the same boat as above. With depths in the range 20–45m, an excellent dive with the same type of rock as at Three Mile Rock. Sonar will be required to find it as this rock is not normally marked. With both of these dives you can get a westward run on the surface during half tides. In these areas the sea is nearly always a little "lumpy". Experienced divers only.

Tramore Dive Sites

In Waterford take the R675 coast road to Tramore about 11km from Waterford. This is the main holiday resort for the area and totally commercialised, plenty of amusements and a 5km long beach.

There is a slipway situated on the pier which goes almost dry when the tide is out. But as cars can be driven on the sand down to the waters edge, boats can be launched without difficulty. The R675 is the coast road to Dungarvan and the pier is situated on the Dungarvan side of Tramore.

Enter the town from Waterford side, avoid the amusement area to your left, go straight up the hill, left at the top, carry on for about 1.5km (still in the built up area) you come to the Ritz pub, a thatched house on your left, at the cross roads take a left turn go left again the Y junction just 25m down. Go down the hill onto the pier, parking is available on either side of the hill.

5. The Metal Man

From the pier head due south along the coastline you will see the three towers of the Metal Man. Go around the big rock and into the little bay just under the towers. Here lies the remains of a wreck called "Oasis", depth 10–12m, and a good interesting dive.

The wreck is located approx. halfway between the big rock and the cliff on the left, it is in close to shore about 10m or so from the rocks where it lies in an east-west direction. Plenty of rocks, sea life with not much weed and a good site for beginners and experienced alike. This is a safe area unless there is a south or southeast wind or a sea running.

6. Green Island

This is not really an island but a large rock outcrop about 500m up the coast from the Metal Man Bay. If there is any wave action you can see a waterspout coming from the middle of the rock. Depth 10–15m, good dive, plenty of sea life, large rocks and crevices plenty of weed, suitable for beginners and experienced. Thirty metres can be obtained a little further out but it is on sand.

7. Newtown Cove

When you reach the Y turn (on the way to the pier) take the right fork and drive along the coast road for about 1.5km and you will come to large parking area on your left, this is Newton Cove. A shore dive, easily accessible with steps down to the pier, then ladders to the water. It is a well frequented bathing area. Snorkel out to the mouth of the cove and take a bearing either left or right. Either is a good interesting dive for beginners and experienced. Depth 10m, large rocks crevices, plenty of weed, plenty of sea life.

If you go right (south) head between the large rock and the cliff, when you come out the other side you can make a large circle and come back into the cove again.

If you go left, go down the coast for about 200m and exit at the Guillamine swimming area. Caution is needed going this way if you are close to the shore as people fish from the rocks and cast out lines up to 15m or so and you can get hooked up. Much the same type of bottom and depth as the other side.

Helvick Head Dive Sites

Helvick is situated on the R674. The N25 is the main road from Waterford to Cork. On the Cork side of Dungarvan about 3km out, there is a junction (R674) for Helvic. This is a small fishing village right at Helvick Head. It is about 16km from Dungarvan and about 1 km from the main road.

The slip is situated in the harbour, which is at the very end of the R674. It is only possible to launch or retrieve a boat for one hour on either side of the full tide.

8. Harbour Dive

In the lower parking lot at the top of the slipway there is a pathway that leads to a small sandy cove right at the head. You can walk this path and do a shore dive by snorkelling out about 100m to the rock at the head. Depth 10–12m, a good dive for beginners and experienced with plenty of sea life, rocks, weed, and gullies. If you have a boat there is a good dive further along the coast to the west or out to sea about 400-500m or so.

9. Black Rocks

These rocks can be seen from the pier in Helvic. Depth 10m, plenty of gullies, weed, rocks, sea life – a good dive for beginners and experienced alike.

Ardmore Dive Sites

Ardmore is situated on the R673 off the N25 approx. halfway between Dungarvan and Youghal. It is a nice seaside holiday resort with a large beach and some amusements.

There is a slipway at the pier. Go down through the main street and you will see the pier on your left. It is only accessible above half tide water. This is a small village, although the street is wide, parking is limited.

The shore diving is not very adventurous and is limited to the back of the pier, however boat diving is good. There is a good dive straight out to sea in the mouth of the bay, 10–12m on rock and sandy bottom with not much weed and some sea life.

10. The Folio (GPS 51.52.86N 7.41.34W)

This is a good wreck dive, 36m and plenty of sea life. The wreck is well flattened but large chunks are still around. It needs fair weather and is a dive for experienced divers only. There is a light current mid-tides 1–1.5 knots approx.

Local Facilities and Information

Compressor:	Wexford Diving Holidays, Riverstown, Murrintown, Co. Wexford Tel./Fax. 053 39373
Tidal Constant:	Dublin +06 05
Local VHF station:	Minehead Radio Ch.16, 67, 83
Chart:	2046, 2049
Maps:	½":1 mile Nos. 23,23. 1:50,000 Nos. 76,82

Lobster ***Photo: John Costello***

South Cork

Around the Cork area there are numerous shore and boat diving sites. The Cork Harbour area has interesting dives which lie some miles off the coast and require local knowledge to avail of these particular areas.

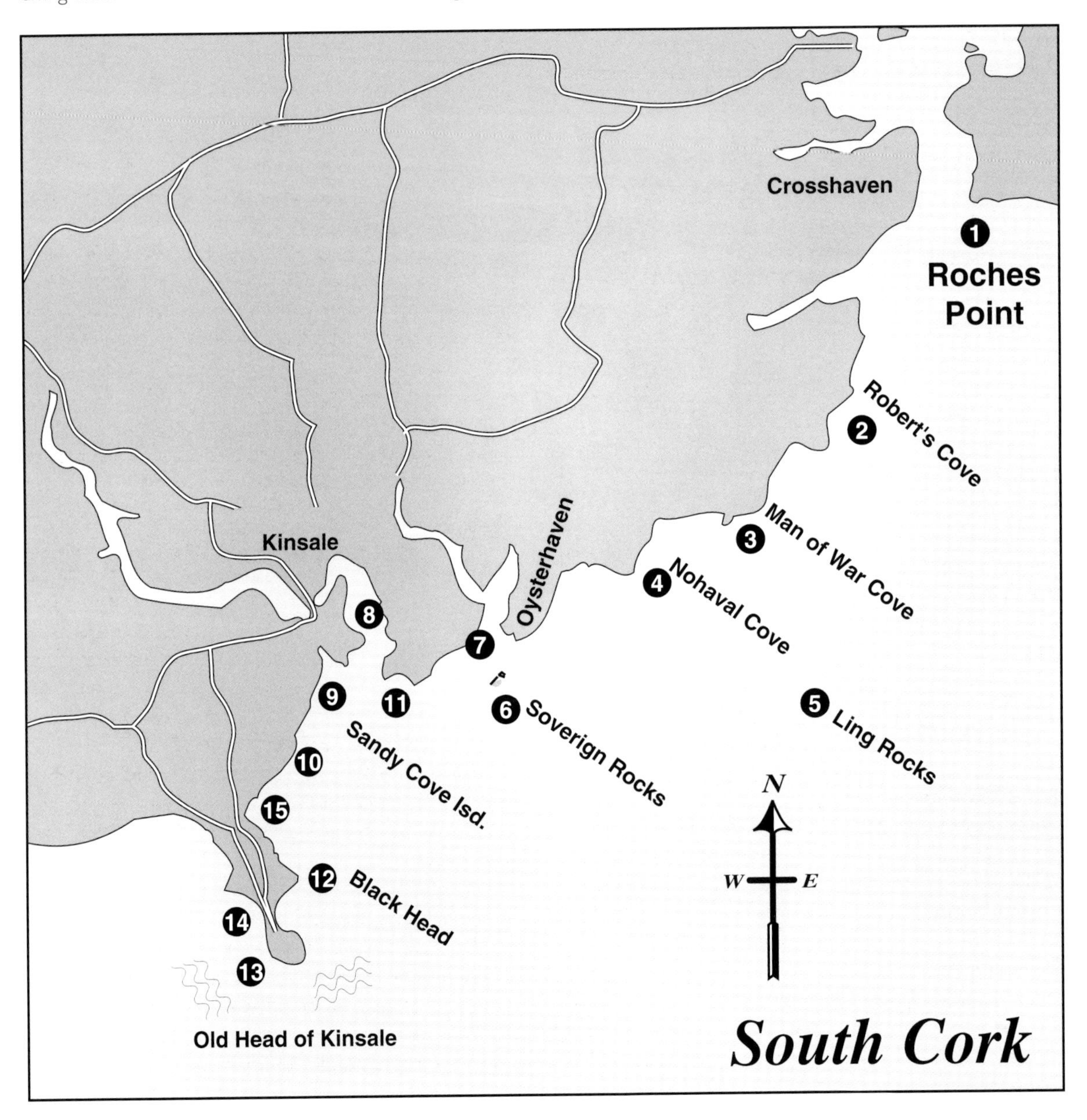

Dive Sites

1. The Celtic

The Celtic lies off Roche's Point and can be located by boat some 15 minutes from Crosshaven, which is well equipped to handle boats having both a marina and a good slip. Local knowledge is required to locate the wreck. The wreck can be affected by a strong easterly current therefore slack water is essential.

2. Robert's Cove

Robert's Cove is situated on the southern approach to Cork Harbour off the L67 Kinsale to Carrigaline Road and is mainly shore diving. Park opposite Robert's Cove Inn on the road and work your way along the cliff, access to be found at the side of a boat house. At the entrance to the cove you can access to the water's edge. Snorkel the width of the cove, and dive in about 6m of water working due south out to the eastern headland.

Boat diving may also be undertaken from Robert's Cove. The Daunt Rock is 5km offshore and well worth a visit but it is very exposed and subject to a strong Easterly current so diving at slack water is essential. The bottom at 30m+ is rough and broken rock with many brittle starfish.

3. Man of War Cove

About 4km south of Robert's Cove is Man-of-war Cove. From Robert's Cove take the road for Nohaval, at the first crossroads turn left and continue for about 1km (through private lands) and work your way down to the cove. The roadway is narrow and little room for parking.

Dive south along the rocks, expect about a depth of 10–12m. The bay is so named because a warship (named the "Zorro")was wrecked there.

4. Nohaval cove

Nohaval Cove is a shore dive, a car may be taken down to the site, but there is no access for boats. Work out of the cove and head east, again expect a depth of 10–15m depth.

Oysterhaven

Oysterhaven has plenty of choices. There is a good slip, which is tidal, for launching boats. Oysterhaven is also a very good venue for shore diving, with easy access to the water.

5. Ling Rocks

This is a very spectacular dive site. The Lings are a series of rocky underwater peaks, some of which sit in 55m of water with the tops of the peaks in only 26m of water, they are some 9km south-southeast of Oysterhaven. This makes any depth from 26–45m available to the more experienced diver and requires slack water. It therefore requires some extra preparation which should include SMBs. This is also a popular angling spot.

6. Sovereign Islands

These two islands are much closer inshore and there are the remains of several wrecks one of which is a Dutch trawler "The Nelly" on the south side (seaward) of the big Sovereign. The small Sovereign has a grotto which is located at the eastern end, this takes some finding, but once found it makes for a sweet dive. One can swim in one end and out the other. Around the Sovereigns depths are approx. 12–15m.

7. Ballymaccus Bay

Ballymaccus Bay directly opposite the slip in Oysterhaven and makes for a good safe night dive, plenty of life to be seen.

Kinsale

Kinsale has a marina and a good slip for launching boats. The choices here are too numerous to mention, but here are some of the good ones. Kinsale is the gourmet capital of Ireland with many first class restaurants to choose from.

8. Charles' Fort

On the north side of Kinsale Harbour, near the Youth Hostel, is Charles' Fort. The route is well signposted with plenty of parking. A good shore dive, plenty to see on a potter.

9. Sandycove Island

Head out of Kinsale Harbour and turn to starboard (left) and head for Sandycove Island. There are plenty of gullies to move in and out of which run in a southeasterly direction with a maximum depth of 15m. Sandycove can also be used for shore diving with easy access by car.

10. Bream Rock

Continue on to the Speckled Door Pub at Garretstown, where a boat can be launched, for a dive on Bream Rock on the eastern side of the Old Head of Kinsale. Watch the tides when diving the rock, always dive on a slack or flooding tide or hello America! SMBs are essential.

11. Bulman Rock

This is a fabulous scenic dive, conveniently located at the mouth of Kinsale Harbour. Ideal for trainee divers, it experiences very little tidal flow. It has a rocky terrain and depth ranges are from 22m–5m. This site is teeming with marine life and is superb for marine biology enthusiasts and photographers.

12. Black Head

Another safe pleasant dive opposite the harbour. Depths range from 10–15m. The tide is not a problem here and the site is well suited to novice divers, but with plenty to interest the more experienced divers. However, if you are allergic to kelp, skip this one.

13. City of Chicago

This is a very safe (12m) and pleasant wreck situated on the west side of the Old Head of Kinsale. There is plenty of wreckage lying about. Make sure you have a permit if you intend to dive this wreck as it dates back to 1892.

14. Holeopen Bay West

This is an exciting dive! Have a flooding tide, a westerly wind and shoot through the hole and find yourself in Holeopen Bay East, the other side of Kinsale Head. This dive varies in depth 12–2m in the middle, but a lot of fun.

15. The Stonewall Jackson

North from the Speckled Door and off the Red Strand the wreck of the Stonewall Jackson is supposed to lie – as it has not been found, there's a quest! This area may also be accessed from Kinsale. Depths around 12m on a mixed bottom.

Seven Heads

Seven Heads have some interest in so much that the "Cardiff Hall" was wrecked there. Take the L42 West from Kinsale and turn off (south) at Timoleague for Barryshall.

Access can be made at Dunworly Bay where there is a tidal slip and a four wheel drive is advisable. This site is also a shore dive but should only be undertaken by the fit, as there is climbing and equipment lugging to be done, before gaining access to the water. Nevertheless a pleasurable dive with depths of about 12–15m.

Local Facilities and Information

Compressor:
Kinsale Dive Centre,
Castlepark, Kinsale, Co. Cork
Tel. 021 774959 Fax. 021 774958
E-mail: maritime@indigo.ie

Cnoc Ard Yard,
Oysterhaven, Co. Cork
Tel. 021 770748 Fax. 021 294808

Tidal Constant: Dublin +05 57

Local VHF station: Cork Radio Ch.26, 67, 26

Chart: 1765, 2049, 2092, 2129, 2424

Maps: ½":1 mile No. 25 1:50,000 No. 87

West Cork
Baltimore to Galley Head

The area between Baltimore and Galley Head is renowned for its wrecks, steep drop-offs and abundant marine life. The area is approached by the N71 where Baltimore, Castletownhend and Union Hall provide excellent natural harbours with good slipways, many pubs and restaurants and fine facilities for the non-diver. There are several good shore dives for the novice but the area is best experienced by boat.

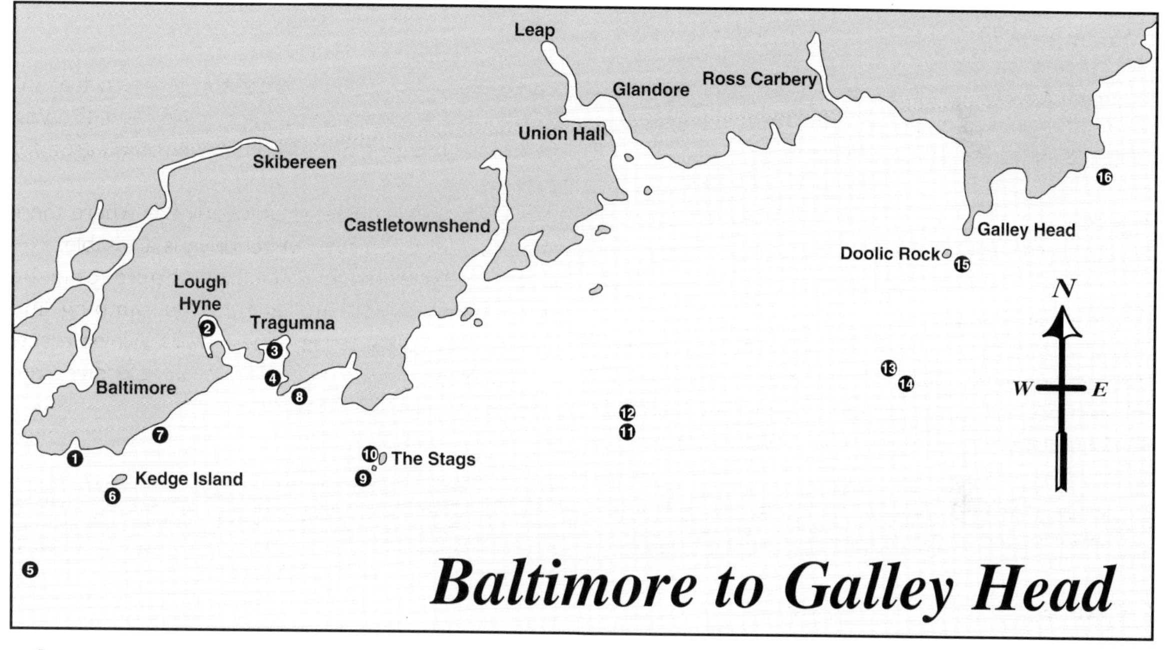

Shore Dives

1. Trafraska

Immediately before Baltimore village, turn left and follow the road about 2km down to a small beach. This steep sided cove provides excellent snorkelling and novice diving with deeper water a short swim further out.

2. Lough Hyne

The calm and clear waters of Lough Hyne provide excellent shore diving to a wide range of depths depending on how far you want to snorkel. Entry to the water can be gained from a number of places along the perimeter. The easiest is from the stone jetty to the north. Please remember that a licence to dive is required which can be obtained from the warden Declan O'Donnell – 028 37347.

3. Tragumna Bay

Take the R595 southeast from Skibbereen for approximately 2.5km then turn right to Tragumna. There are excellent shore dives from both sides of the bay.

4. Gokane Point

About 1.5km further south from Tragumna, turn right down the track immediately before Gokane Marine Services. The cove gives easy access to the water and excellent shore diving.

Boat Dives

5. Malmanger

Also known as the "tanker" this 5671ton/100m long Norwegian vessel was torpedoed whilst in a convoy from New York. One of the escorts towed her towards shore but she sank 3 miles off Baltimore Beacon on 12th March 1917. She sank into soft ground in approx. 65m so it can be quite a dark dive if stirred up.

6. Alondra

This wreck lies on the south side of Kedge Island having run aground in thick fog on 29th December 1916, The wreck is well broken up in the gully that runs into the south side of the island. Her boilers are still prominent in about 20m and there is a fair amount of hull plating which now house large conger eels. To the east you will find excellent gulleys and walls teaming with life.

7. Dido

About 5.5km east of Kedge Island, close inshore lies this barque which sank on 26th August 1883. She lies at 18–20m and is spread over a large area just off two oblong rocks running W-E. Some of her anchors are still visible and plating runs away to the east.

8. Carnavonshire

About 400m east of Gokane Point lies this three masted barque that sank on 1st April 1896. The area around her has fantastic arches and gullies that make this a memorable dive.

9. Kowloon Bridge

The largest wreck in Europe went aground on Stag Rocks on 24th November 1986 having drifted several days without steering. Her forecastle with impressive anchor winches rises to 6m. It is possible to swim down the anchor fairlead where the starboard anchor is missing. This brings the diver out over the massive bulbous bow, the bottom of which sits in 35m. The bow section is of interest to both ardent wreck and reef divers. Its spectacular size has created a 'reef' festooned in anemones, patrolled by wrasse and is home to cavorting shoals of pollack. The stern section at 46m is a wreckies paradise and is now breaking up to expose gargantuan machinery. Strong tides at the Stags dictate that slack water diving is a must. Diving the top of the bow section at 6m with any swell running can be dangerous.

10. Asian

This 125m long steamship ran aground in fog on the south of Stag Rocks on 17th September 1924. She lies in 18m of water at the entrance to a large gully between rocks on the southwest side. She is broken forward of No. 2 hatch and is well spread out.

11. '78 Rock

Twin offshore pinnacles rising sharply from 50 to 17m. Home to abundant reef life, washed by clear offshore water and sparkling with jewel anemones. Dive at slack water only. Watch your depth.

12. U-260

Having struck a mine some 32km off the Fastnet, this VIIC class submarine headed inshore but eventually became unmanageable. She was scuttled on 13th March 1945 and now lies in 45m on a rocky sea bed. She is virtually intact apart from damage caused to her bow by the mine and is an exciting dive. Her periscope, Walter snorkel and DF aerial are all intact which make her a unique dive.

U-260 was a type VIIC U-boat and 568 were commissioned from 1940–1945. Type VIIC was a slightly modified version of the successful VIIB. They had basically the same engine layout and power, but were slightly larger and heavier which made them not quite as fast as the VIIB. Five torpedo tubes (four at the bow and one at the stern) were installed.

The VIIC was the workhorse of the German U-boat force in WWII from 1941 onwards and boats of this type were being built throughout the war. The first VIIC boat commissioned was the U-69 in 1940. The VIIC was an effective fighting machine and was seen in almost all areas where the U-boat force operated ,although their range was not as great as the one of the larger IX types. The VIIC came into service as the "happy days" were almost over and it was this boat that faced the final defeat to the Allied anti-submarine campaign in late 1943 and 1944. Perhaps the most famous VIIC boat was the U-96 which is featured in the movie Das Boot.

13. Robber Bank

This shoal rises from 35m–18m with a steep face on the SW side. Like many offshore reefs the visibility can be fantastic. Being close to Galley Head it is best dived at slack.

14. Ludgate

This WWI vessel was mined 3.2km SSW of Galley Head carrying copper on 26 July 1917. The wreck lies in 50m – the copper was grab salvaged.

15. Crescent City

She struck Doolic Rock in dense fog on 8th February 1871 and sank within 400m to its east in 30m. Also known as the "silver dollar wreck" because she was carrying Mexican coins, she is spread out but there are several big sections that are home to large conger eels.

16. HMS Mignonette

A flower class sloop mined and sunk about a mile (1.61km) SE of Sands Cove on 17 March 1917. The bow section fell away in 46m, the stern section eventually sank in 33m. Large boilers and extensive debris field, this is generally a "dusty" wreck as tides are not strong in this area.

Local Facilities and Information

Compressor: Aquaventures Dive Centre, Baltimore
Tel. 028 20511 Fax. 028 20511

Baltimore Diving & Watersports Centre, Baltimore
Tel. 028 20300 Fax. 028 20300

Tidal Constant: Dublin +05 30

Local VHF station: Cork Radio Ch. 16, 67, 26
Bantry Radio Ch. 16, 67, 23, 85

Chart: 2129, 2092

Maps: ½":1 mile No. 24, 25 1:50,000 No. 88,89

Roaringwater Bay
West Cork

Roaringwater Bay lies between Crookhaven to the west and Baltimore to the southeast and includes the 'Carbery 100 Isles'. It is these islands that offer the varied and sheltered diving which makes this area so attractive.

Schull is the ideal base for diving the area and is 20km west of the town of Skibereen on the N71/L57. It is a very popular holiday destination and in the high season accommodation should be booked well in advance, however it has an excellent range of facilities with many pubs, restaurants and shops including the area's only dive shop. It also has a fine harbour with the best slipway in West Cork.

There are a variety of dive sites ranging from shore dives for the absolute novice to demanding dives off the famous Fastnet Rock 12km out to sea. Tides need to be watched at a few exposed points, but in general diving can be carried out at any state of the tide.

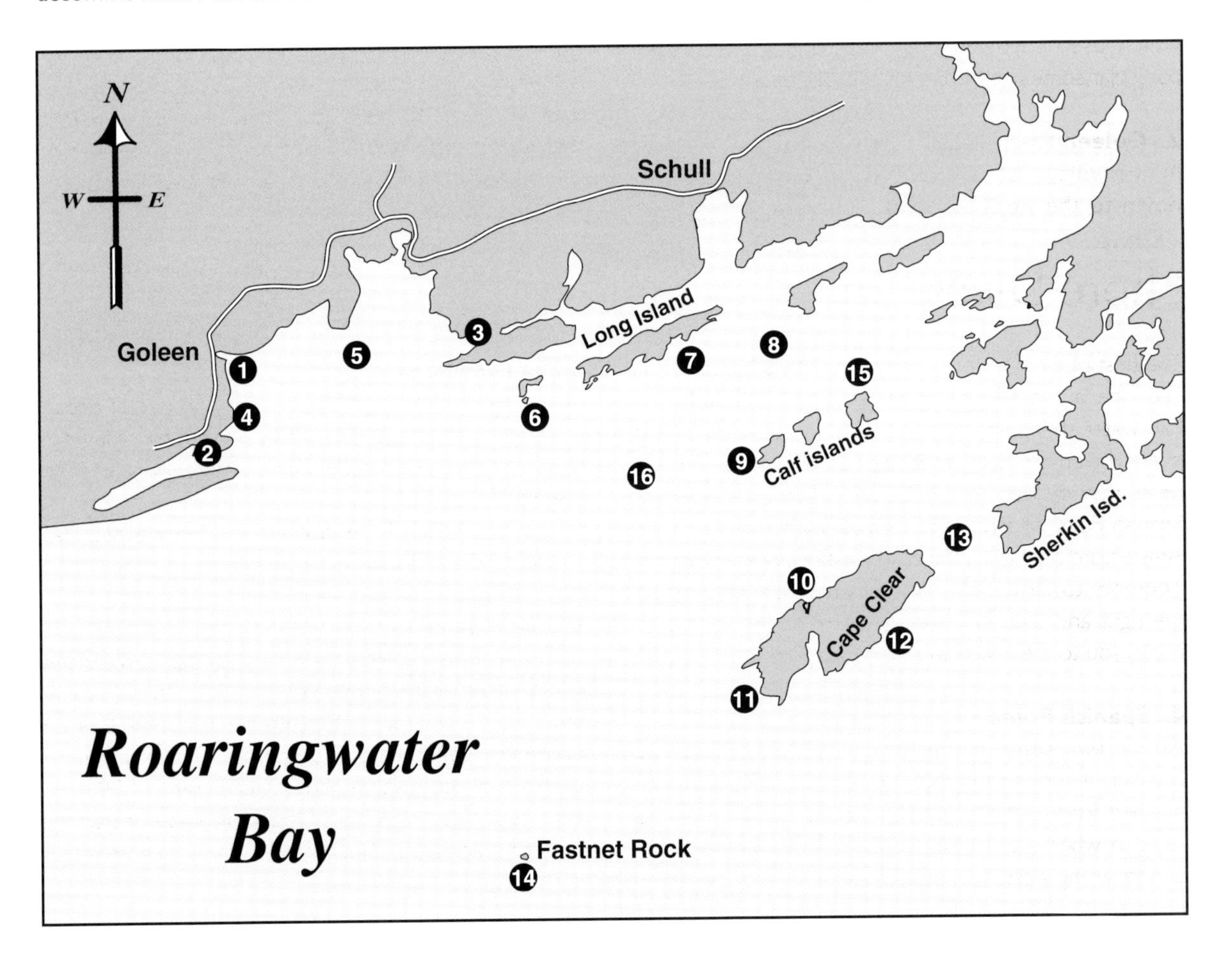

Shore Dives

As the main attraction of the area is the range of islands there are few interesting shore dives, however some are worth mentioning

1. Rock Island

Travel about 2km beyond the village of Goleen, west of Schull, on the Crookhaven road take a junction on the left to 'Rock Island', which overlooks Crookhaven Harbour. Access to the shore is private, but there should be no problem using the small pier at the western end of the island and the Irish Lights caretaker will usually allow you to dive off the pier at the lighthouse complex at the eastern end, but do ask.

The area is well sheltered from all but easterly winds. Although the bottom rapidly runs into mud/gravel there are some pretty outcrops covered with plumose anemones. However, the main reason for diving here is to search for items dropped off the old sailing ships which used to tie up here in the last century, in particular some fine bottles have been recovered.

2. Goleen Pier

In the village of Goleen take a turn to the left down to the small pier and slipway, which dries at low water, continue on the narrow lane to the outer pier where there is always water and is close to the open sea. Access is easy and the scenery reasonable and improves if you swim out further into the bay where depths of 15m can be found. This site is well protected from westerly winds.

3. Castle Point

Travel 5km west of Schull on the road to Goleen, take a left turn signposted "Schull, via Coast Road". After 1.5km the road swings round to the east you will see a castle on a spit of land off to your right. Take a narrow road in the direction of this castle for 500m until you reach a sheltered little pier. Access into the water is easy and the little cove offers excellent conditions for real beginners with a shingle bottom and rocky walls with good marine growth.

Although exposed to strong westerly winds the visibility is usually very good and it is an excellent location for night dives. It is best when the tide is in, as the slippery lower steps are covered. Depths of 10m can be obtained.

Shore Dives

The best place to launch boats of any size is Schull where even the largest of RIBs can be easily launched at all but low water spring tide. It is also possible to tie off a boat overnight on a running mooring beside the pier. Smaller boats may be launched at Goleen (above half tide) for Spanish Point or across the sand at Ballyrisode beach for Amsterdam Reef (take the road west out of the village of Toomore towards Goleen for 1.5km, past a gift shop on the right and then take the next turn to the left which brings you to the beach and car park in 1km)

4. Spanish Point

About 1km south of the village of Goleen is a low headland and reef well protected from the west. It is easily reached from Goleen pier and fair diving can be found close in when more adventurous sites are not available due to strong westerly winds. An easy site for beginners.

5. Amsterdam Reef

About 1km south of Ballyrisode beach is a small group of rocks and outlying reef where interesting diving can be had on the eastern flank and in the shallows of the reef itself.

The remainder of the dive sites in Roaringwater Bay are best reached by boat from Schull.

6. Goat Island

Heading west out of Schull harbour up Long Island Channel for 4km brings you to Goat Island which appears to be split into two pieces. There is an excellent reef running southeast from the southern most tip of the island where water depths of 20m on either side. Start right under the small white beacon on the island and watch out for the current when the tide is running.

Close in, the western side of the island has nice diving when it is too rough to dive off the point itself. The small islands and rocks which spread west from here have excellent diving on their south side but rapidly run into sand on their north sides. These sites are more suited to the experienced diver and trainees would do better off Long Island.

Lady Charlotte

Somewhere in the vicinity of the Barrel Rocks, 1km west of Goat Island, lie the remains of the Lady Charlotte which floundered in shallow water on 23 October 1838 en route from Peru to Liverpool with a valuable cargo of silver bullion. seventy thousand pounds worth of silver was promptly salvaged, but it is likely that not all was recovered. Indeed many years ago a silver dollar was found washed up on a beach on Long Island. Many divers have tried their luck with looking for this wreck, but without success so far!

7. Long Island

The white beacon standing on Copper Point at the eastern end of Long Island can easily be seen 2km from Schull Pier. The whole of the south side of the island offers good, easy diving in the range of 10–20m close to the shore, with the diving getting better and a little harder as you move west along the 3km coastline, so it is easy to select a site to suit your party's experience.

8. Amelia Rock

This rock, lying about 1km southeast of Copper Point, comes to within 3m of the surface at the end of the reef which runs out south-west from Castle Island. Beyond it the depth drops rapidly to the sandy floor of the open bay at 25m. There are impressive breakers here during rough winter weather but lovely gullies and marine life at 15–20m in the summer.

There is a green navigation buoy about 100m SW of the rock, but as it wanders a bit, an echo sounder or dragged anchor should be used to find the edge of the reef. As divers will surface at least 1km from any land it is not really suitable for beginners.

9. West Calf Island

Half way to Cape Clear Island and about 6km from Schull Pier lie the three Calf Islands. A few hardy families lived on these wild islands until the 1930s and some ruined houses still remain. The best of the diving is on the western end of West Calf, where the jagged rocks take the full brunt of the Atlantic weather. In 1848 a wooden ship, the '"Stephen Whittley" struck these rocks and a few encrusted remains can be found in the gullies just north the tip of the island in about 15m of water.

A little further off from here are marvellous deep broad gullies heading down gradually to 30m where there is an abrupt drop of 5m to the sandy floor of the bay. There is a tidal flow across this point and care should be taken when the tide is flowing hard, but the scenery is magnificent with extensive beds of dead-man's fingers and jewel anemones.

Just south of the point one gully has a massive rock jammed in it making a spectacular archway to swim through. Due to the potential problem of drifting off into wide open sea, good boat cover is important and use of SMBs is recommended. The north and south sides of West Calf offer good diving when it is too rough to dive the point itself. There is an interesting sheltered dive in the lee of the small group of rocks on the northern side of Middle Calf.

10. Cape Clear Island

Lying some 10km south of Schull is the large island of Cape Clear on which some 100 people still live. It is reached from the mainland by passenger ferries from either Schull or Baltimore. However, on a calm day it is no problem to make the journey from Schull by dive boat, but a convoy of two boats would make sense.

The main landing place is North Harbour which is in the hollow midway along the otherwise hilly island. It is a charming little harbour with several pubs, shops and guest houses. There is excellent diving out west from the harbour, under the cliffs and headlands right around to South Harbour, which is only a short walk across the narrow neck of the island back to North Harbour. Continuing east along the south cliffs there are good dive sites right up to the Gascanane Sound which separates Cape Clear from Sherkin Island.

11. Nestorian

This 120m long 2400 ton ship carrying steel ingots and empty shell heads foundered under the cliffs south of the "Bill of Cape" in 1917. The wreckage is well spread out very close under the cliffs in 10–20m, but makes for an interesting wreck dive with nice scenery as well. Due to the closeness of the shore and the exposed westerly position, this is a dive for very calm days only!

Directions: Coming from the north, after passing the distinctive "Bill of Cape" head across the small bay for the next headland, which is actually the cape of Cape Clear but in fact is not very dramatic. One gully before the cape there is a large flat rock about 4m long looking like the sole of a shoe perched at the top of the cliff face and the wreck is directly below this. On the chart No. 2184 it is at the point where there is a depth sounding marked "12.8m"

12. Illyrian (Lighthouse Wreck)

About 1km east of South Harbour there is a large rock scree running down the cliffs below the old lighthouse. The ship seems to have ran bow first into this cove with the wreckage running out eastward. There are anchors and chain to be found in the bottom scree at about 8m and the boilers are still intact at about 22m along with a lot of plate.

13. Gascanane Sound

The area between the islands of Cape Clear and Sherkin offer some marvellous diving with large pinnacles ranging from 10m down to 40m at the southeast corner of Cape Clear. There are superb areas of marine growth on the southern side of the Carrigmore rocks that are mid way across the sound. There are very strong tidal flows through the sound and the sea can get very rough when the wind is against the tide. The surface can appear to 'boil' as it surges over underwater rocks and ledges. Plan to dive either at slack water or well within a tidal shadow of the rocks and use a surface marker buoy whenever possible.

The best of the gullies at Carrigmore are close to the rocks in about 10–15m. There are a few dull patches especially to the west, so if you land in one move east a bit till you hit the right spot. For the advanced diver drift diving around these rocks to the east is spectacular but very demanding and requires excellent preparation. The other small islands close to the eastern side of the sound also offer excellent diving, as does the south side of Sherkin Island itself.

14. Fastnet Rock

The world famous Fastnet Rock with its impressive lighthouse lies 5km southwest of the end of Cape Clear Island and offers some of the best diving anywhere in Ireland. As there are strong and sometimes erratic tidal flows and deep water all around the rock, it means diving at the Fastnet is only for the experienced and then only with reliable boats and very calm weather.

It is 15km from Schull and it is advisable to charter a hard boat for the trip to give extra security and to benefit from local knowledge. For those "going it alone", two substantial dive boats, both with reliable engines and radios should be considered the absolute minimum. As it is very difficult to assess the weather conditions around the rock from shore, be prepared to abandon the dive and head for a less demanding spot and keep a sharp watch out for changing conditions when the tide turns.

All that said, when the conditions are just right, a trip to the Fastnet can give you a day to remember for many years. The visible rock is in the middle of a narrow reef running SW-NE about 1km in each direction with depths of 45m being rapidly reached on either side should you get swept off by the tide. The section of reef towards Cape Clear is the simpler to dive on and close to the rock itself there is some shelter from the tide if you have missed exact slack water.

The section of reef outside the rock should be approached with great care as the tide rarely stops flowing and the diving is very demanding. Being an isolated rock, the underwater scenery is spectacular with huge shoals of fish and fantastic growths on every rock face. Due to the clarity of the water and the excellent scenery it is easy to misjudge depths and durations, so don't get too carried away!

A suitable method of spotting divers who have surfaced a long way from the boat must be used, though due to the deep narrow gullies and tidal flows, a SMB can be difficult to use effectively. If the sea is absolutely flat calm, it is possible to land on the rock and inspect the lighthouse at close quarters, to marvel at the high quality of the stone masonry which has withstood 80 years of Atlantic storms. This is only for those who are nimble footed and prepared to swim back out to a boat if the swell suddenly picks up!

15. Mystique (GPS 51.29.276 N 009.29.609 W)
To the north of Calf Island Fast a 20m long fishing vessel called the "Mystique" was sunk deliberately to provide a sheltered wreck site close to Baltimore. She sits upright on a sandy bottom in the 22m hole shown on chart 2129 on the north of the island. She is an easy dive and is acquiring fauna rapidly.

16. Pinnacle (GPS 51.29.276 N 009.29.609 W)
This is an excellent pinnacle that rises out of Long Island Bay from about 40m to 20m. This should only be dived in calm weather as any swell makes for an uncomfortable dive.

Local Facilities and Information

Compressor:	Schull Watersports Centre, Schull Tel. 028 28351/28554 Baltimore Diving & Watersports Centre Baltimore, West Cork Tel. / Fax. 028 20300 E-mail jkdiving@iol.ie Aquaventures, The Stone House, Baltimore, Co. Cork. Tel./Fax. 028 20511 Email aquavent@aquaventures.iol.ie
Tidal Constant:	Dublin +05 20
Local VHF Radio:	Bantry Radio Ch. 16, 67, 23, 85
Local Chart Nos.:	2184, 2129
Maps:	½":1 mile No. 24 1:50,000 No. 88

Mizen Head
Co. Cork

Mizen Head – the Land's End of Ireland is situated at the very southwestern point of Ireland and approached by the N71 via Skibereen and onwards through the villages of Schull and Goleen. The last village on the peninsula is Crookhaven.

There are several good shore dives, but to appreciate the area at best boats are required. Due to their exposed locations, many of these dives are suitable only for experienced divers and in calm conditions.

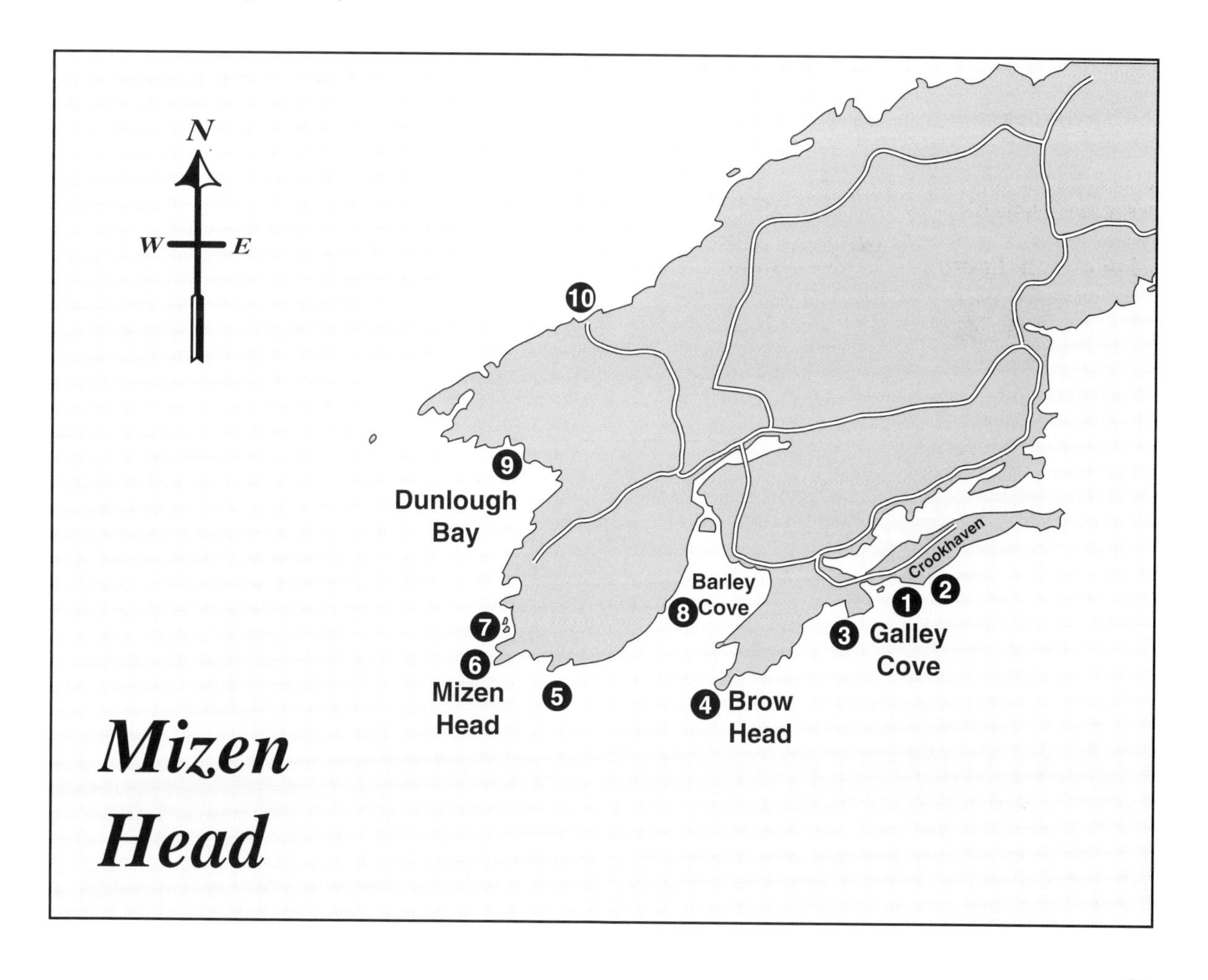

Galley Cove Dive Sites

The most westerly access point on the south coast is Galley Cove, about 2km before Crookhaven, where a fine sandy beach opens up on your right with a good view of the Fastnet Rock 10km out to sea. Small boats can be launched across the beach, while large RIBs should be launched at Crookhaven, where there is a good slip, and motored the 5km around Streek Head to meet the rest of your party at Galley Cove beach. From here there is a selection of sites ranging from simple shore dives to deep spectacular boat dives under cliffs for the very experienced diver.

1. Galley Cove Rock.

Just 100m from the beach there is excellent snorkelling inside the rock over a gently sloping sandy bottom with rocky outcrops. Beyond the island there are interesting gullies in a depth range 10–25m suitable for the less experienced diver or for those without a boat.

2. Carrigadeavaun

About 1km east of Galley Cove is a rock that looks like it has just split off from the mainland. There is some shelter from a westerly swell behind it which can make kitting up more comfortable. There is an interesting bottom at 20m usually covered with feather and brittle stars. Swimming towards the point of the rock and out to sea the bottom tumbles down to 35–40m with loads of life all the way down. This site is suitable for intermediate and advanced divers as you can easily select your depth.

3. Reen Point

Heading west from Galley Cove the first headland reached after only 400m is Reen Point. Here the depth drops off rapidly to 40m just offshore in several jagged steps. There can be a gentle tidal current and excellent walls of jewel anemones.

The bay between Reen Point and Brow Head was known as a mating ground for basking sharks, but they are rarely seen now. However, there is good 30m diving all along under the cliffs heading west to Brow Head with no noticeable current. An old anchor was spotted a couple of years ago about 800m short of Brow Head in 20m of water but there is no sign of any wreck.

Take note: The Mizen Head area offers some of Ireland's best diving but can be dangerous. Make sure your equipment is up to scratch, two reliable boats and a VHF radio should be considered the minimum. Even then be on the watch out for changing conditions when the tide turns.

The following dives are only suitable for experienced divers and calm weather.

4. Brow Head

There is spectacular diving under the towering cliffs at Brow Head, the southern most point of Ireland. The tide can be very strong here so it should be only dived at slack water. However, for those capable there is a stunning drift dive from the tip of the headland going west towards Mizen Head when the tide has just turned to ebb.

There is a reef at about 20m which runs parallel to the flow and lasts for at least 1km. With a gentle current and good visibility you can cruise from ridge to ridge which due to the high energy environment, are carpeted with dead man's fingers and jewel anemones. Taking care not to slip off the top of the reef into deeper water on either side, you can get a full half hour drift while keeping above 24m, excellent boat cover is essential.

Every diver should also carry some additional method of signalling in case of separation (sausage, flags, flares, etc.) as being alone 1km off the end of Ireland is very lonely!

5. Carrignagower

This rock, which is awash at high water, lies 50m offshore about 1km before Mizen Head. Even in the calmest weather the swell breaks against it. The outside of the rock is an excellent wall with marine growth on every square inch. This is a slack water dive only! There is a safe passage inside the rock for those heading for the Mizen.

6. Mizen Head

When the weather is very calm this is the place to head for, but conditions north of the point can be very different to those on the approach. If you are unhappy about rounding the point there is a lot of good diving close in between the point and the bridge where 35m is easily reached. On the mainland side of the bridge the water is shallower and the diving less demanding. For those who have the necessary permit, the cannons and anchors of the "L'Impatient" (sunk 1796) lie off the small headland which also has a small pier and access steps.

Back to the tip of the Mizen, right under the lighthouse (which is now unmanned) there is a deep gully where at least three boats have been wrecked, two trawlers, "Ribble" (1906) and "Manoes" (1908) along with the yacht "Taurima" (1975). The weather must be flat calm to allow divers to venture right up the gully, but who knows what may be found amongst the rocks!

The reef out from the tip of the Mizen offers diving that is hard to beat anywhere with stunning scenery and large shoals of fish. However, since the tide runs across the reef (rather than along it as at Brow Head) you can only dive here at exactly slack water, so plan to arrive a little early and be prepared to wait.

North of the Mizen is a graveyard of many steamers and coasters from around the turn of the century. "Irada" (1908), "Oswestry" (1899), "Bohemian" (1887), "Mephis" (1896) and several more. Very little structure has survived the ravages of a century of winter storms but wreckage can be seen on almost every dive in this area.

7. The Copper Boat

The remains of the "Oswestery" lie wedged on the north side of a towering stack 500m north of Mizen Head. Sometimes mistakenly called the "Irada" the wreck got its name from the 40kg copper ingots that were in its cargo and could still be found up to a few years ago. A couple are still visible but have resisted all attempts to move them! There is little structure left but the wreck is easy to find, only 15–20m deep and it is the most impressive site for a rummage you could imagine!

Shore Dives

Apart from the straightforward shore dive at Galley Cove, there are several advanced shore dives at exposed small piers around the Mizen headland. They all require a walk from the car to the access point and it would be wise to check the conditions before getting kitted up. If there is a significant swell do not enter the water as it can be difficult to get out after a dive when you are tired. There are no significant tide runs at these sites, but at low tide the access steps will be high and dry.

8. Vaud Cove

Follow the road west from Goleen towards Mizen Head, 800m past the Barley Cove Hotel the road widens on the left. Turn down here towards a farmhouse. Just before the house turn right through a gate along a track towards an isolated modern house. From here the footpath goes off to the left before swinging round and down to a small pier after 200m. Entering the water it is worth snorkelling across to the right-hand point and diving on the cliffs beyond. This site is exposed to S and SE winds.

9. Dunlough Pier

Approaching Mizen Head pass Barley Cove Hotel and continue straight on up to the T junction. Turn right and follow the road on until it ends after about 3km. To reach the pier, walk straight ahead, cross the steep slipway and clamber about 3m and you will see the steps leading to a small pier about 50m away. In the water snorkel across to the point opposite before going down and out along the gullies where 30m depth can be easily reached. This site is very exposed to westerly swells and wind.

10. Toor Pier

While technically in Dunmanus Bay, this site is grouped under Mizen Head shore dives due to its similar exposed and spectacular location. Approaching Mizen Head, about 1km before the turn off to the Barley Cove Hotel, there is a national school on the right. Take the next turn to the right after about 100m. Follow the road up and over the hill and down towards Dunmanus Bay until the road ends, from where there is a footpath 100m down to the pier.

In the water the best diving is along the cliff to the right of the pier where ridges run out to meet the sand at about 30m. For the more energetic the diving around the right-hand point of the island is well worth the effort, while the tunnel through the headland and surrounding area is shallow but quite interesting, but the gullies run in all directions making navigation difficult. It is an excellent spot for the advanced snorkeller.

Local Facilities and Information

Compressor:	Schull Watersports Centre, Schull, Co. Cork 028 28351/28554 Baltimore Diving and Watersports Centre. Baltimore, Co. Cork Tel./Fax. 028 20300 E-mail: skdiving@iol.ie Aquaventures Ltd., The Stone House, Baltimore, Co. Cork Tel./Fax. 028 20511 E-mail: aquavent@aquaventures.iol.ie
Tidal constant:	Dublin +05 20
Local VHF Radio:	Bantry Radio Ch. 16, 67,23, 85
Local Chart	No: 2184
Maps:	½":1 mile No. 24. 1:50,000 No. 88

Tompot blenny ***Photo: John Costello***

Dunmanus Bay
Co. Cork

Dunmanus Bay lies between Mizen Head to the south and Bantry Bay to the north. It is out of the main tidal flows and has no significant river flowing into it. Hence it has above average visibility and little silt. The isolation of Dunmanus Bay should be taken into account when planning dives as there is little other traffic in the bay to help you if you run into problems. The small village of Durrus lies at the head of the bay on the R591 (Bantry to Goleen Road). The north side of the bay is more populated with a couple of villages and a gentle shoreline.

Turn off in Durrus on a smaller road to reach Kilcrohane after 16km. The south side is very isolated with towering cliffs and a dramatic coastline. Follow the R591 towards Goleen about 16km beyond Durrus until reaching a junction to the right signposted "Goleen via Coast Road" which brings you to Dunmanus Harbour after a further 1.5km.

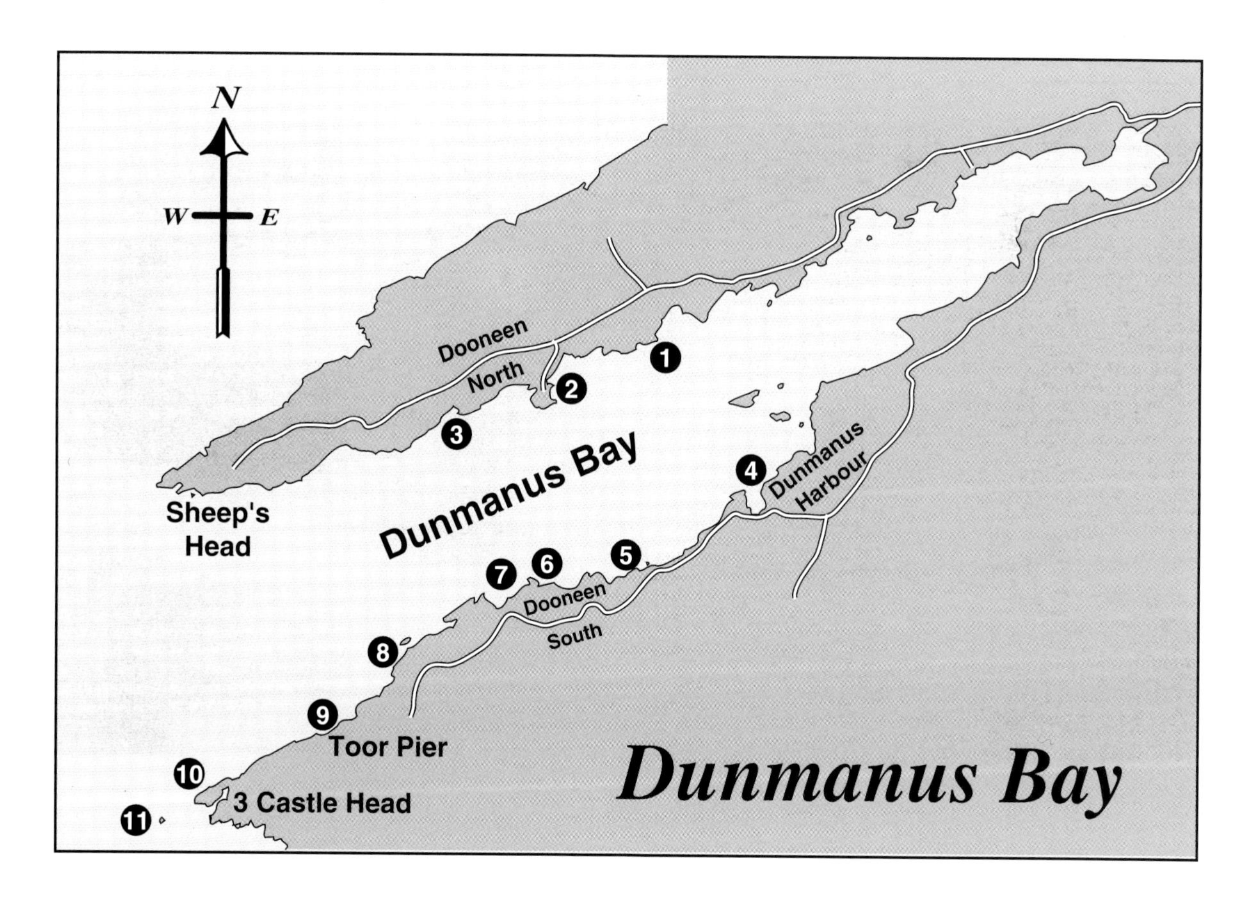

Dunmanus Bay North Dive Sites

1. Kilcrohane Pier

Turn left at the western end of Kilcrohane village by the children's playground and follow the road along to the small pier and slipway. Boats can be launched here above half-tide to access dive sites further west along the coast. The area around the pier is suitable for shore diving for the less experienced and also night diving with depths of 5–15m.

2. Dooneen North

Head west out of Kilcrohane for 3km until you spot a solitary bar on the left side of the road. After a further 200m take a turn to the left by a large red barn. Follow the narrow road down to a substantial pier. There is no possibility of launching boats here but they can easily be brought from Kilcrohane Pier only 1km away. With a boat you can explore the area around the headland where intermediate dives with depths of 20–30m can be reached.

The area in the vicinity of the pier is well protected from the prevailing westerly winds and can be dived when other sites are too rough. If shore diving the area, out and to the right of the pier are the most interesting with rocky outcrops and ridges. Depths of 20m can be obtained after a reasonable fin before the bottom runs into sand. Watch out for subsurface mariculture frames and ropes. About 25m to the left of the pier there is a narrow cleft which runs back 50m into the cliff. The cave is never narrower than a metre wide and has an air space above it at all times. At high water the cave is 10m deep and there are extensive vertical walls which are carpeted with jewel anemones, particularly near the entrance. A torch is useful for exploring the end of the cave where you should also watch out for a surge if there is any swell running at sea. This site is suitable for novices and less experienced divers.

3. Ballybroom Pier

About 5km west of Kilcrohane there is a small museum by a junction where the road splits, straight on heads towards Sheep' s Head and right continues along the "Goats Path" back towards Bantry. A small road leads down to the left here and runs to a surprisingly large pier and slipway after about 1km. This is the last access point on the northern side of Dunmanus Bay, high cliffs run on from here to Sheep's Head 7km away.

As the little bay faces southwest it offers little shelter and is only useful in calm weather, when shore dives and short distance boat dives are rewarding without being too demanding. Diving under the high cliffs close to the headland is not as exciting as you would expect and hardly worth the effort involved in getting to this very remote place.

Dunmanus Bay South Dive Sites

4. Dunmanus Harbour

The substantial pier is used by local fishermen and has just enough water off the head for a boat at low tide, but at low springs it may be necessary to paddle a short distance before lowering the engine. Boats may be launched across a hard gravel shore via a short track about 100m east of the pier. There are no steep gradients and boat trailers can be easily manhandled into the water, however for larger boats launching would need at least half-tide. The harbour is sheltered except for strong north-westerlies and it should be safe to moor a boat if several days diving in the bay are planned.

The harbour itself is suitable for snorkelling or training but for diving it is best to head west out of the harbour. There is good intermediate diving close to the headland only 100m beyond the harbour mouth. Further around the headland there is deep water close in where advanced divers can easily find depths of up to 40m. It is wise to drop a shot line to assess the depth before diving as the deep water comes very close to the shore in places!

It is possible to shore dive this general area on a calm day by driving 1km west along the coast road where there are access points down to the shore across the fields for the nimble footed diver.

Carbery Island about 2km out in the middle of the bay may look promising but in fact has nothing special to offer the diver.

5. Canty's Cove

Head west along the coast road from Dunmanus Harbour for about 5km until the small hamlet of Dunkelly is reached. The road takes a sharp turn to the left after the fourth house on the left which has a derelict lean-to. Turn down to the right 20m before the sharp bend onto a narrow gravel road which twists and turns for 1km down to a charming cove with pier and slipway. The steepness of the access road demands a vehicle that can pull the boat easily. If you did run into problems, the boat could be recovered at Dunmanus Harbour 4km away.

The bottom of the cove is coarse sand and the water is usually crystal clear with loads of life on the rocky sides of the cove. Access into the water is very easy and it is the ideal spot for trainees, snorkellers and night dives. On the left of the cove there are three fissures in the rock that lead to an open space with a hidden waterfall. One entrance is 2m wide and open to the sky, another is narrower, closed overhead but with ample air space. The third is quite a wriggle but is dry at the highest spot at low water and it all makes for interesting exploration.

Canty's Cove is the most westerly launching place for boats for those heading for the spectacular dives along the cliffs running west to Three Castle Head 10km away. However, it is possible to collect divers from piers further west for those groups with more divers than boat space. However, there are interesting intermediate dives from a boat close to the shore, particularly around to the left leaving the cove, where depths down to 30m can be selected.

6. Dooneen South

Head west from Dunmanus Harbour as for Canty's Cove (see above) but at the sharp bend do not take the gravel road but take a tarred road to the right 20m further on. After 1.5km turn down right again at a group of farm houses and head for a large solitary white house by the shore about 1.5km away. A small pier and slip are reached just before the house. Parking is tight here and the track is often used by local farmers, so be considerate. The slipway is very rough and only suitable for the smallest of inflatables. Larger boats can easily be brought from Canty's Cove only 2km away. However the pier is very handy for shore diving as the little cove faces NE and is quite sheltered.

The bottom is very interesting with depths of 5–15m to the right of the pier or across towards the point opposite and is an ideal site for intermediate divers. For those with even the smallest of boats, there is excellent diving around the headland to the left.

7. Dooneen Wall

Just 50m off the cliff that forms the outside of the promontory that protects Dooneen Pier is a spectacular wall that plunges from 25–43m. For those coming by boat direct from Canty's Cove, the white house at Dooneen is clearly visible as you approach. There is an archway through the headland which can be used by boats when it is very calm, however to find the wall ignore the archway and carry on around the headland to its NW point.

Drop divers about 25m due north of this point to land in about 20m of water. Swimming due north will bring you rapidly to the edge of the wall after a distance of about 50m and at a depth of around 26m. The rim of the wall is quite abrupt and actually overhangs in places. Since it is 17m straight down and below 40m at the bottom, going "over the edge" is a dive for experienced divers only. For those using computers it is possible to swim back up the wall and return gradually to shallow water, finishing up with an ascent from only 10m without incurring any decompression requirement, thus making for a satisfying and safe deep dive. Continuing around the headland a little more, close to the exit of the archway, there is very good intermediate diving close in to the rocks if there is no westerly swell.

8. The Iberian.

The 2000 ton cargo ship, the Iberian, was en route from Boston to Liverpool when she sank on 20 November 1885 after getting lost in fog and striking a reef south of Bird Island. She was carrying cattle and general cargo along with 54 passengers and crew. No lives were lost in the accident and the ship slipped back into deeper water after 2 days, where she lies today in 30–38m. Due to the depth the wreck has not been totally flattened by a century of storms and some sections still stand several metres clear of the rocky bottom. The underwater scenery is also very good at this site making this an ideal spot for a group of divers with varied aspirations! As this wreck is now more than 100 years old, a permit is required to dive on her.

Directions: Bird Island lies 5km west of the last boat launching site of Canty's Cove. The wreck lies 500m beyond the island just off the low rocky promontory that continues westwards while the main cliffs turn south. It is possible to pass between Bird Island and the mainland, but watch out for a nasty couple of rocks mid channel that only just show at high tide.

The simplest way to find the wreck is to start your dive close in about midway along the low pile of rocks in about 15m of water and then fin out into deeper water heading NW. The stern section of the ship with the (iron) prop still in place is in about 35m and stands 5m proud of the bottom. Note that no wreckage has been found below 40m at this site, so if you find yourself this deep, turn back!

9. Toor Pier

This site has been described under "Mizen Head" as far as shore diving is concerned, but it is a handy place to collect divers from if diving on the towering cliffs that run west towards Three Castle Head, rather than make the long journey from Canty's Cove with an overloaded boat. Having a boat at Toor Pier also allows you to dive on the outside of the island without having to worry about a long swim back to the pier. The coast just to the west of the island is not exceptional but if the weather is calm a trip of 3km brings you to the very end of the bay and some spectacular diving.

10. Three Castle Head

The southern end of Dunmanus Bay is reached at Three Castle Head where the 50m depth contour almost touches the shore and in fact the drop off is so fast that it is hard to find water shallow enough to drop anchor! The last 100m offers the very best of the diving with massive cliffs above and below water.

Below the surface extensive rock faces are covered in every kind of life and large shoals of fish abound. The best of the scenery is in the range 25-35m with the rocks tumbling down a further 25m below this again. A strong tidal current flows across the point so be careful not to venture into it if the tide is running. This site is exposed and isolated and requires calm weather, experienced divers and reliable boats to be dived safely, however the rewards well justify the extra effort.

11. South Bullig Reef

This very tricky site is actually an underwater extension of the cliffs of Three Castle Head. A narrow reef runs south west about 1km from the headland before finally giving way to the deep waters offshore. The last rock rises to within 6m of the surface with rock faces cascading down on three sides to 50m and beyond. As this is a very high energy site the fish life and underwater scenery is spectacular, but of course it can only be dived in very calm seas. It is also critical to dive only at slack water as with the steep drop offs the consequence of drifting off the rock on the descent means an aborted dive as you will never see the bottom before you reach your depth limit!

By lining up Bird Island and the cliffs at Three Castle Head so that they just touch, you will have the line of the reef and for those without an echo sounder the end of the reef can be found by dragging an anchor. Do not guess and be sure to use a shot line when divers go down. The nearest access point for picking up divers is Dunlough Pier which is about 1km southeast of the headland. (for directions – see Mizen Head, shore dives)

Local Facilities and Information

Compressor:	Schull Watersports Centre, Schull, Co. Cork Tel./Fax. 028 28554 Bantry Bay Divers, Glengarriff, Co. Cork Tel. 027 51310 Fax. 027 52175 E-mail: divebantry@aol.ie
Tidal Constant:	Dublin +05 10 min
Local VHF Radio:	Bantry Radio Ch. 16, 67, 23, 85
Local Chart No:	2552
Maps:	½":1 mile No.24 1:50,000 No. 88

Bantry Bay
Co. Cork

Bantry Bay is the longest of the many narrow bays that cut into the coastline of West Cork. The town of Bantry is situated at the head of the bay and the major fishing port of Castletownbere about halfway along the northern shore. The south shore is accessed by a minor road called the "Goat's Path". Turn right just after the West Lodge Hotel when leaving Bantry on the N71 heading south the road heads out to Sheep's Head some 30km away. The north side, which is more than 50km long, ends at Dursey Island with Kenmare River to the north. There is deep water right up the bay and this was the reason for siting a major oil terminal on Whiddy Island as it could accommodate the largest oil tankers in the world, however this is now effectively closed.

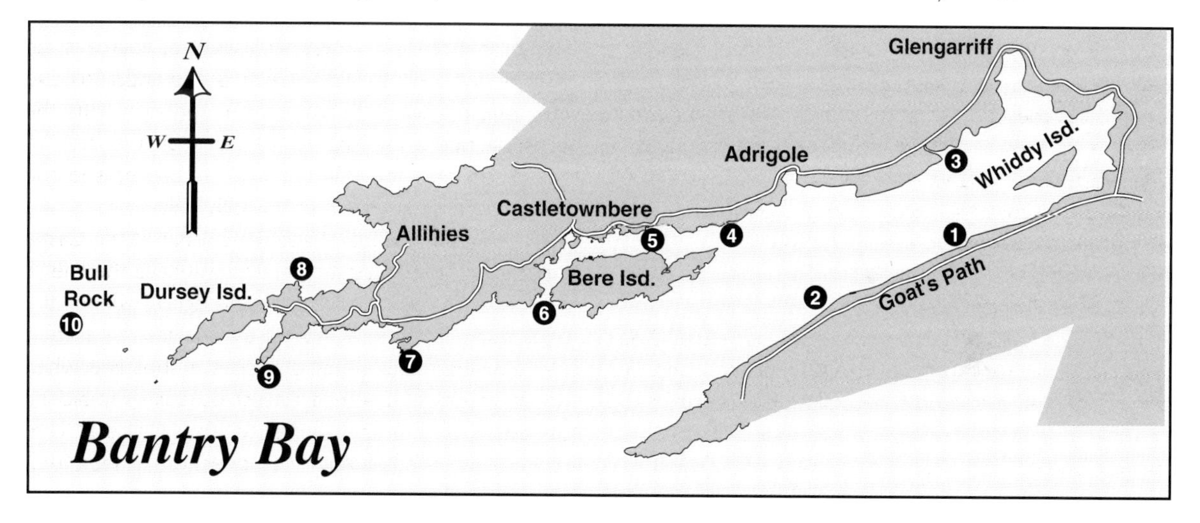

Bantry Bay South Dive Sites

The diving on the south shore is not spectacular with bare rock faces plunging rapidly into the depths with little growth. However, there are a couple of locations worth a mention.

1. Gerahies Pier

About 8km along the Goat's Path from the West Lodge Hotel is the small harbour of Gerahies with a good slip usable after half tide, giving access to the coastline to the west where there are some interesting gullies just beyond the pier. It is also possible to shore dive by entering the water a little east of the pier across a rocky reef.

2. Collack Pier

A further 8km along the Goat's Path there is a turn off to the right down to the water at Collack Pier. The access road is a little rough, but it should be possible to launch a medium sized boat here. There is no shelter from westerly winds, but on a calm day shore diving around the pier can be rewarding.

Bantry Bay North Dive Sites

It is 16km on the T65 from Bantry to the picturesque village of Glengarriff, where the road splits and the L61 heads off towards Castletownbere along the northern shores of Bantry Bay.

3. Zetland Pier

Seven kilometres beyond Glengarriff take a left turn marked "Zetland Pier" and follow the road down to the shore for 2km until you arrive at a charming open spot with a simple pier. While there is no slipway, it is possible to manhandle an inflatable into the water without much problem, while RIBs would have to be launched in Glengarriff (8km) or across the bay at Gerahies (5km). The area around the pier is suitable for snorkelling while the attraction for divers is Sheelane Island about 800m offshore.

At the western end of the island is a small outlying rock with a splendid open cave to explore. Beyond which the rocky bottom is covered with brittle and feather stars as it runs down into deeper water and life begins to peter out at around 30m.

4. Lonehort Point

About 16km beyond Glengarriff lies the straggling village of Adrigole dominated by Hungry Hill beyond. Five kilometres beyond the centre of the village (that part by the shore) take a left turn down to Bank Harbour which has a small pier suitable for inflatables. This is the best location for departures to the rocks and reefs to the east of Bere Island. There is a wreck of a Spanish trawler here, but it is completely dry on the rocks!

5. Bardini Reefer

Continuing west past the large campsite there is a left turn signposted for Bere Island Ferry, which brings you after 800m to a pleasant little harbour with a good slipway. About halfway across the bay towards Bere Island lies the wreck of the factory ship "Bardini Reefer" which sank about 10 years ago in 15m of water after catching fire while at anchor. Finding it is no problem as the masts are still showing above water! .

The wreck is almost complete and it is possible to poke your nose into some of the openings. Due to the gentle currents that bathe the wreck there is loads of growth on the superstructure. Given the shallow depth it is best to plan you dive for high water, when you can spend as long as you like exploring without going below 10m. Bere Haven can be dived when it is far too rough to dive in the open bay, however to appreciate it at its best, a day with good visibility is needed.

6. Spanish Trawler

This 30m long fishing boat struck the rocks just west of the entrance to Castletownbere and sank in 30m. It is still substantially intact and lying on its side. There are two slips at Castletownbere Harbour. The one at the far end of the pier complex is less public and more suitable for a group of divers and all their gear.

Directions: The wreck lies at the narrowest part of the western entrance to the harbour about 3.5km from the pier, exactly on the leading lights, which can be spotted in daylight by the fluorescent orange backing plates. Continue out to sea along this line until Sheep's Head appears across the bay from behind the cliffs of Bere Island. About 100m further and a house will appear between the rocks on the mainland and this is the second transit for the wreck. It is easily picked out with an echo-sounder.

Watch out for heavy trawler traffic that comes through the narrow channel, avoid Sunday afternoons when they all put to sea after the weekend!. Be sure to have your A-flag flying and your divers have SMBs and be on the constant lockout. It is possible to launch a smaller boat at Dunboy Castle and thus halve the journey to the wreck (head west out of the town on the L61 and turn left at the signpost after 1.5 km).

7. Black Ball Head

Head west out of Castletownbere on the L61, passing a junction to the right to Allihies after 10km. About 1km further a national school is passed on the right. Take the next left turn and then quickly right onto a narrow lane and Black Ball Harbour is reached after 1km. It is possible to launch medium sized boats across the rocky beach about 100m before the pier.

Heading out of the harbour and turning left, after 300m, brings you to the dark imposing cliffs of Black Ball Head. Here the cliffs rise 60m above the sea and plunge 45m underwater with hardly a pause. Finding a bottom to anchor in is quite a problem! The underwater scenery is marvellous with massive walls of rock carpeted with life running down to a sea floor of massive boulders. Enter the water very close to the cliffs in order to find 'shallow' water. This is obviously only suitable in calm conditions and slack water.

8. Garnish Pier

Continuing along the B61 westwards, the scenery gets wilder and wilder, but after driving through a narrow pass a valley opens up on the right with a road heading down at a junction signposted "Garnish Pier" (continue straight on here and after 2km you will reach the end of the road and the unique cable car connecting with Dursey Island).

Arriving at the pier there is lots of space with a good pier and slipway usable except at low water. There is even a nice sandy beach for relaxing on! The bay is quite sheltered and if it is too rough to dive 'outside' then interesting (and quite deep) diving can be had in the vicinity of the rocks, with a bollard on them, out to the right.

There are the remains of an old coal boat here. However when the conditions are right, the long journey to this remote spot is rewarded with superb diving around to the left beyond Garnish Point. If the tide is high it is possible to pass directly from the pier to the open sea, otherwise you must motor 1km around the islands. The whole area between the point and the entrance to Dursey Sound offers excellent diving with rock faces tumbling down to 40m and beyond. It is a very high energy site and thus rarely calm, however this also means the rocks are ablaze with life to 35m. This whole area offers a multitude of other top class dive sites suitable for the advanced diver when conditions are very calm.

9. Crow Head

After about 6km from Garnish Pier by boat, passing through Dursey Sound, you reach the long headland of Crow Head sticking out into Bantry Bay. There is a rock just awash just offshore and the whole area is an amazing jumble of massive rocks and boulders, some over 30m high in an area that is generally 40–45m deep. Great care is needed to avoid too much ascending and descending, but when the visibility is very good this is the nearest you will get to "flying". Obviously slack water is essential.

10. Bull Rock

For a major expedition off shore for a group with the right boats and personnel, look no further than Bull Rock, 5km beyond the end of Dursey Island and some 15km from Garnish Pier. This very impressive rock rises almost vertically from the sea on all sides to a height of 80m and is topped by a lighthouse. There is a large archway right through the middle of the rock, through which it is possible to take a dive boat, but watch out for the thousands of sea birds that nest on the cliffs! Although it is probably possible to dive in a tidal shadow, it makes sense to plan a dive here for slack water to reduce risks.

Excellent deep diving is assured here wherever you enter the water with the life running on well beyond safe diving depths. The helicopter landing pad, 60m above sea-level, was washed away by a wave during a storm some years ago, needless to say it needs to be exceptionally calm to dive here. There are two other offshore rocks nearby, the Cow and the Calf, equally impressive.

Local Facilities and Information

Compressor: Schull Watersport Centre,
Schull, Co. Cork
Tel. 028 28351
Fax. 028 28554

Bantry Bay Divers,
Main Street, Glengarriff,
Co. Cork
Tel. 027 51310
Fax. 027 52175
E-mail divebantry@aol.ie

Tidal Constant Dublin +05 02

Local VHF Radio: Bantry Radio
Ch. 16, 67, 23, 85

Local Charts Nos: 1838, 1840, 2495

Maps: H":1 mile No. 24
1:50,000 Nos. 84,85

Derrynane Co. Kerry

The name conjures up tales of smuggling and daring do in the times of Daniel O'Connell. The area offers a great deal to the visitor in terms of scenery and history as well as diving. Being on the famed ring of Kerry, Caherdaniel is easily found. Turn off the main Ring of Kerry road by Freddie's Pub and continue for 3.2km – bearing left – until you get to Derrynane pier. Alternatively if you find yourself at Derrynane House, Dan O'Connell's abode, turn left on exiting. When towing a boat choose the former route. There is one slipway; this allows you to launch the boat on all but the highest of tides. There is ample parking nearby. The diving is varied and will suit all tastes.

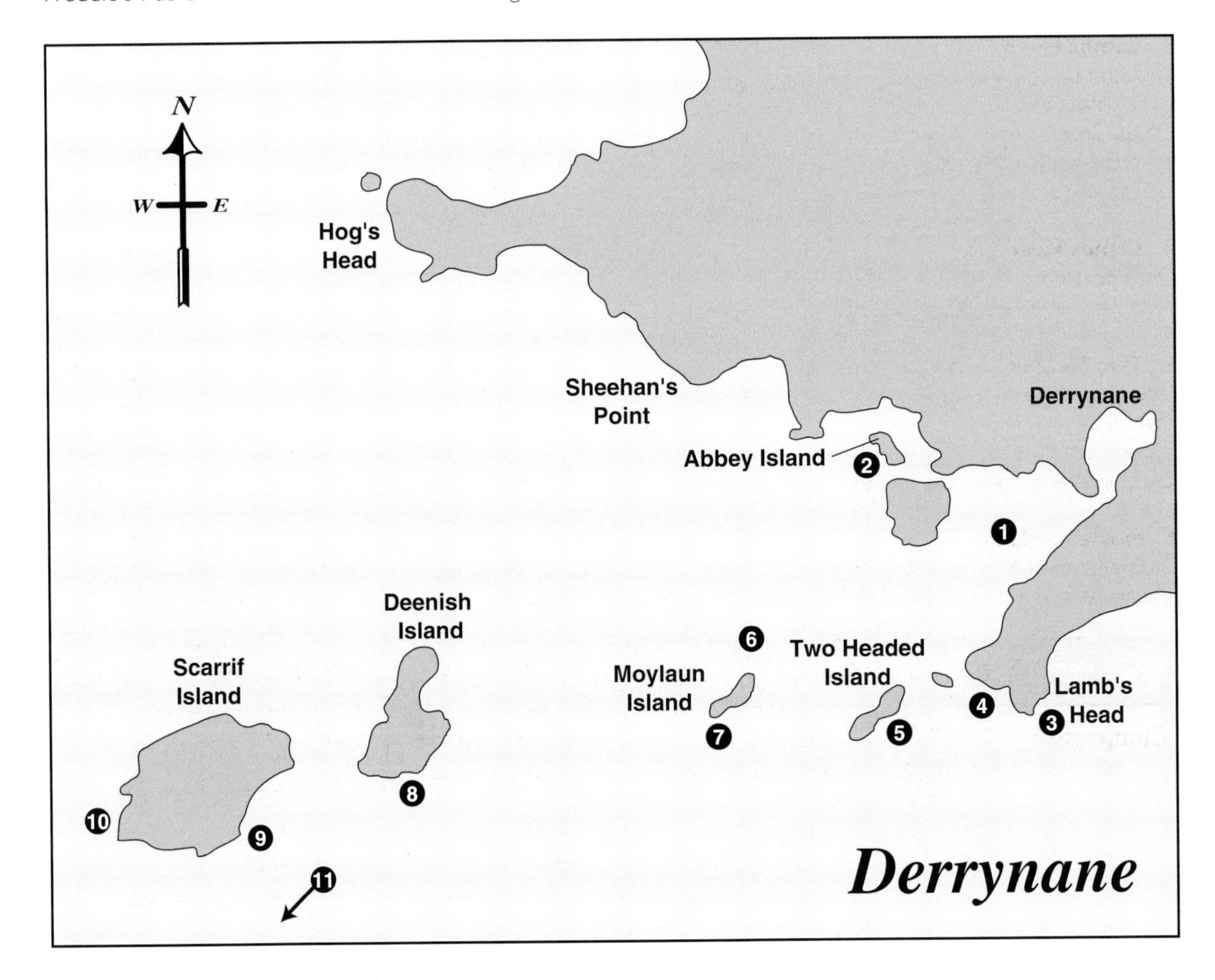

Dive Sites

1. Derrynane Harbour

An ideal site for a first trainee's dive. If the tide allows begin at Lambs Island at the harbour mouth, head inwards following the shoreline. Who knows what you might find. A cannon and anchors were found here a few years ago from a previously unknown shipwreck. It is a safe night dive in 3–10m with plenty of life. There is marvellous snorkelling about here as there is an interesting rocky bottom at about three metres on the seaward side of the harbour. A narrow channel leads to the sea in the SW corner of the harbour This is a great snorkel as it is full of life.

2. Abbey Island

From the boat you can see a major vertical crack in the rock face. Enter this, continue to a T junction. Look out for iron bars from an ore ship at 10–20 metres. A schooner, the "Ethel B Jacobs", was wrecked on Abbey Island in 1899. A handy night dive is a circumnavigation of the island. The bottom is sand at six metres but there is life in the rocks.

3. Lambs Head (1)

This must be one of the best shore dives in Kerry. It makes a fine default dive if you end up with less than a boat crew. On the Sneem side of Caherdaniel make a right turn down an incline and continue to the road's end. There is a pier with parking space and an easy entrance or exit.

4. Lambs Head (2)

On a boat from Derrynane dive the southern tip of the head. The odd seal and porpoise has been seen here.

5. Two Headed Island

One third of the way along the SE side there is a lovely cave. Stay at the 6m level to find the entrance. Even without a lamp you can enter and see the exit on your left. Continue on for a comfortable dive to 20m.

6. Moylaun Island

Drop in at the NW corner and head south. You will find a ledge at about 14m with a vertical drop off to 40m. Look for a gully further down the west side. Bring a lamp as it is a dead end. On the way out about 3m to the left side look out for "Andy" the resident conger.

7. Moylaun Rock

Southwest of the main island it does not look much from the surface but is a hive of activity below. Dead mens fingers cover the rock. All types of schooling fish mill around. Find the lee side and dive a zig zag course back up from the maximum depth of 31m.

8. Deenish Island

Steer clear of the fish farm and dive the southern side to 25m if conditions allow. Seals are often to be seen.

9. Scarriff Island – Lamb's Cove

Drop in on the southern side close to the cliff into about 6m with some kelp covering the rocky ledge, at about 8m a cliff edge comes into view which descends to over 30m. Swim east towards Lambs cove. It is sheltered both for kitting up and recovery of divers.

10. Scarriff Island – The Hedges

There are good gulleys to explore at the Hedges on the west side of Scarriff. The depth is up to 30m.

11. The Bull

The Bull Rock just off Dursey Island, is only about within range of Derrynane. The Bull is the largest of three rocky islands called The Bull, The Cow and The Calf and is dominated by a light house. A feature of the rock is the large cavern through which trawlers and other fishing boats can pass under the lighthouse. The wide range of potential sites is obvious.

One interesting site is a reef to the North of the Rock. The reef is made up of a series giant steps of about 5m and descends to over 35m. The edge of the reef was serrated like a saw with an abundance of life. Like most dives in the area all the rocks are covered with jewel anemones, sponges and soft corals. Currents can be strong in the reef area and SMBs are recommended.

Local Facilities and Information

Compressor: Skellig Aquatics Ltd.,
Caherdaniel, Co. Kerry.
Tel. 066 75277
Fax. 066 75277
E-mail: skelliga@iol.ie

Tidal Constant: Dublin +05 58 min.

Local VHF station: Valentia Radio Ch.16, 24

Chart: 2459, 2423.

Maps: ½":1mile No 20, 24
1:50,000 No. 83, 84

The Skelligs

The Skelligs are one of the dive jewels in Ireland's crown. Every dive boat available, trawlers, half-deckers, RIBS, inflatables from every creek between Dingle and Derrynane wants to make the journey there. Little wonder that they do, this magical place still amazes and excites like a new-found discovery time after time. It is here that the warm Gulf Stream first touches the Irish coast, bringing its frequent, international visitors to the Skelligs, trigger fish, basking sharks, minke whale, and the occasional leatherback turtle. A wreck-fish which may have followed a piece of flotsam half way across the Atlantic could suddenly decide that the shadow of your boat offered a better habitat for the day.

But, apart from exotic visitors, Nature has run riot in local fish life – in colours, in jewelled walls, in grey seals who will always arrive wide-eyed and curious to inspect the latest human intruders; in feathered fellow-divers – guillemots, razorbills and puffins, who 'fly' on elbow-bent

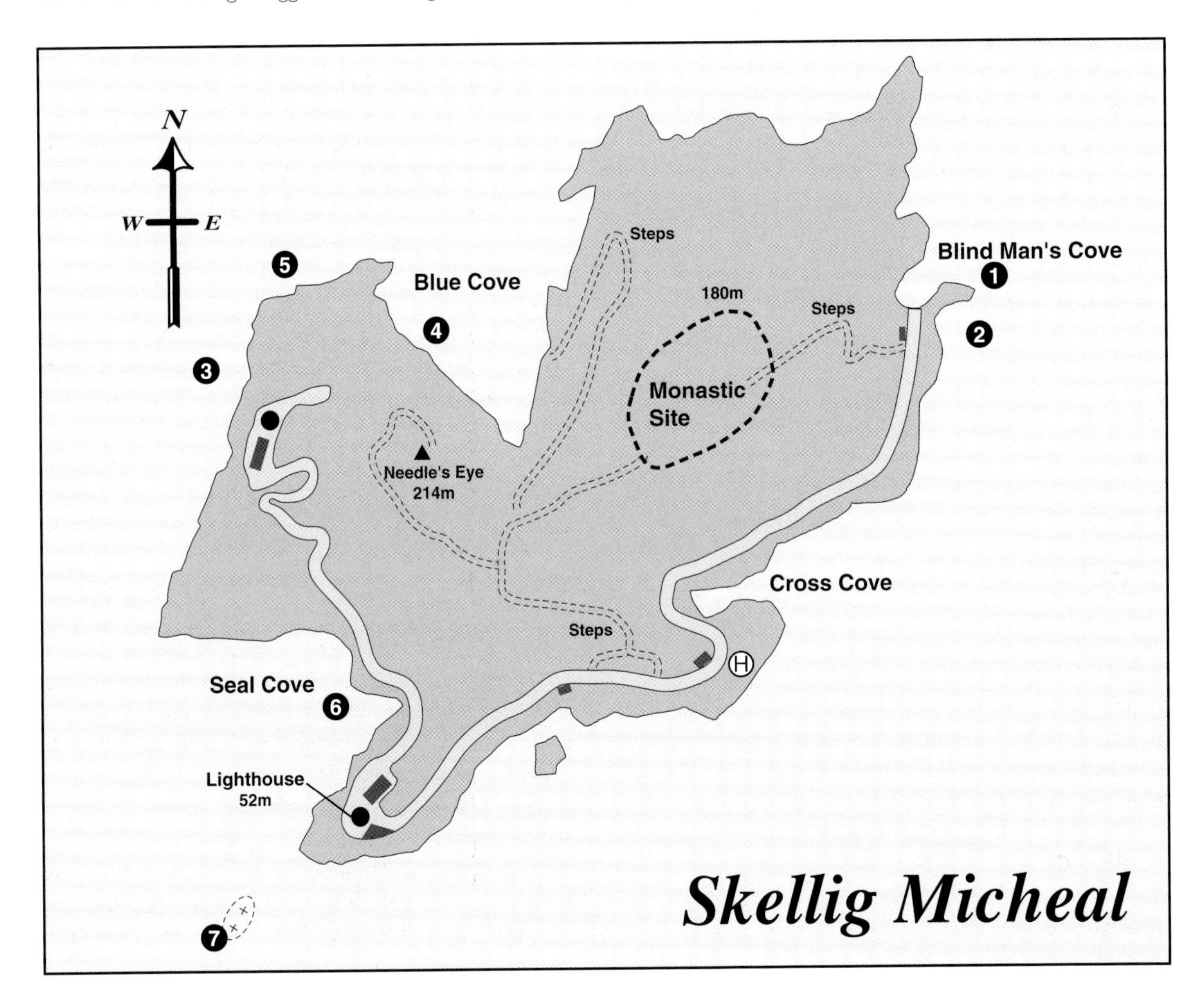

wings as adroitly, or perhaps better, underwater than they do in air. And gannets, the Little Skellig is home to 25,000 pairs, which will create an aerobatic fuss above your head and thus signal your presence to the skipper if you surface too far away from the dive-boat

At the Skelligs, what you see is what you get, the landscape overhead is a good indication of what lies below. Steep cliffs continue as sheer walls, bird-filled ledges continue as jagged steps, reaching down to 40m. on the south side of the island and 55m on the exposed north side before any trace of the bottom appears. Most visitors need look no further than these obvious sites, but given slack water and good conditions, the more adventuresome may wish to seek out some of the islands' offshore reefs.

At the summit of Skellig Micheal, which is accessed by climbing almost 700 steps, are the remains of a monastic settlement dating from the eighth century. This settlement is well worth the long climb. However, a permit is required to land on the Skelligs and not all dive operators have one. Check with them before hand if you wish to see the settlement and there is no point in going to the Skelligs if you do not! A landing permit may only be obtained from the Office of Public Works.

Skellig Micheal Dive Sites

1. Blindman's Cove

Skellig can be a shore-dive! You can step off the landing place at Bind Man's Cove and glide down into a vast field of rose coral in a minute. But this fairway is busy with passenger boat traffic in season and it would be better to settle for any of the many, many boat-dive options.

2. Landing Pinnacle

An easier, more sheltered pinnacle – built, it would appear, of mauve, lilac and lime-green corinactis – stands about 50m south of Skellig Michael's Blind Man's Cove landing place. Well hidden, since the sea never breaks on it, the tip of this column is about 15m from the surface and 45m from the sea bed. Nearby shore marks for this reef are convenient. A particular handrail stanchion which unlike its immediate neighbours has a cube-shaped concrete base will be in transit with the southern gable of the nearby flat-roofed Rope Store.

3. Old Lighthouse Reef

About 100m NW of Skellig's old, ruined North Station lighthouse lies another sunken reef which is almost awash at low water. Even on a very calm day, the telltale swirl of water will advertise this site. Again, seldom fished, it is another shellfish outpost – except on its western face where only a crab could cling to its 60m. drop off!

4. Blue Cove

You must dive Skellig Michael's Blue Cove, keeping an eye out for a cross-inscribed stone slab which disappeared – presumably fell – in recent times from the monastic hermitage archaeological site at the island's sheer, overhanging South Peak, 219m above the sea.

5. US Navy PB4Y-I

The cliff face about 100m west of Blue Cove is a must. Here there is a chance, an off-chance, of finding something, anything, from a US navy PB4Y-I Liberator bomber which hit the South Peak and plunged into the sea without survivors or wreckage in February 1944.

6. Seal Cove

Another un-missable dive is Seal Cove! Seals, yes, but this is also where a complete lighthouse, together with all its history, was dumped into the sea in 1963! An engraved lighthouse telescope of 1950 found here at 30m. by local diver Billy Rafter and is now a treasured exhibit at the Skellig Experience visitor centre on Valentia.

7. Washerwoman's Rocks

The Washerwoman's Rocks situated 1 cable southwest from the Lighthouse Point are a very visible outcrop of rocks indicating a reef which runs southwestwards and are an excellent dive site. It is recommended to dive these at slack water to avoid tides. Descending at the middle rock, underwater the pinnacles merge into a reef which is both colourful and abounds with fish life. Depths range from shallow to 40m and at a leisurely rate the reef can be circumnavigated in one dive. Lobster, crayfish, squat lobster, crab, shoals of pollock, wrasse and many anenomes are to be found on this dive. Care must be taken as nets and pots are often placed in this area. Use of the diver down flag is essential on this, as on all sites at Skellig.

Little Skellig Dive Sites

8. Cannon Cove

But enough of reefs! We must do a dive to inspect the ancient iron cannons and anchors in Small Skellig's western cove. These 18/19th century artefacts are scattered on the jagged ledges from 16m onwards. But wondering what may lie hidden in the rough gravel 35m down is still the stuff that diving dreams are made of.

9. Crawfish Reef

Another reef worth considering lies about 50m NW of Small Skellig's NW point. With a conspicuous daylight slot visible through the heart of the island, your echosounder will easily find this reef, which soars from 60m to 10m. Seldom fished because of its exposed position, this reef appears to be the home of all crawfish.

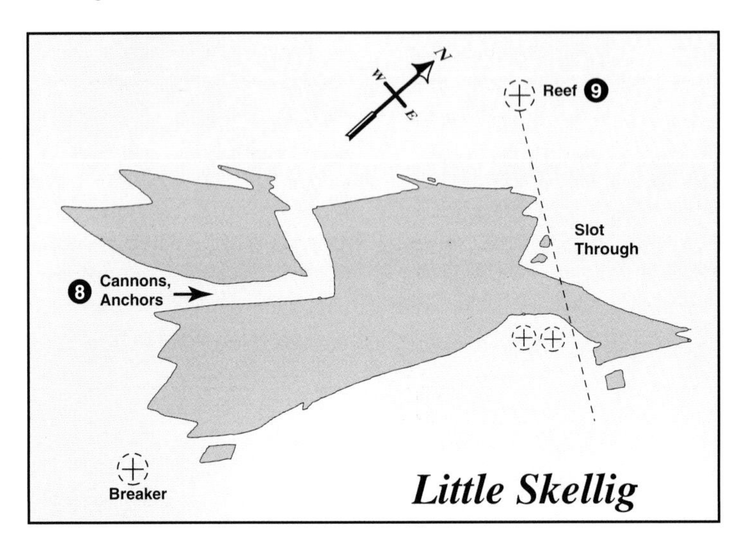

Local Facilities and Information

Compressor:	Des & Pat Lavelle Valentia Dive Centre, Valentia Tel 066 76124 Fax. 066 76309 Valentia Island Sea Sports Knightstown, Valentia Island Tel. 066 76204Fax. 066 76367 Ballinskelligs Watersports Dungegan, Ballinskelligs, Co. Kerry Tel. 066 79182 / 025 32531 Fax. 066 79303 / 021 509907
Tidal constant:	Dublin +04 33
Local VHF station:	Valentia Radio Ch. 16, 67, 24, 28.
Chart:	2495
Maps:	½":1 mile No. 20 1:50000 No. 83

St Finan's Bay
Co. Kerry

St. Finan's bay is situated in the heart of the Ring of Kerry, it is the stopping point for the tourists and divers of many countries. The area offers spectacular scenic, adventurous and as yet, many unexplored dive sites, an ideal working ground for the serious photographer and naturalist. The crystal clear, unpolluted waters are home to a variety and abundance of life that is hard to equal. There are also a limited number of wreck sites for the wreck diver. There is a great deal to do between dives and the non diving members of the party will not be disappointed either as a lovely unspoilt beach is one of the main local attractions.

The local pier, which is situated in an extremely sheltered inlet, is suitable and safe for the overnight mooring of boats. There are two slipways off the pier, suitable for the launching of RIBs and inflatables. The lane way leading to the pier is a little narrow and caution should be observed while travelling on it, especially while towing a boat as the turning points are limited. However, a little prior planning can ease the situation.

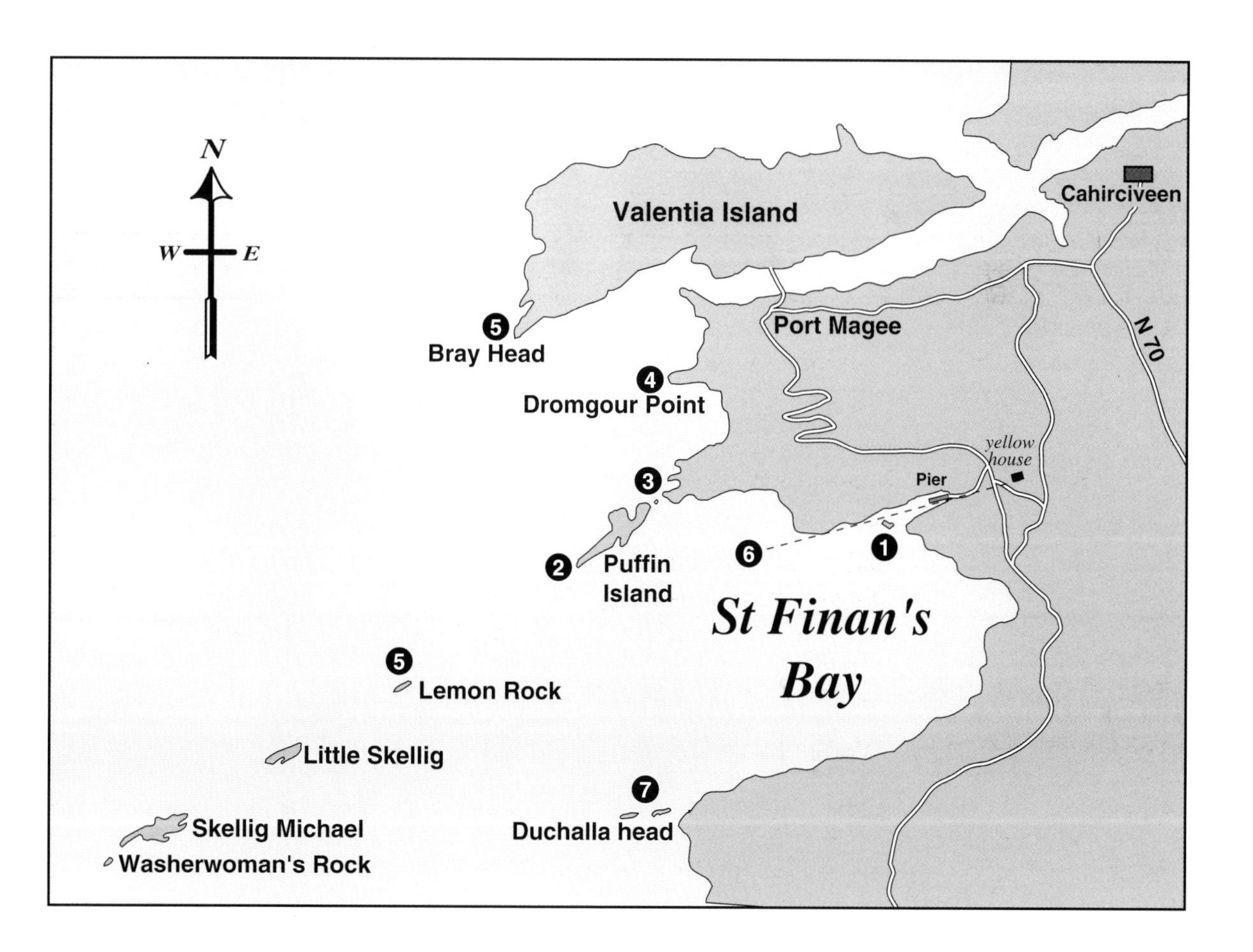

Dive Sites

1. St. Finan's Bay

Diving in the area is centred on the local pier which is situated in an extremely sheltered and clean inlet. The inlet itself is eminently suitable for introductory dives and beginner training. Its clear waters and sandy bottom are full of life and flatfish are plentiful. The waters vary in depth from 5–10m and it is very suitable for swimmers and snorkellers.

A large rocky outcrop protects the narrow inlet -- like a stopper in a bottle. The depth here varies from 10–25m. From the outcrop, rocky fingers spread down and out into the sandy bottom like the arms of an octopus. The sheltered gullies between them provide a haven for many species of fish and crustacean. As the distance from the pier is only about 500m, it makes an ideal location for an evening or night dive. The well lit pier makes night diving a joy and safety is guaranteed.

The diving all along the coast west from the pier and on to Puffin Island is excellent, with depths from 10–30m on a white sandy bottom. Ridges and reefs abound with a multitude of gullies interrupting the underwater landscape. The waters here are generally calm except in strong south westerly winds with virtually no current and it is an excellent location for novice and experienced divers alike. The fish life in the gullies and on top of the reefs can be prolific due to the shelter offered by the ragged rock faces.

2. Puffin Island

Puffin Island is 10 min. by RIB from the pier, it offers an endless choice of dive sites in relatively sheltered waters. All areas of the island are diveable and the underwater landscape mirrors the overwater landscape, sheer rock faces and craggy outcrops. The island which is a bird sanctuary is home to many seabirds, in particular puffins, during the breeding season. The diving is relatively safe and sheltered on most sides of the island.

WARNING! The currents on Puffin Head at certain times and states of the tide can be treacherous and instantaneous. Puffin Head is for the experienced divers only and should be treated with care. The Atlantic swell at Puffin Head and on the northern side of the island can be enormous, depending on the weather conditions. Again, common sense is required. Diver SMBs are essential here.

Having issued the words of warning, the diving on Puffin Head is spectacular. Two large reefs splay south-westwards from the tip of the island, plunging down sheer cliff faces to about 50m at the bottom.

Slack tide, with strong sunlight streaming through crystal clear waters makes this a most memorable dive site. The strong currents have "close shaved" all the algae from the rock, and one gets the impression of a "bald head' while diving on the top of the reefs. The sheltered nooks and crannies are covered in an abundance of sponges and "bejewelled" anemones of all types. The fish and crustacean life is outstanding. Early mornings often see dolphins and pilot whales on the surface. Puffin Head is guaranteed to provide an exciting and spectacular dive every time.

3. Puffin Island Sound

The other spectacular diving on Puffin Island is in the area of the sound. Obviously, current and wave states dictate if it is diveable. A drift dive from the north side through the sound is magnificent given the proper conditions of sunlight and water clarity, it is the closest to "tropical" diving you can come across in European waters. The variety and quantity of fish and sponge life is phenomenal. In September and October, huge shoals of mackerel and scad circle the sound incessantly, while legions of huge pollack wait on the far side of the sound, like a phalanx of Greek warriors, holding in the current, and waiting to attack any food coming their way. Seals also maintain a permanent presence in the sound and add their measure of excitement to the diving.

4. Dromgour Point

Diving anywhere west of the sound, along the coast to Valentia, is also excellent. Special attention should be paid to Dromgour Point. This ended up as the final resting point of the "Crompton", a four masted barque, which ran aground and was wrecked in 1910. It is now badly broken up, but beautiful visibility and fish life make it an ideal second dive as she lies in relatively shallow waters. Travelling time from the pier is about 15–20 min.

5. Lemon Rock

Lemon Rock lies about half-way to the Skelligs and is also well worth a visit. The rock itself is a microcosm of the whole surrounding area. Off the south face there is beautiful scenic diving down to 37m. Two light iron anchors lie together on a large flat rock, evidence of a mishap at sea some time in the past. More evidence lies on top of the rock itself. To the north side there are beautiful terraces for a stepped descent as far as you want to go.

6. The Montana Bank

The loveliest and calmest of the local offshore reefs is the uncharted Montana – 18–55m. First dived about 1993, it got its name because a popular member of the dive-crew, hailed from that US state! The Montana Reef lies 750m SE of Puffin Island Sound, with the 'Glen' pier in transit with Florry Moriarty's two-storey, yellow house.

7. Duchalla Head

Duchalla Head, about 20 min. distance by RIB, and southeast from the pier in Finan's Bay, is also well worth noting. The outer rocks are only suitable for experienced and fit divers as the currents and swell can be difficult. The ledges drop straight down to 50m in places and again, as in the rest of the area, the fish and crustacean life is abundant. There are a multitude of canyons, gullies, rock outcrops, drop off's and holes.

One of the greatest pleasures is to stop on a ledge at about 20m and look down into the clear dark depths below. After a few moments the pollack, ballan and cuckoo wrasse rise out of the depths. They have not learned to be afraid of the diver and are very inquisitive. The cuckoo wrasse in particular are very curious and adventurous. Conger eels, ling and angler fish are common among the many cracks and fissures in the rocks, particularly in the deeper, clearer waters. It is also common to find large cod and conger cohabiting in the same crevice. It's hard to know what they find in common, but there is some mutual bond between them.

Local Facilities and Information

Compressor:	Atlantic Divers, St Finan's Bay Valentia Island Sea Sports Knightstown, Valentia Island, Co. Kerry Tel. 066 76204 Fax. 066 76367 Des & Pat Lavelle's Valentia Diving Centre, Valentia, Co. Kerry Tel 066 76124 Fax. 066 76309
Tidal Constant:	Dublin +04 58
Local VHF station:	Bantry Radio Ch. 16, 67, 23, 85 Valentia Radio Ch. 16, 67, 24, 28
Chart:	2495
Maps:	½":1 mile Nos. 20,24 1:50,000 No. 83

Valentia Island
Co. Kerry

Launching Sites

Valentia harbour is well served with launching and berthing facilities.

A. Knightstown village has three slipways and a good pier with shelter from the south, west and north. Be careful not to obstruct the slip as access is a vital part of the lifeboat operation.

B. Renard Point on the nearby mainland has a deepwater pier which is in a derelict state, but its related slipway is spacious and uncluttered.

C. Carriglea, on Valentia's southern shore boasts a small slipway although the room to manoeuvre a car and trailer is rather limited. Turn left at the top of bridge road and travel 100m, turn left and continue to bottom of the road.

D. Portmagee village has safe deepwater pier and a good slipway, but again, car access to this slip may be a little difficult in a busy season.

All these local piers are well used in commercial activity

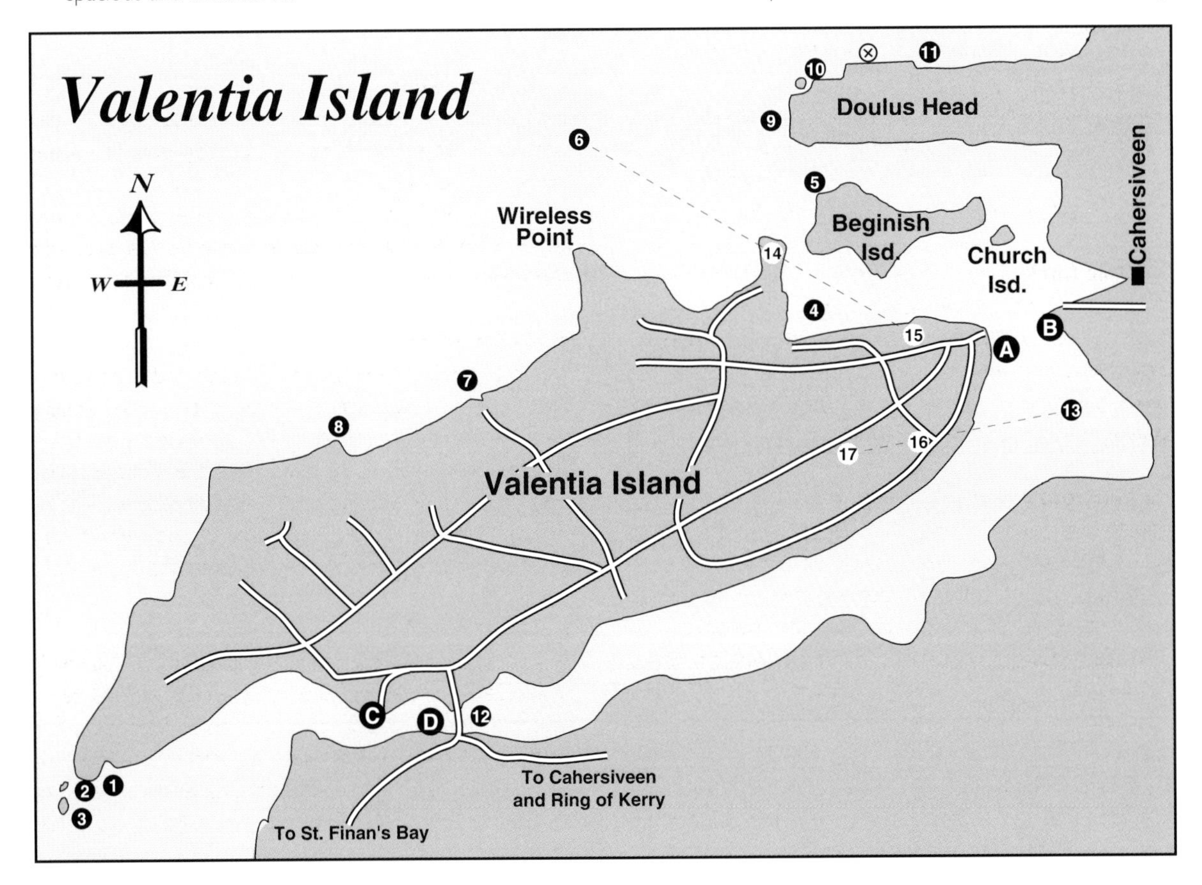

Dive Sites

and visiting boat-handlers should be considerate in the occupancy of berths for any extended period.

Valentia is mostly boat-diving territory. One can enter the water on foot from any beach within the 6 mile (9.66km) long harbour area and from a few rock faces, but a boat is essential for access to the best cliff faces.

1. Cubs Diarmuid (Divela)

On the southern side of the island and 150m east of Bray Head is Cubs Diarmuid. Depths vary from 16–30m and beyond. The terrain is boulders with cliff face, drop offs and ledges. Kelp is plentiful and may be avoided by swimming southwards from the cliff face to a depth of 20–25m. Strong tides prevail if one swims too far south. Flood tides sweep in and eastwards. An SMB is advisable. Rose coral is found below 25m. Wrasse, pollack, conger eel, velvet crab, brown crab, lobster and crabs are plentiful. It is a photographers paradise.

2. Bray Head

To the west of Cubs Diarmuid, Bray Head is more exposed to the elements and the diving is similar. A feature, however, is the presence of diving seabirds. These can be razorbill, guillemot and puffin. Seals also regularly check out the intruders and can nibble a fin when in playful mood, which is the only time they are evident.

3. Spit Rocks

Another great dive and many of the species encountered in the previous locations occur here. At Bray Head and Spit Rocks the tides differ in that they tend to sweep outwards and north in a flood tide and outwards and south in an ebb tide.

4. Harbour Rock

Situated within the harbour this rock is marked by a metal perch and light. Depending on the state of the tide a depth of 12m is attainable. It is an ideal location for a novice or trainee dive. Visibility varies from 4m after rainfall to 12m. The life includes anemones, deadmen's fingers, wrasse pollack, lobster, conger eel, shrimp, starfish, urchins, scallop, squat lobster and shoals of mackerel in season.

5. Basalt Cliffs

On the NW side of Beginish Island the cliffs offer depths from 8–30m. There are dropoffs, ledges, boulders, caves and fish life. If a swell is running caution is needed especially in a NW wind.

When leaving the harbour it is advisable to stay close to the Valentia (lighthouse) side. The eastern corner of Beginish is dangerous to all vessels if white water is evident.

6. Coastguards Patch

This is a rather inaccessible location marked on the charts. The bank is easily found with an echosounder and a transit of the lighthouse tower (14) and Jeremiah O'Connell's house (15). It is governed by tides which can be strong. The best time to dive is at slack water on neap tides. A marked shot line and depth sounder are advisable. As the pinnacle begins at 24m and continues to 45m+ a shot line is necessary to avoid missing the peak. If conditions are suitable and the tides slack the rock can be circumnavigated. The visibility is usually 20m+. The area is frequently fished so nets and pots may be encountered.

7. Black Islands

This is an interesting but shallow dive. Gullies run westwards from the shore. It is best to enter between the islands, submerge and swim northeast in a flood tide or southwest during an ebb tide. The ridges vary in depth from 4–12m and deeper away from shore. Kelp abounds and visibility is usually good. Fish life is profuse.

8. Culoo Head

This is a famous shore angling location and a good dive site. Entering just west of the head (to avoid angling tackle) and swimming WSW you come upon a crater like bottom. Some very large holes have the stone in place which caused the crater. Shoals of mackerel are common in season. It is possible to encounter a shoal which lasts the duration of the dive, this is an exhilarating experience.

9. Dolus Head

This is the most prominent head just north of Valentia in Dolus Bay. Descending close to the cliff one will see a cavern at 9m divided in two by a column of rock. It is possible to enter on one side, swim into the interior, and exit the other side. The floor of the cavern is covered by a carpet of mussels. The column is home to jewel anenomies. In good visibility no torch will be needed. There is a shelf at 18m and further shelves continue to beyond 30m. On ebb tides descend at the headland and swim southward while on flood tide swim northward.

10. Oilean an Iasc

North of Dolus head is an inlet with a large rock in the centre. There is ample room for two boats to manoeuvre in safety on the south side. In ideal conditions this is a wonderful dive site. There is spectacular scenery in every direction. Fish life is abundant and the anenomies are a particular feature. It is possible for divers to swim around the rock, and swimming from the inside, keeping the cliff face to the left, an old mast can be seen close to the rock.

11. The Birds

Hugging the coast NE from Dolus head and avoiding the reef (X) you come to a cliff face which is home to razorbills, kittiwakes and guillemots (hence the name). The sea bottom at the eastern end of the cliff is at 16–18m. The underwater cliff face is covered with life. Little ledges are host to many species of crab, lobster and crayfish; pollack swim nonchalantly by, wrasse are plentiful, and many cuckoo wrasse are inquisitive. In late spring or early summer it is possible to find intact bird's eggs which have fallen from the nests above. Properly treated these make a lovely memento of your visit. Continue to swim westwards as the terrain and the life change. To the north the depth increases to 20–25m but the sealife is less interesting.

12. Valentia Bridge

So, the worst has happened: it is blowing westerly force 8! Do not retire to the pub in dismay; Valentia bridge is eminently divable in these conditions. Make your boat fast to the bridge's central pier at 1 hour and 20 minutes before high water. Let the hurricane now blow as it will, you can dive in clear, still water between the plumose-anemone clad pier piles. The depth is only 8m, but the sea-life is even deeper! Mussels grow on the wooden fenders, and then fall to the bottom where every other creature of the sea assembles for the feast!

13. The Granat

Within the shelter of Valentia harbour at a depth of 11m, this wreck is ideal for an easy second dive, and only 650m southeast of Knightstown Pier. The wreck of this wooden trawler is home to congers, lobsters, and shoals of colourful small pouting. It is the only echosounder blip on an otherwise flat bottom. Miss Smith's house (16) in transit with Daly's new barn (17) is the line for this.

Night Diving (A)

The Main pier at Knightstown is an excellent location for safe, shallow night diving. The pier itself is alive with fish. Lobster, shrimp, conger, crab, pouting, mullet, starfish, octopus, sand dog and bearded rockling can be seen. It is the ideal place to introduce divers to the pleasures of sea life at night.

Local Facilities and Information

Compressor:	Des & Pat Lavelle's Dive Centre Tel 066 76124 Fax. 066 76309 Valentia Island Sea Sports Knightstown, Valentia Island. Tel. 066 76204Fax. 066 76367
Tidal constant:	Dublin + 04 59
Local VHF station:	Valentia Ch. 16, 67, 24, 28
Chart:	2125, 2423
Maps:	½":1 mile No. 20 1:50,000 No. 83

The Skelligs *Photo: Nigel Motyer*

Fungie the Dingle dolphin *Photo: Nigel Motyer*

Jewel anenomies *Photo: Nigel Motyer*

Angler fish – Valentia *Photo: Nigel Motyer*

Plaice – Derrynane *Photo: Nigel Motyer*

Blenny – Carraroe *Photo: Nigel Motyer*

Nudibranch on feather duster worms – Killary ***Photo: Nigel Motyer***

Juvenile whiting in lion's mane jellyfish ***Photo: Nigel Motyer***

Plumose anenomie *Photo: Nigel Motyer*

Diver and overhang – Connemara   *Photo: John Collins*

Dingle and the Blaskets Co. Kerry

Located approximately 40 minutes drive west of Tralee, via either the main road (N86) through Annascaul or the spectacular Connor Pass (not recommended for trailers), it has some of the finest restaurants and drinking houses in the country. Divers will be impressed with the warmth and efficiency of the local people. The new Dingle Harbour Marina provides an excellent base with a massive slip way and ample car parking.

A snorkel with Fungie, the famous "tame" dolphin, can be enjoyable early in the morning or late in the evening. Because of the amount of spectator boats, caution needs to be exercised by coxswains and divers.

Diving in the area is very much affected by the weather and careful attention must also be given to the local tide conditions which can be very treacherous. For best visibility around the Blaskets, the first hour of the flood tide seems to be the time to dive.

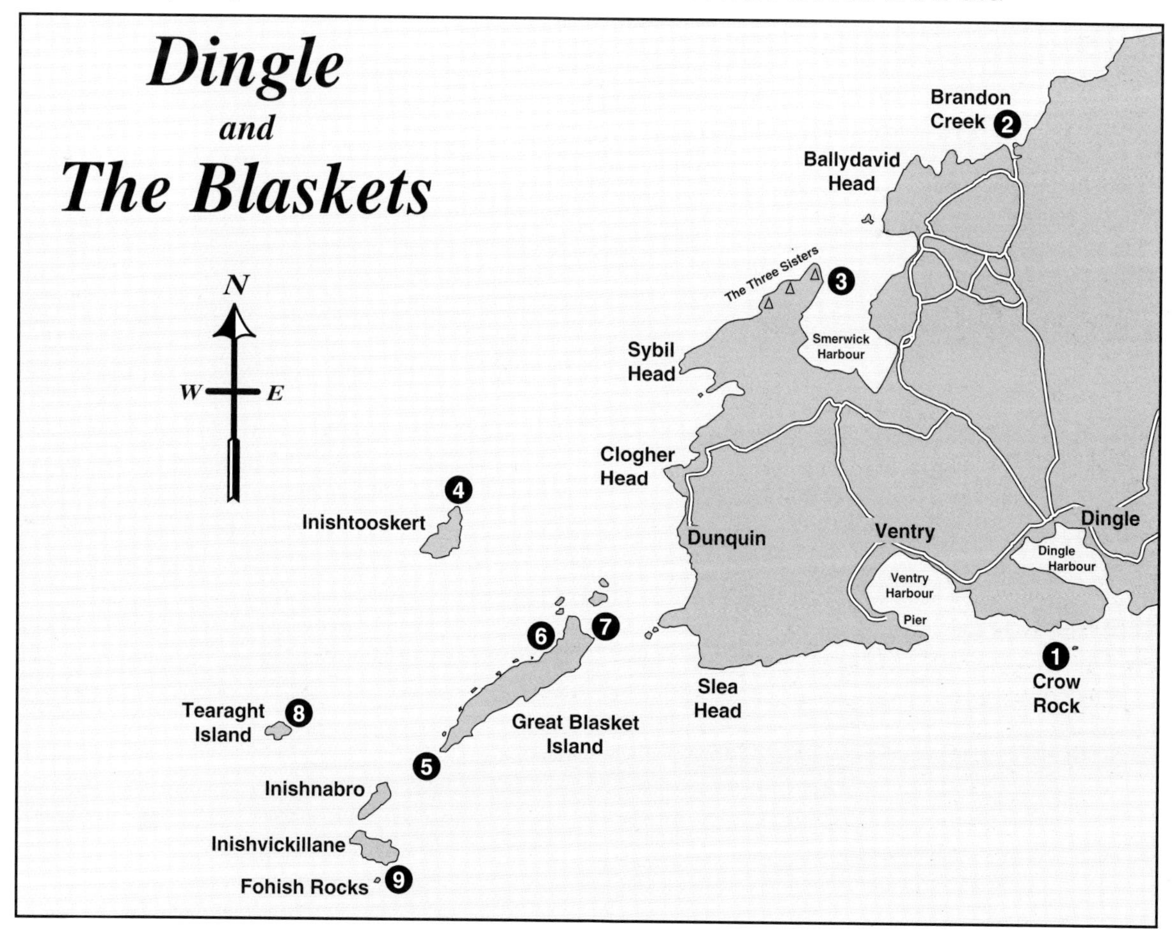

Dingle Dive Sites

1. The Crow Rock

Located approximately 800m southwest of the Dingle Harbour entrance the Crow Rock provides a comprehensive range of diving in calm southwesterlies or strong northerlies. It is generally clearly visible being awash through all but the highest spring tides. The north face of the rock has a ledge at 15m sloping down to sand at 20m. A colourful 15–20m dive is available moving west from the rock while the south face slopes down rapidly to boulders at 35 m.

2. Brandon Creek

Twelve kilometres from Dingle on the north of the peninsula Brandon Creek provides excellent diving in strong southerly winds. It is a beautiful cove with a reasonable slip and pier which is usable 2 hours after low water. Just at the head of the creek on the west side there is a sea arch which provides lovely snorkelling and leads down to a 18m dive towards the centre of the creek.

Moving either east or west out of the cove there is excellent wall diving with the bottom generally starting at 30m and dropping away deeper very quickly. Visibility in settled conditions is generally 20m plus and marine life is plentiful and varied.

3. Smerwick Harbour

As a strong westerly wind will make most dives around the Blaskets and the peninsula uncomfortable your only escape may be Smerwick Harbour on the north coast. Launching from Wine Strand, interesting shallow dives, maximum depth 15m, may be made along the western side of the harbour. If you need to log deep dives then you can generally get whatever depth you require in the middle of the bay, on sand. The further out you go, the deeper it gets. Outside the harbour to the southwest under the Three Sisters and Sybil Head there is excellent wall diving.

Blasket Island Dive Sites

Those looking for more adventurous diving should consider an expedition to the Blasket Islands. I say expedition as diving here should not be taken lightly. The Blaskets, the most westerly islands in Europe, is a cluster of seven islands, islets and rocks.

Looking out at the archipelago from Slea Head on the mainland; Inisvickillane is to the southwest; Inishnabro to the west; and further west, behind the Great Blasket, is Tearaght Island, with its lighthouse; to the north lies Inistooskert; and off the east are Beiginis and Oilean na nOg. The Great Blasket sits in the centre of this cluster of islands.

They are exposed to swells from southeast right around to north, the southwesterly and northwesterly swells being the most serious. Strong tides run in the sound, and western passage. The 100m contour is located only 5km west of the Terraght, with a result that whales are a common sight from August to October.

If you prefer to travel by inflatable then a convenient launching place is the beach opposite the Dun An Oir Hotel near Sybil Point. RIBs can be launched from the slip in Ventry Harbour. For obvious reasons it is recommended that no fewer than two well-equipped boats be used.

4. Inishtooskert

The most northerly island has excellent diving on the easterly face (drop off from 15–40m) and in the cove on south west face 15–20m with nice gullies and lots of life including seals.

At the most northerly tip of this rocky pinnacle there is a most spectacular dive. Starting at the tip (during slack water as there are rip tides in this area) and heading in a southwesterly direction with the reef to the right you will descend to 15m, maintaining this direction you come after a few metres, to the top of a wall which is covered in jewel anemones, sponges, cracks and crevices for crabs and crayfish.

The maximum depth here is approx. 40m. Following this wall the direction swings more NW and you enter a gully which eventually narrows into an undersea cave. With the aid of a torch one can follow this cave for a short distance to find it blocked by a boulder.

Keeping the reef wall to your right, the gully begins to open at about 20m. Here there is a series of outcrops and ledges with plenty of life. The general direction of the dive is SW and these ledges and small gullies fade away into a flatter but craggier terrain. In general this is a terrific dive site, with good shelter from most winds, and a range of depths making it suitable for all types of divers.

5. The Three Brothers

One of two good wrecks lying off the Great Blasket Island this is a 30m steel fishing boat lying between 18–30m near the southwest point of the island. The hull is sound and clean and so provides an excellent introduction to wreck diving to the uninitiated. The exact position of this wreck is not known, to the writer, so local knowledge is required to find it.

6. The Quiebra

The second Great Blasket wreck is a WWI munitions ship which sank on the north face. The "Quiebra" lies in 15–27m of water starting in a gully just off a rock known as "Speir Cuas Faill Beag". This wreck is well broken up but as the dive site is relatively sheltered from most winds it offers a good, safe and interesting dive.

The cargo consisted of wire and artillery shells and these can be seen in the gullies to the west of the wreck. On the wreck the boilers are standing upright while the recoil spring of a ship's gun is still to be seen. Heading north out into deeper water (30m+) the gully, containing the main bulk of the wreck, falls away.

7. The Island Harbour

Just off the slip and out of the small natural harbour of the Great Blasket, the area has a maximum depth of 12m and is suitable for trainees. Heading east out of the harbour you can follow the reef which acts as a breakwater for the slipway. The bottom is on white sand with a wide variety of sea life and the reef is frequented by seals.

Returning along the original dive path instead of re-entering the harbour proper head northwest across the sands to another group of rocks and some shallow gullies. This is an excellent shore dive for the trainee or casual pottering diver. During the day it is advisable to use an SMB as the ferry boats operating to and from the island have to travel over this dive site in order to reach the slipway.

8. Terraght Island

This island has excellent diving and large schools of fish especially beneath the lighthouse (the most westerly lighthouse in Europe) and along the ridges and gullies of the north face. There are two landing stages to serve the lighthouse on the north, and south of the spectacular sea arch and it is possible to get ashore there from inflatables.

9. Inishvickillane

This most southerly island is privately owned but has excellent diving along its south shore, most notably at Fohish Rocks. There are three pinnacles joined by a reef with a ledge out 20m on the northeast side but dropping rapidly to 40m. Fish life is abundant with plenty of drop off.

Local Facilities and Information

Compressor:
Wine Strand Holiday Centre,
Dingle, Co. Kerry
Tel. 061 325125 Fax. 061 326450

Waterworld,
Scraggane Pier, Castlegregory, Co. Kerry
Tel. 066 39292 Fax. 066 39557 E-mail: dive@iol.ie

Dingle Marina Dive Centre,
On the Waterfront, Dingle, Co. Kerry
Tel. 066 52422 Fax. 066 52425 E-mail: lfarrell@tinet.ie

Tidal Constant: Dublin +05 01

Local VHF station: Valentia Radio Ch. 16, 67, 24, 28

Chart: 2789, 2790, 2254

Maps: ½":1 mile No. 20 1:50000 No. 70

The Maharees
Co. Kerry

The Maharees Islands are situated approximately 30km from Tralee on the tip of the isthmus which divides Tralee and Brandon Bays.

The nearest launching point is from the slip at Scraggane Pier to the north of Castlegregory off the N86 Tralee to Dingle road. Launching a boat presents no problems as there is a wide gradually sloped slipway. There are also toilet facilities and ample parking. The Maharees consist of seven islands in all and they offer completely different types of diving with depths from 3–40 m, all within 20 minutes of the pier.

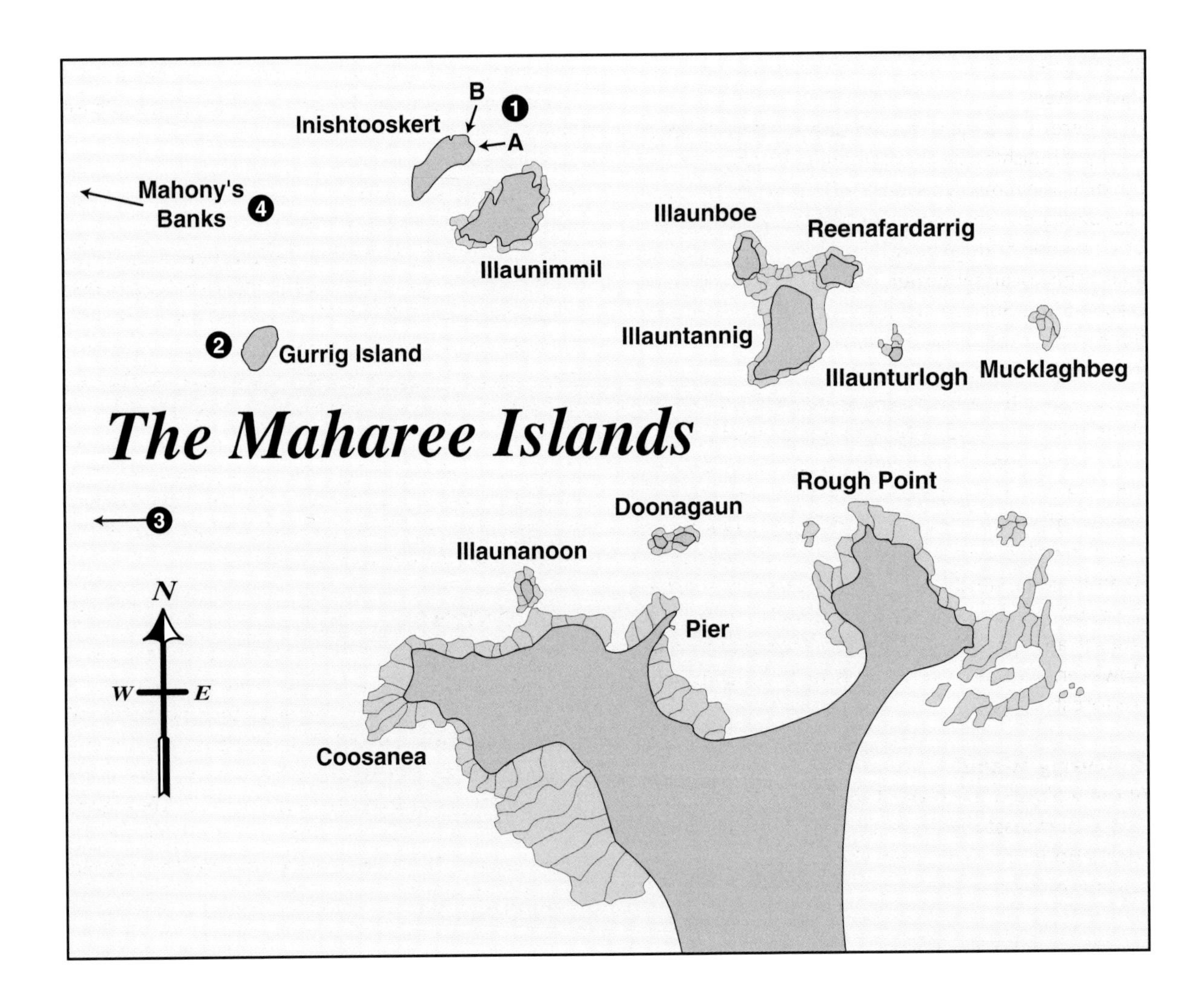

Dive Sites

1. Illaunimmil and Inishtooskert

To one's left from the pier is Illaunimmil and behind it is another island – Inishtooskert, which is not visible from the shore. To the NE of Inishtooskert is the wreck of a Spanish trawler, in 10m of water, which is marked by a buoy.

A. Starting here, follow the contours of the island in a northerly direction where the depth increases to 20m. This brings you to an area of large overhanging rocks worn away by the currents. This is a photographer's paradise, with yellow, brown and green breadcrumb sponge, sea anemones which look like fields of daisies – crayfish, lobster, flatbacks, pollock and wrasse in abundance. The journey here takes about 10 minutes by boat. On the third and fourth hours of the tide, there is a good current so it is preferable to dive only during slack water.

B. There is a very nice dive about 200m from the NE tip of Inishtooskert when lining up the southerly tip of Illaunimmil. This area offers acres of gullies, approximately 3m wide, 5m high in 25m of water. The number of dogfish in this area is quite unbelievable. The local fishermen sell the dark red spider crabs to the Spanish trawlers who call about three times during the summer months. On the way back from these dives, one can visit Illauntannig, which has a monastic settlement including oratories and stone huts, surrounded by a large stone wall.

An indication of the different types of diving in the area is that these two dives are within 200m of one another and yet are so different. During the winter months, these islands get the full force of the Atlantic gales which have a sand blasting effect on the south-westerly sides of the islands, leaving very little, if any, growth, but still an abundance of life. However, on the easterly sides of the islands there are forests of kelp.

2. Gurrig Island

About 2.5km to the NW of the pier is Gurrig Island. At the northeasterly tip of the island there is a large rock about 6m from the shore. Using this as a starting point descend between the island and the rock. This brings you through a gully 9m deep to an area thronged with lamargh sea urchins and walls of sea anemones. Again, follow the contours of the island in a northerly direction where the depth increases to 20m. About 5 minutes from the starting point you will come to a number of flat rocks, here change your direction to northwest. This will bring you to a plateau of unbelievable rock formations, sculptured by years of erosion.

3. Deelick Point

From Scraggane Pier go WSW by boat to Deelick Point which takes 25 minutes. This area offers superb diving. One could fill a book describing it, sheer walls 20m high in 30m of water. In summer it is quite common to see shoals of mackerel swimming on the surface in and out of the shallow caves. Rose coral can be found below 20m – please leave it there!

4. Mahony's Banks

(GPS 52.19.05N 10.09.03E)

The pinnacle of ones diving on the islands is a dive on Mahony's Banks. These banks are 3.2km due north of Brandon Point. This dive requires a trawler with a depth sounder, local knowledge, excellent planning, slack tides and experienced divers. The sea bottom is at 65m and the top of the banks are at 28m. The local fishermen do not fish here, because there is a wreck and their nets and pots could foul. About 20 years ago an ore boat, the Lola, coming from Foynes sank here. Basking and blue sharks are common during the summer months.

HOLIDAYING

For anyone thinking of holidaying in the area, there are four caravan and camping sites within half a mile of Scraggane Pier, the departure point for all dives in the area. Directly across the road from the largest caravan site is Sandy Bay Beach. This is an ideal family beach patrolled by two lifeguards during the summer months. In Castlegregory, 2 miles away, there are numerous hotels, guest houses and pubs.

Local Facilities and Information

Compressor:	WATERWORLD, Harbour House, Scraggane Pier, Castlegregory, Co. Kerry Tel. 066 39292 Fax. 066 39557 E-mail: dive@iol.ie WINE STRAND HOLIDAY CENTRE, Ballyferriter, Co. Kerry Tel. 061 453582 Fax. 061 326450
Tidal Constant:	Dublin +05 15
Local VHF station:	Valentia Radio Ch. 16, 67, 24, 28
Chart:	2739, 2254
Maps:	½":mile OS No. 20 1:50,000 No. 70, 71

Grey seals on the Little Skellig ***Photo: Nigel Motyer***

Kilkee
Co. Clare

Kilkee is probably the most popular dive site in Ireland at present. Situated on the southwest Clare coastline it owes its existence to a natural break in the cliff wall facing the Atlantic. It is renowned for its deep, clear water and abundance of flora and fauna. Because of its exposed location the elements have ensured that Kilkee is well preserved and not over dived as many a more sheltered location tends to be. There are more than 20 surveyed dive sites some of which are described below. Kilkee has a Dive Centre and Marine Rescue Centre which is manned on a voluntary basis.

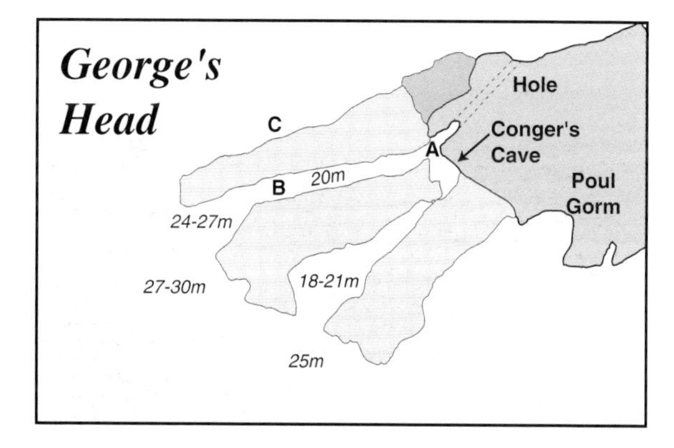

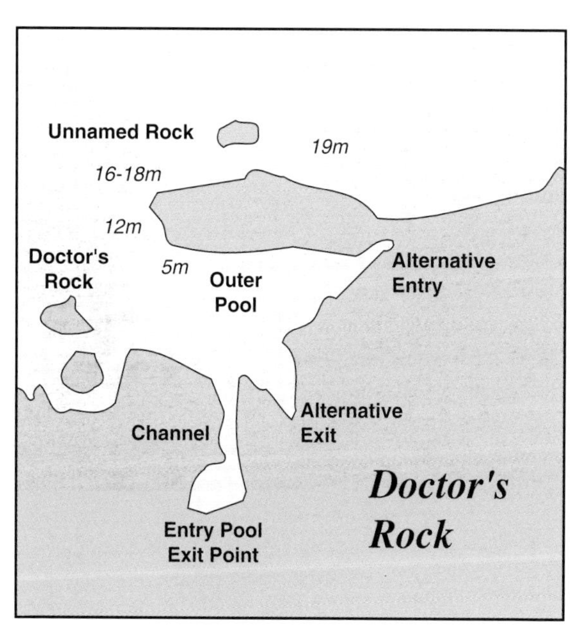

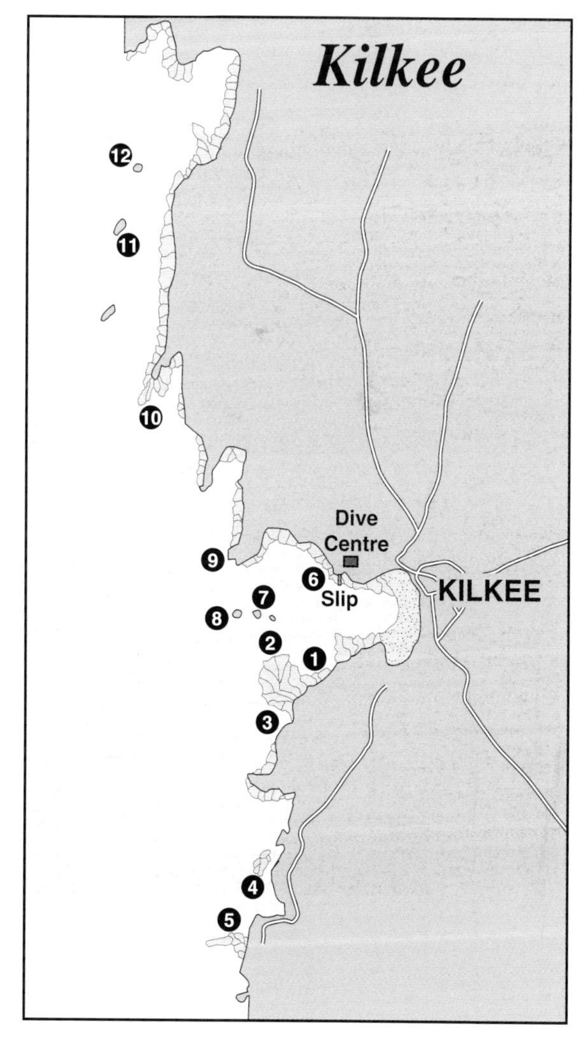

Dive Sites

1. Newfoundout

Near the car park on the south side of the bay, down steep steps, Newfoundout is the most sheltered of all Kilkee dive sites and is usually accessible in all but the worst conditions. It is ideal for trainees and the inexperienced diver. The best course is to proceed over kelp 30° west of north towards the inner face of Duggerna Head. There is a rock reef on a sandy bottom and has a max. depth of 10m.

2. Myles Creek

Myles Creek is a north-facing inlet on the top of the Duggerna Rocks, a large reef covered by tides at the mouth of Kilkee Bay. It is accessed by road on the south side of the bay and trekking over the rocks at low water. Beware of slipping and allow plenty of time in your planning.

Except in very calm conditions, when it can be dived from a boat, the site is otherwise very tide sensitive. For shore diving, it is essential to enter the water before low water, preferably 30 minutes before. This gives you a dive in calm water. If there is white water out there, or a bad forecast, don't dive it.

The creek is initially shallow (3m) with a ladder for bathers in summer time.

There is a drop off to about 14m into a sheltered valley, often with startlingly clear water, given reasonable conditions. This has spectacular colour on the floor and walls covered with anemones and is generally populated by a variety of fish. If one follows the left-hand cliff, this turns round a corner and the protection ceases. You are now on a more normal dive site with kelp on the floor. Go north to the next drop, about 20m. Again follow the cliff on your left and you will eventually encounter a large cave in usually clear conditions at about 33m. You should check your air and perhaps start back.

This dive can be made from the sea. However, there are submerged rocks both sides of the entrance. The shallow valley is ideal for novices in very calm conditions at only 14m and clear water. An excellent site for snorkellers too.

On a shore dive, you have to exit in exactly the same place and must navigate back correctly. The alternative is an almost impossibly long swim around the reef to Newfoundout.

3. Doctor's Rock

Dive 1

Located on the face of Duggerna Reef this is a pleasant shore dive that begins in a sheltered rock pool, proceeds through a narrow channel into a wider bay of water and drops at the beginning of the main reef face. It is generally necessary to return by the same route for safety, so a sense of navigation and monitoring of air consumption are required. The pool which is easy to enter is shallow and weedy, with occasional pockets of depth. The channel has deep grooves each side of the shallow centre rock, which provide access to the sea. The northern side is more interesting, save this for the return journey.

The outer pool starts at about only 5m, but is beautifully coloured with a carpet of anemones. Depth increases seawards until one reaches a drop-off face to about 15m, there is a small cave on this face which is often home to very large conger eels. These eels sometimes move around the general area and may even pass you during the dive. They are not dangerous just big!

Follow the rock face to the north (keeping it on your right), when the floor changes from solid to stones and eventually back to solid rock with a light carpet of anemones and moss, **check your air supply**. If all members have enough air proceed further along cliff face which gets better and better. Air is really the big factor here, if you have to surface before the pool, you will not get back easily except in very calm conditions.

Dive 2

Follow same course until you sight a large rock on the seaward side, circle this and return along face towards pool drop-off. If the air supply is sufficient, continue south along the rock face to yet another offshore rock. Circle this (go under the fallen rock arch) and then return along the rock face to the pool drop-off, ascend and navigate back. If your group has enough air, you can explore around the north area of the outer pool or through the caves on the north side of the channel on the way back. This can be a very simple and pleasant dive. Flora and fauna vary throughout the year, even from year to year. Diveable only in calm conditions, it can be ideal for trainees, but be aware of the potential problems of the site.

Dangers: slippery rocks, the site is very tide sensitive, the turning tide may make return difficult. The best entry is about 30 minutes before low tide, also it is necessary to exit in the same place, due to more difficulty elsewhere. Air awareness is essential for both these reasons, surfacing in breaking waves can be dangerous.

Dive 3

In suitable conditions, you can jump off the rocks in corner of the Outer Pool and swim for the open sea, where there is a drop to 19m approx., with an overhang cliff covered in anemone patterns and crab colonies. Return with the rock face on your left until you come to the cave drop-off (first dive above), signposting your return route. This dive needs calm seas, low tide and a knowledge of the area. Beware of sea urchins!

4. The Diamond Rocks

The name comes from the quartz in the rocks, which glistens in the sunshine. This dive is accessible by land along a path leading to nearby Lookout Hill overlooking Intrinsic Bay, named after the ship which was wrecked there at the end of the 1800s. An anchor and some metal are believed to remain in the bay, if you care to search it.

Underwater, there is a reef about 6–9m deep, which protects a deep valley about 30m deep between itself and the shore. This protection can sometimes give rise to exceptional visibility within the valley. There is a nice approach from outside the reef, which crosses over two circular holes at the narrow entry which are about 6m deeper than the floor and are often full of both edible and spider crabs.

The sea face of the reef falls in steps from about 20m down to 40m+. It is interesting and varied. Avoid the reef in any type of white water, wave action etc. This is a fair weather dive only.

5. Bishop's Island

South of Kilkee accessible only by boat is Bishop's Island. Sheltered from S and SW swells, the terrain consists of large boulders, gullies and a cliff face.

6. Black Rocks

This is a shore dive, very suitable for trainees, on the north side of the harbour opposite the golf club. There is a pathway and some steps to the inlet with a short climb to the water. This site is affected by the prevailing westerly winds.

A long narrow and deepening channel leads (about 2m down to 10m at its mouth) towards the centre of the bay. The best approach for a dive is single file. The mouth of the channel is its lowest point with some kelp-covered rocks and a few wrasse. The area outside is broken and not too interesting. Return through the same channel as there is no other easy exit, so navigation is essential.

7. Middle Rock

Located in the mouth of Kilkee Bay this is one of the finest dive locations in the area, a very large hunk of indented rock, the middle rock of a group shown on the charts as "Black Rocks". That just about describes the colour of the exposed peaks visible at low tide. This is the most diveable of the three and is well worth a visit or two, there is more than one good dive here! Three of the four faces, all except the east, are worthwhile. The north face is the easiest to approach, but is less well lit particularly in the evening. The ideal approach is in calm conditions at low water, when the rock is visible.

Find the trench near the Cnap (peak), follow this southwards. The trench widens and deepens, as you near the south face of the rock. On the right-hand side of the trench you will notice a slotted hole, this slopes downwards and exits at the back of a cave facing deeper open water. Beware of the occasional strands of coral as you come out at about 27m deep on the bottom which then slopes away to the south.

There are a few more features on the south face where the light is best. A different approach is to try to find the Arch Hole. This is an impressive cathedral vault opening to the west, it is hard to find as prevailing weather conditions don't always allow shallow water searches. Approached from below the effect is noticeable.

After leaving the arch or on any other dive you can work along the rock face at your choice of depth, crossing over the west face. Depth increases rapidly towards Outer Rock. There are indented low caves on the seaward face where you can see many prawns, squat lobsters and the occasional resting monkfish. Pollack hang just off the rock in mid water.

Dive boat hints: Beware of the swell over Middle and Outer Rocks. Know the tide times and weather forecast. Sometimes the swell off Outer Rock is quite high, when divers are dropped off on the north face, they often surface to the south. where they may not be visible. **dive to a plan**, but the cox'n should be aware of possibilities.

8. Outer Rock

As its name describes this is the most seaward rock of the Black Rocks and is only visible at low tide and may only be dived in good weather even then there can be a large swell. It is a good site with sheer cliff faces rich in fish and plant life. There is an arch on the inner face and the maximum depth is over 35 m.

9. George's Head

George's Head at the mouth of Kilkee Bay has more than one dive. The force of the Atlantic has shaped the terrain to give a number of saw-toothed ridges with a vertical face on the exposed side and a sloped back on the landward side. There are a number of canyons, cliff faces and a tunnel running into the head itself. It is the terrain, rather than flora in this exposed location, which is the real attraction of the area. Diving is possible in most reasonable sea conditions, avoiding areas of breaking waves.

Area A

This is a 15m exploration of the channel which cuts into the head, you can see through the cliff above water level. This needs reasonably calm water. You can explore the channel, which is longer than it seems, the bottom of which is covered in huge boulders. No plant life, but often shellfish and the occasional tope. On leaving, if air allows, follow the cliff to the left. A very large conger occupies (or fills!) a low wide hole near a large rock, worth a look!

Area B

This dive is possible in almost all except the most severe weather conditions. Once the inner line of the head cuts off the view of the hut in Burn's Cove and if the boat stays 100m+ from the land, avoiding the waves formed at the corner, it is even possible to anchor. Drop into the nearest valley and work from there. Navigation skills are recommended. In rougher conditions it is better towards south or west. In calm conditions all directions give pleasing results.

The Valley marked B is worthwhile and leads to a nice open cliff face. The cliff which faces southwest, is usually well lit and has good fish life. There are some caves and varied terrain with a few strands of coral.

The cliff face C reminds one of Arizona, it is stark and majestic in its form and colour. To find it cross the ridge from B. The valley leads back towards the head and Chimney Bay and is not shown here in full detail.

Outside this cliff line are a number of interesting canyons both blind and connected by narrow passages. At this time no definite information is available.

Wave patterns at head: In extreme conditions a large breaking wave, known by the ancients as the 'Beam' practically cuts off access to the Bay. In more normal conditions, the swell forms waves over the various peaks. The shallower inner corner should be avoided. Storm waves reflect off the head across the bay.

In reasonable seas the head is quite safe and easily dived. In rougher conditions, a pull will be noticed in the narrower valleys. Avoid surfacing in waves or close to rocks, plan your dive so that you will surface away from the rocks and surf.

The southern and western part of dive site is in the path of boat traffic so be careful, when surfacing, use SMB and Diver Down flags.

10. Illaunabaha

The headland just before Biraghty Mor has a reef running westwards. It is sheer on its south side and sloped on its north side. The rock bottom on the South side varies from 25m to 35m+ and the ground away from the rock is deep. The plant and fish life is very colourful, the north side slopes away to 40m+. The reef is diveable up to Force 4 winds but be careful in strong swells. A good site for "diving spiritual renewal" and almost always a satisfying dive.

11. Biraghty More

About 1km North of Kilkee Bay this island is worth a visit. With a sheer face on the landward side and sloped on the sea face it is sheltered from the westerly swells. It has a rock bottom on a sheer face varying from 25–35m+ with the ground away from the rock very deep. The plant and fish life is excellent. The shelter of the rock allows diving inside a large cave at its SW corner.

12. Biraghty Beg

A rocky island about 1.5 km north of Kilkee, smaller than Biraghty Mor and thus more exposed to the prevailing winds. Dived only in calm water the site is not well known. The ground is more varied with channels but there is less life then Biraghty Mor.

Warning: Beware of nets!

There are a lot more sites further along the entire length of coast south to Loop Head but with few places for shore access.

Local Facilities and Information

Compressor:	Kilkee Dive & Watersports Centre Kilkee, Co. Clare Tel. 065 56707 Fax. 065 56020
Tidal Constant:	Dublin +05 34
Marine Rescue Centre:	Kilkee 065 56211
Local VHF station:	Shannon Radio Ch.16, 67, 24
Chart:	3338, 2173

North Clare

Mutton Island

Mutton Island stands roughly halfway between Loop Head and Black Head on the West Clare coast. The coastline in this region is quite flat, in sharp contrast to the cliff formations to the south around Kilkee and to the north around the Cliffs of Moher. Maybe this lured the Captain of the Spanish Armada vessel to seek shelter in the area 400 years ago. His ship lies on the bottom (protected by the National Monuments Act) testimony to the fact that no such shelter exists. Spanish Point, to the north, gets its name from this historic event.

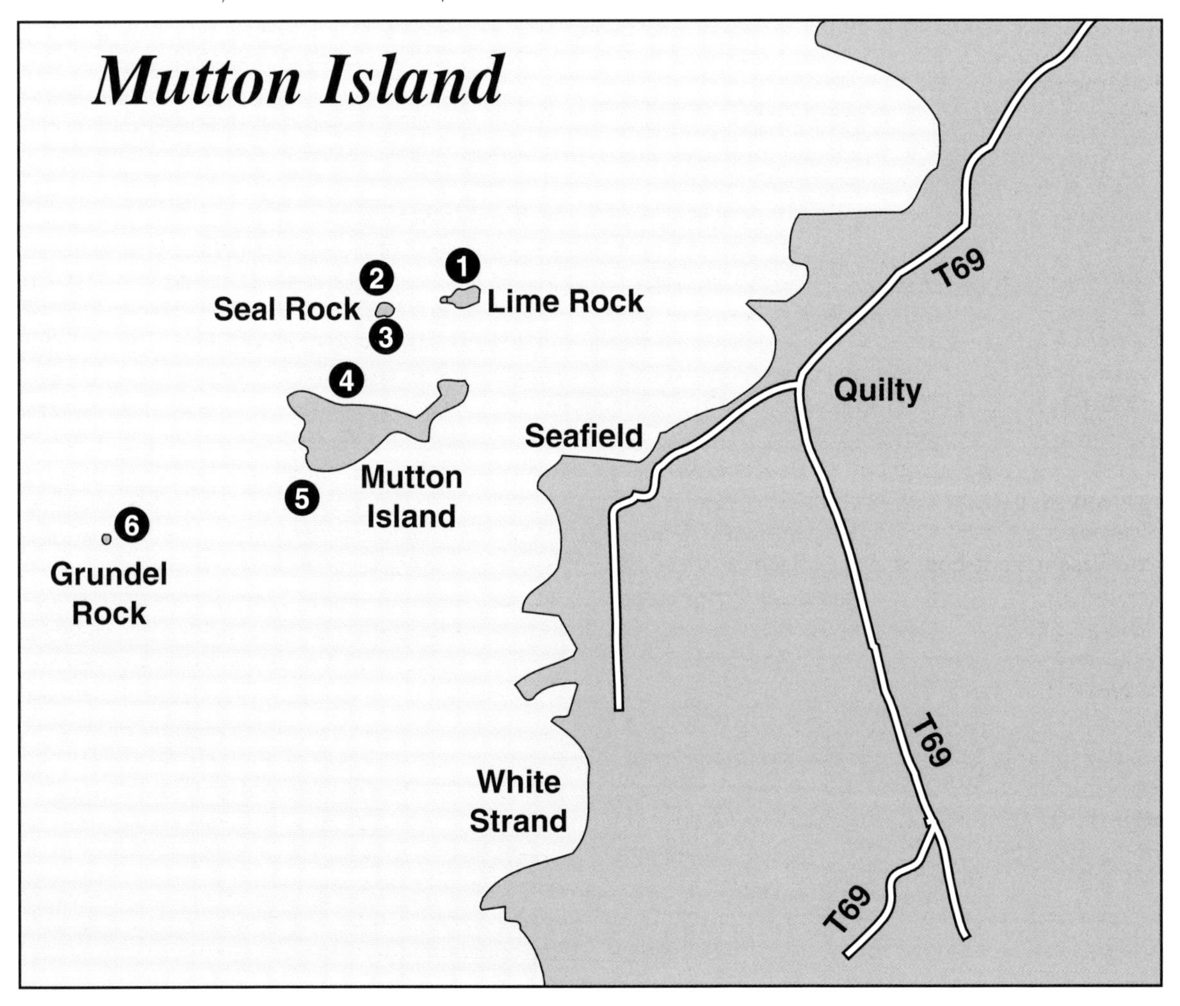

Quilty, 32km north of Kilkee on the road to Lahinch, is the nearest village (and pub). Turn left and proceed to Seafield Harbour (Lurga Point on ½ inch map). Boats can be launched on the slipway two hours off low tide or across the sand with a four wheel drive vehicle.

All dives are boat dives and should only be undertaken in fair weather as the area is exposed to westerlies from all directions. Mutton Island, with its distinctive look-out tower, can be seen about 1,5km off shore westwards. In the past locals used to travel to the island to partake of its special healing qualities for which it was renowned.

Shallows run from Seafield Point westwards for approximately 400m towards the island. To avoid these, boats should always steer a course NW before turning W. Watch out for lobster pots which are in abundance in the area.

1. Lime Rock

This is a long, low, rock running east-west about 1000m to the NE of the pier. On the map it is called Carrickaneelwar, but is known locally as Lime Rock.

Diving is on the north face of this rock, which remains above water even at high tide. Depths from 15–30m are available at most points along the rock, although it does get shallower with heavy kelp at the eastern end. To the north, away from the rock, it gets very deep quickly. There is a broken drop-off for most of the length of the rock, with depths up to 30m. Of interest are several very large steep-sided "pots", some are up to 10m deep, close in to the rock. These were caused by the action of boulders being whirled around on the softer rock by wave action. They are usually clean of kelp inside, but well worth a look, there is often the large boulder at the bottom which caused the hole to be made.

2. North Seal Rock

This site lies on the northern side of the rock and there is a sheer cliff dropping from the waterline to 30m or more in places. One can start from either end and move to the other and still get a very fine dive. If moving east, it is possible to find the opening between Seal and Lime Rocks, passing under a large overhang into shallower sheltered water on the SE of the Rock. A very large tuna was sighted there.

3. South Seal Rock

This site lies at the SW end of Seal Rock. On descent just off the tip of the rock, there is a sharp ridge at about 17 m, which runs away to the SW towards Mutton Island. There is a steep fall off on both sides into 30m This very interesting ridge probably runs all the way to the Island, while gradually getting deeper.

4. Brandon Point

Brandon Point lies at the NE corner of Mutton Island, which can be sheltered even in fresh SW winds. There is a fine wall and "amphitheatre" dropping to 30m, with many ledges and some small caves. The wall can be followed to the east, probably getting into shallower water eventually.

5. Brandon Rock

Brandon Rock is south of Mutton Island and only can be dived in fair weather as it is very exposed to the open Atlantic. Dramatic underwater scenery with plenty of sealife and depths to 40. Beware of sudden swells and changing sea conditions.

6. Gander Rock

Shown on the charts as Grundel Rock, it is known as Gander Rock to divers. It is situated well out into the Atlantic to the SW of Mutton Island and can only be dived in the best of conditions. The central part of the reef breaks at low tide, or in large swells, so cox'ns must be very wary. To locate the rock, use must be made of lobster pot markers first and then by watching for the large breakers that indicate the site. It is an underwater reef running roughly North-South with a sheer wall on the outer side which goes down in places to 50mplus. The wall seems to run for about 1000m and is broken in some places.

Divers should approach from the open-sea side and swim in underwater on a compass bearing to meet the wall, which because of its size is very hard to miss! Circle the rock in any direction and expect to find west coast life at its best. Rare fish such as large angler, sunfish and the odd blue shark have been seen in the area. End the dive swimming out to sea westwards before surfacing. SMBs or surface flags are essential for ensuring that they are seen and picked up. This is an outstanding dive, but more than one boat is advisable and it is not for trainees. It is at least 20 minutes by RIB and more by inflatable from Seafield Pier.

Liscannor Bay

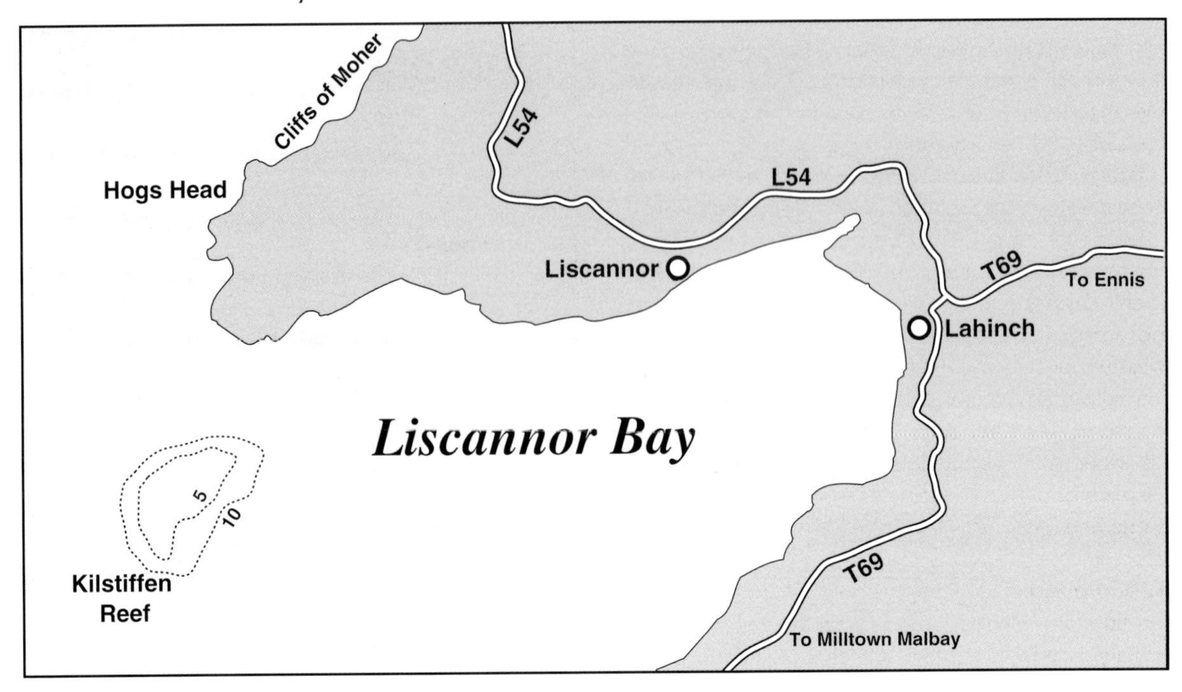

Kilstiffen Reef

If you stand on the promenade at Lahinch and look straight out to sea, Kilstiffen Reef lies on the horizon and can only be spotted in rough weather. The top of the reef lies in about 10m and is not exposed at low tide. It is difficult to locate and use must be made of an echo sounder, or by searching for lobster pot floats, or by waiting for the occasional large breaker that arises, even in fair weather.

The reef appears to be quite long, possibly as much as 1500m running from north to south, and it has a shallow plateau that extends towards Lahinch for about 1000m. The nearest headland is about 1500m away to the NE. The dive site lies on the outer side, nearly on a line running from the Cliffs of Moher, which can be seen away to the north. The impression when on site is that you are diving in the open Atlantic. It takes about 20 minutes in a RIB, or longer in an inflatable, to reach the reef from the nearest launching site, which is at Liscannor, on the northern side of the Bay. This harbour dries out at low tide, but sufficient water remains just at the pier's end for diving boats.

There is a drop-off on the western side, but it is broken and not always defined clearly. At mid-tide, 30m plus can be found at the foot of the drop, on the outer side of which the sand starts. Two very distinctive features have been identified, well worth diving on, if they can be found! One is a narrow and dramatic canyon cut into the reef, which runs towards Lahinch for about 300m, the sheer sides reaching to the bottom at 25m. At no point is it any wider than about 10m, with many "shelves" lined with the best of what the Atlantic can offer. The cleft ends in a large cave at the inner end. Another site, again on the outer edge, could well be called the "ruined cathedral", as a number of buttresses can be found close together at 20m which look very like those found supporting the side walls of cathedrals. Reaching from the top to the bottom of a small rockface, they are quite large and look almost manmade. On the reef generally, the fish are large and abundant, and blue sharks have been sighted.

Kilstiffen is a difficult site, not for trainees, because it is ill-defined, much time, (and petrol), can be lost in locating it, and because of the manner in which very large breakers can rear up out of calm seas without warning. It is not suitable for poor-weather diving, and the use of SMBs or flags are advised at all times. Because there is little shipping in the area, apart from a ferry to the Aran Islands, it is preferable to have more than one boat for additional safety, and even then, the cox'ns must be very vigilant for those surprise breakers.

Ballyreen, Fanore

This dive site is not easy to find, but is well worth the effort if the weather conditions are right. From Ballyvaughan on the N67 Galway-Lisdoonvarna road take the L54 for Black Head. The site is 6.4km south of Craggagh Post Office or 8km south of Fanore Strand. There is a large rock just at the entrance to the car path.

Being open to the Atlantic it is not always possible to dive this area unless there has been settled weather for several days as the site is exposed to the south, west and north. The area is strongly affected by Atlantic swells which can have their source far out in the ocean. The best prevailing weather is easterly winds or calm conditions. The main difficulty encountered is in exiting the water and it is not a dive recommended for the inexperienced. It is best to dive from one hour before to one hour after high or low water

Before kiting out survey the entrance/exit. Access to the water is through the gully to the left of the blowhole. At high tide the gully fills and access to the water is easier than at low tide. Do not jump from the cliff face except at high spring tide, after surveying the entrance point from below. Observe the swell, as this causes the most difficulty when leaving the water.

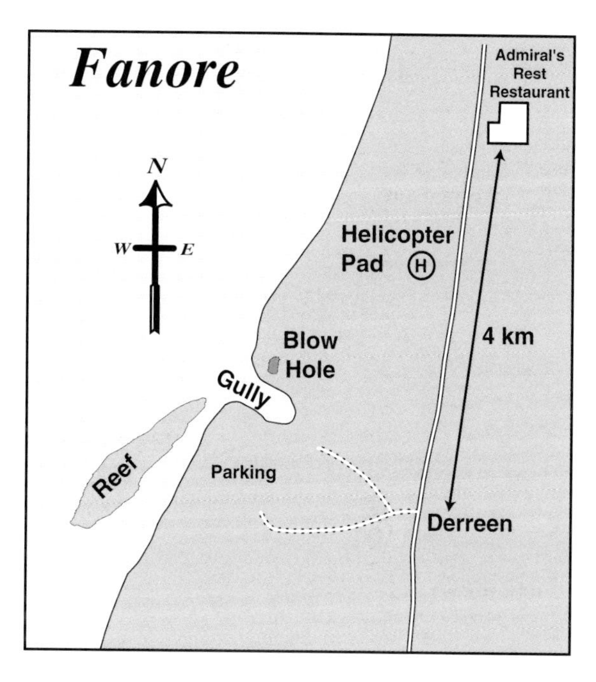

The Dive.

Enter the water through the gully and continue out to sea for approximately 50m. You are now in about 10–15m water and you can begin your descent. You should see the northern end of the reef to your left. Follow along to the corner and turn south. You will notice at this stage the numerous fish that are in close proximity to you. They are quite used to divers and are fed by divers breaking white sea urchins. Follow along the reef face at either the 15m or 18m level. There are numerous nooks and crannies along the length of the reef, which overhangs at several spots. A torch is quite useful for picking out the numerous fish which shelter in the overhangs. The bottom consists of a mixture of sand, shale and rock.

About 100m along the reef face there is a large opening which leads to"The Cathedral", a semicircular cavern open at the top. Avoid swimming over the reef as it is quite shallow and you can easily get caught in the swell. If you do find yourself on top of the reef, head NW back out to sea and down the reef face.

The preferred way to plan this dive is to dive the bottom of the reef on the outward leg, turn back when half your air is left, and swim along the middle section surfacing in the gully at 10–6m.

Avoid surfacing on the outside of the reef if possible and do not attempt to dive between the reef and the shore. When ready to leave the water, observe the wave pattern when approaching the gully and time your exit between waves. Do not linger in the water when you have gained a foothold, as the surge has claimed countless masks, fins and is responsible for several torn suits.

Moving out to sea, away from the reef, there are large clusters of rocks. However, the sealife is quite sparse and the shale bottom just stretches out for several hundred metres, at a depth of 18–20m. A variation on this dive is to dive to the right of the gully along the cliff face. It is not as interesting and beware of the shore anglers overhead.

For the non diver there are a variety of walks in and around the Burren close to the dive site. It is also a favoured site for rock climbers. There is a long sandy beach in Fanore, 6km north of the dive site, but beware of the undertow!. The Fanore area is famous for it shore angling and has hosted many national and international competitions. There are several castle and church ruins in the area.

Local Facilities and Information

Compressor:	Kilkee Dive and Watersports Centre, Kilkee, Co. Clare Tel. 065 56707
Tidal Constant:	Dublin +05 30
Local VHF station:	Shannon Ch. 16, 67, 24 Clifden Ch. 16, 67, 26
Chart:	3339
Maps:	½":1 mile OS No. 14. 1:50,000 No. 51

Sunburst over diver ***Photo: Nigel Motyer***

Aran Islands
Co. Galway

The Aran Islands are renowned as one of the prime tourist attractions on the west coast. From a heritage point of view they are remarkable in that many of the uniquely Irish traditions and ways have largely been preserved. Here the Irish language remains the first language for most of the 1,100 islanders.

Geographically the islands are unique. Located at the mouth of Galway Bay the limestone rock islands have more in common with the harsh landscape of the Clare coast, although administratively the islands are actually part of Co. Galway. The islands form a chain running in a northwest-southeast direction across the mouth of Galway Bay. During winter they form a sea barrier protecting Galway Bay from the Atlantic storms which have been known to lift seaweed off the rocks on the west side of Inishmor and to hurl it into the air, where it could be seen being blown over the islands!

While the islands share many of the characteristics which makes the west coast generally so good for diving, it is the abundance of life and unique limestone scenery which often leaves divers truly amazed, caves, sheer walls to 40 m, deeply undercut rock faces, tunnels connecting pools to the sea and swim-throughs under giant boulders the size of two-storey houses. The pitted limestone rock provides a surface for life to cling and attach itself to, giving a density of marine life unusual even to the west coast.

A landscape of limestone, stripped bare by the glaciers of the Ice Age, sculptured by the Neolithic tomb maker, the monastic architect, and the farm wall builder, with one material STONE. A sight that endures in the mind, and makes a visit plus good diving an unforgettable experience.

The three islands, Inisheer, Inismeain, and Inismor, as a group form the Aran Islands. It is possible to cross to them from Galway (long route), Rossaveal (short route to Meain and Mor), and from Doolin in Co. Clare to Inisheer, by ferry.

It is also possible to travel by air (Air Aran) from close to Rossaveal, but problems may arise with both diving cylinders and weights.

Accommodation on all islands is very good, but of the bed and breakfast type, similar to the mainland. It is strongly recommended that local contact be made in order to ensure a smooth trip.

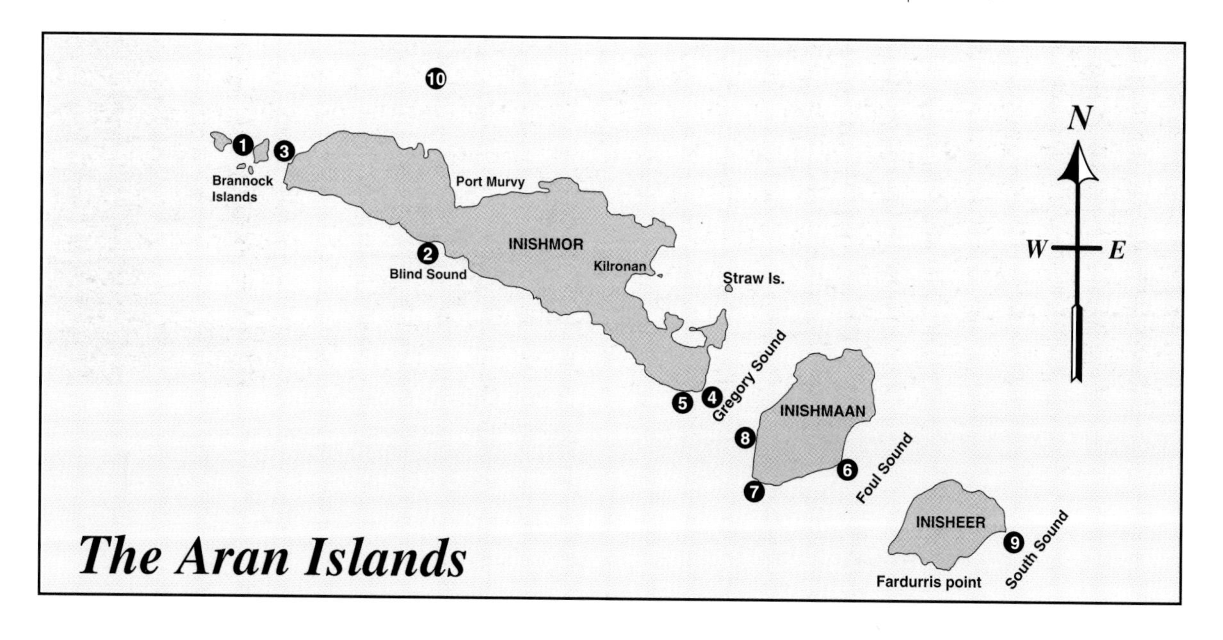

Inismor Dive Sites

1. The Canyon

This site lies between the Brannock Rock and the North Light. The area between these two islands is flat limestone about 9m deep. Opposite the landing stage for the lighthouse there is a vertical canyon about 30–45m wide, 400m long running east-west, with the bottom at 33m. As this is a limestone area, the walls of the canyon are fissured and abound with all sorts of fish life. Visibility will frequently permit divers on one side to see divers on the other side of the canyon. There is a slight current, the site is partially exposed. Max. wind Force 3. Find the canyon with an echosounder.

2. Poll Na bPeist (Worm Hole)

This is on the Atlantic side of Inismore about 1.6km south of Dun Aengus, the famous cliff top fort on the west side of the island and consists of a rectangular opening in the flat foreshore, it looks like a man made swimming pool. Entry is through a wide underground cavern about 25m long, depth in the pool is about 15m. Outside the pool the bottom is strewn with huge boulders and slopes away to 45m deep after about 300m. This site is located under Dun Angus, which is perched on top of vertical cliff 90m high. There is good shelter here in winds from the north to east, but is not divable in westerly winds above Force 2.

3. Brannock

Located between Brannock Rock and the main island, this site is made of a series of steps starting at 8m at the shore reaching 32m after 60m out. The steps are approx. 3m high, and are fissured and undercut, perfect abodes for various life forms. This is the most sheltered site and is exposed only to north to east winds, winds up to Force 4 are no problem, there is no current and it is protected from the Atlantic swell.

4. Aill na nGlassog (Glassan Rock)

This dive is at the southwesterly tip of Inishmor. Begin slightly to the north of the tip where there is a cave above the water. The depth here is 15m but quickly drops to over 30m. The vertical rockface has an overhanging ledge 3–4m deep cut into it at a depth of about 12m. This runs around the tip of the island and into Gregory's Sound. The ledge narrows towards the back and provides a perfect home to congers, lobsters and wrasse. The occasional crayfish can be found hanging upside down in a recess in the ceiling. Swim around the tip of the island to where a spectacular collection of giant boulders carpeted in dead mans fingers are propped up against the side of the island. It is possible to swim beneath some of these, stopping to look out at shoals of pollack swimming by.

5. The Puffing holes (Cave dive)

This dive is an underwater chasm in the limestone which extends for at least 120m and is closed at one end. Although they cannot be seen from underwater, it is believed that the cave eventually leads to the puffing holes which are visible high on the shore above. Divers should not venture more than 10 or 15m into the entrance without advanced training and planning and using appropriate cave diving techniques. Under the right conditions this dive is exhilarating and unrivalled, but is definitely not one for the faint hearted.

Inishmaan Dive Sites

6. Gob Na Fearbhai (Farvey Point)

A dive site stretching for about 2.5km long, beginning 800m south of the Island Pier, at the point of Gob Na Fearbhai. There are ledges at 10m, 20m, and 30m running parallel to the shore, and the shallow ledges are very suitable for trainees. As one moves out into deeper water, 30m plus, the area is covered in great boulders with excellent colour and fish life. This site is protected from the prevailing south-westerly winds. Currents are 1.5 knots at full flow.

7. Poll Seidte (Puffing Holes)

This is a dive site for the quiet (windless) day or a wind from the north, which is rare during the summer months. Situated on the southern point of the island the drop-off, close to shore, is sudden and dramatic. Dive on the rising tide as this gives greater comfort to the diver.

8. Poll Gorm (Blue Pool)

Dive site on the exposed side of Inismeain facing Inismore, under steep cliffs (the spot known as Synge's chair is directly above the dive site, this was Synge's favourite place for meditation). Very colourful drop-offs and wonderful colour, depths to 45m. As with all dive sites facing the open Atlantic, diving can only be safely undertaken in good weather conditions.

Inisheer Dive Sites

9. Finnis Reef

The dive site is 4.8km west of Innisheer Pier, halfway between the east marker of the reef and the island, depth 15m. The reef stretches east from the Island for just over 1km, and levels out on to a sandy bottom. The colour, plant and marine life is very varied, dive on the rising tide.

10. Brocklinmore

This is an underwater ledge on the east side of Inishmor which runs for most of the length of the island. It offers some superb dives in waters that often are diveable when westerlies don't allow you out behind the islands. The ledge itself can be very difficult to find without accurate GPS reading (ask Galway Bay Scubadivers!). The ledge occurs along the contour where the seabed shelves up from 30–20m and follows the general lie of the island. There is normally a gentle current (0.5–1.0 knots) along the ledge which makes it an effortless dive with good boat cover. Drift along with the tide, swimming up and down the ledge which is dotted with rose corals and large white sea fans. The ledge is undercut and in places this can reach back 5 or 6m – too narrow to allow a diver in but a perfect home for the occasional crayfish.

Other Dive Sites

As all the dive sites are on the more exposed open Atlantic side of the islands it is essential that great care is taken in the planning of all dives. The minimum requirement is two large inflatables, radio, and that elusive calm weather. Most of the sites are only suitable for the more experienced diver.

The above sites are just an introduction to the diving in this vast uncharted area, an examination of the marine chart shows many areas of great potential. The Aran Islands represent some of the most spectacular and beautiful underwater terrain to be found anywhere in Ireland. It remains remarkably little dived perhaps due largely to the difficulty in finding many of the better dive sites and a previous lack of facilities for divers. Hopefully this information will be helpful to people wishing to dive the islands and will encourage groups of divers to consider a trip to the Aran Islands. Charters and assistance in diving the Aran Islands can be had by contacting Galway Bay Scubadivers.

Local Facilities and Information

Getting there:

Aran Ferries Teo., Galway	Tel. 091 68903	Fax. 091 68538
O'Brien Shipping, Galway	Tel. 091 67283	Fax. 091 67672
The Doolin Ferry, Doolin, Co. Clare	Tel. 065 74455	Fax. 065 74417
Island Ferries, Galway	Tel. 091 61767	
Inter Island Service	Tel. 091 61767	
Aer Aran, Inverin, Co. Galway	Tel. 091 93034/93054	Fax. 091 93238

Compressor: Galway Bay Scubadivers,
Inverin, Connemara, Co. Galway
Tel. 091 553065 Fax. 091 553065

Tidal Constant: Dublin +05 50

Local VHF station: Clifden Ch. 16, 67, 86

Chart: 3339

South Connemara

The part of Connemara to the west of Galway city is a Gaeltacht (Irish speaking) region and is often referred to as South Connemara or the Connemara Gaeltacht. Places such as Spiddal, Inverin, Carraroe and Rosmuc are already familiar to many Irish people, particularly those who spent time at one of the many Irish colleges in the area.

The Connemara Gaeltacht is Ireland's largest Gaeltacht region. Commencing at the village of Barna, it is mostly a coastal area and stretches almost as far west as the fishing village of Roundstone. The landscape comprises much of the north shore of Galway Bay and towards its western end this becomes broken into a series of islands separated from each other by a series of large bays and narrow tidal channels. Most of the islands are connected to the mainland by a series of causeways allowing access to most places by car.

The many bays, islands and inlets offer excellent opportunities for sheltered year round diving – a selection of sites is nearly always guaranteed, no matter how bad the weather is. Further offshore lie the Aran Islands and, more to the west, the Skerd Rocks which offer truly stunning offshore diving and are best accessed from South Connemara.

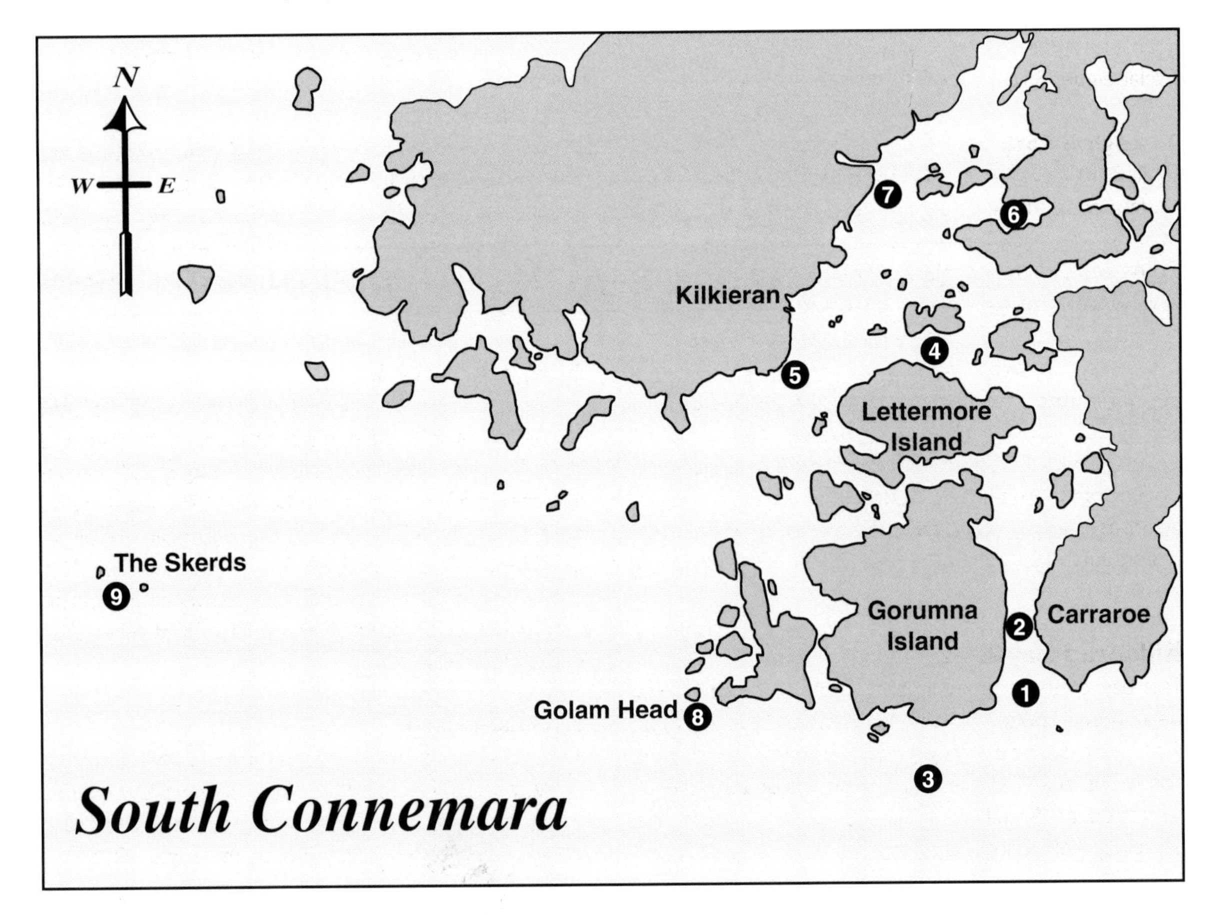

Dive Sites

1. Coral Strand

The Blue Flag Coral Strand or Doilin, is approximately 3km from the village of Carraroe. This is an excellent site for trainees with a clear sandy bottom and lots of life. Diving is best timed for a slack tide, although little if any tidal current will be encountered unless you venture too far into the channel. Maximum depth here is 9m at high water. It is possible to launch an inflatable here.

2. Reef Dives

These reefs can be dived from the shore at the small pier at the end of Bothar na Bui and are straight out from the shore. Currents tend to be stronger here, but if diving other than at slack water it is possible to exit the water at almost any point along the shore. Currents are north-south. The reefs are home to several huge congers and lobsters and are fantastic for night dives. Max. depth is 17m at high water. Boats are best launched from Callaheigue, 800m away.

3. English Rock

English Rock is accessible by boat only. These can be launched at Callaheigue and loaded at the Coral Strand. The rock lies about 1.2km SW of Trabawn Point on Gorumna Island. The rock uncovers at low water but can also be found with an echo sounder. Caution is needed if searching for this reef in even a light swell as it may break occasionally and without warning. The best dives are on the west and southwest side with depths to 25m ending on a coarse bottom with sand and boulders. In the right conditions this dive is as good as many west coast offshore sites with often spectacular visibility and lots of life. Two sunfish were seen here in 1996.

Kilkieran Bay Area

This bay offers some exceptionally sheltered sites with very unusual sponge-covered bottoms and heaps of fish life. Drift diving is very good here with flat calm conditions in all but the worst weather. Boats are best launched at Anaghvaan, having driven across the causeway from Carraroe.

4. Gurraig Sound

The best dives are on the south shore of Inishtravin Island. The dives can only be done from a boat, although the actual sea journey is less than half a mile from the pier. These sites can be dived as drift dives at any state of the tide. The west end of Inishtravin has depths of 45m within 50m of the shore and makes for an interesting unusual dive with lots of congers. The channel between Inishtravin and Bird Rock has a max. depth of 26m and makes a spectacular drift dive along the Inishtravin side. Currents run west on ebbs and east on filling tides.

5. Kilkieran Point

Operating from Anaghvaan, Kilkieran Point makes a pleasant 20m dive. Slack water is best but it makes an excellent drift dive too. A boulder slope meets the corralline algae bottom at 20m. Great fun, drift dives with large lobsters and scallop beds to be seen (remember, it is illegal to take shellfish on scuba!).

6. Roskeeda

A tricky boat journey from Anaghvaan as there are plenty of reefs to fall foul of. This site is a spectacular drop-off into a 35m hole in a surrounding area only 6–8m deep. Diveable in any weather – no matter how bad! Renowned for the rare and large Pachycerianthus anenome.

7. Kylesalia Creek

Not far from Roskeeda on the west side of Kilkieran Bay, Kylesalia makes for a great shallow night dive and drift. The inlet is approximately 500m long and only an average of 50m wide. It can be dived from the shore, entering at the bridge crossing the inlet near the village of Kilkieran. One of the best drift dives in the area. This site is known for some very rare seaweeds and some recorded species occur in only a handful of other sites in the North Atlantic.

8. Golam Head

This is the tip of land that forms the eastern entrance to Kilkieran Bay. It is recognisable by the tower on top of it. There are good dives to 30m on the west and south sides of the head. This site can be classed as an offshore site as it is completely open to the Atlantic and westerly or southerly winds. Diving on the south side is spectacular with granite rock being carved out into gullies leading down to large boulder slopes ending in coarse sand at about 28m. Crayfish, lobsters, wrasse and congers hide amongst the rocky crevices and in the kelpy shallows. The south side can be dived from the shore by driving to the end of the road on the island of Lettermullan, heading for the obvious tower on the headland. There is a fairly major walk down the shore and conditions must be at their calmest for the entry/exit. A boat launched in Callaheigue or Anaghvaan can be driven to the headland down either Greatmans or Kilkieran Bays and allows the site to be explored when shore diving isn't possible.

9. Skerd Rocks

The Skerd Rocks are perhaps the jewels in the crown of diving on this part of the coast. They lie to the very western limit of the area described and approximately 9.5km SW of Mace Head near Carna or a similar distance NW of Earaght Lighthouse on Inishmore. It is a long boat ride from any location but nevertheless can be accomplished by RIB or hard boat from several points in south Connemara.

The Skerds really are the last outpost and you are a long way from land. The view back towards Connemara on a clear day has to be seen to be appreciated. The rocks themselves are granite pinnacles rising from 50m below to a height of almost 30m. During winter the rocks are completely engulfed in spray and white water. In summer they make truly exceptional diving with memorable encounters with nature practically guaranteed.

Only a very few people have dived the Skerds in the past. Hopefully more will be encouraged to dive here, however proper expedition type planning is necessary for those wanting to dive here without chartering a hard boat. Good weather, equipment, planning and local knowledge on getting there is essential for safety but more than worth the effort.

The Skerds consist of two peaks – Doonguddle and Skerdmore. Diving on the south, west or east side of either is first class, although Doonguddle has the most spectacular drop-offs.

Advice, assistance and facilities for diving this area are available by contacting Nick Pfeiffer at Galway Bay Scubadivers.

Local Facilities and Information

Compressor: Galway Bay Scubadivers,
Coill Rua, Inverin, Co. Galway
Tel. 091 553065 Fax. 091 553065

Aran Islands Dive Centre,
Inishmain, Aran Island, Co. Galway

Tidal Constant: Dublin +05 51

Local VHF station: Clifden Ch. 16, 67, 26

Chart: 2096, 3339

Maps: ½":1 mile No 10 1:50,000 No. 44, 45

North West Connemara

In good weather these sites are well worth a visit for the experienced diver, with a boat.

How to get there: From Clifden, take the Westport Road (N59), turn left at the signpost for Claddaghduff. This road runs parallel to Streamstown Bay. Go through Claddaghduff past the Strand Bar and Sweeney's shop. Turn left at the Y fork and take the next left down a narrow lane which lead down to the pier at Aughrus More and the beach. Inflatables and RIBs can be easily launched from the beach. First check that there are no large rocks on the lane down to the beach. Please remember that this pier is used by fishermen so don't block the roadway.

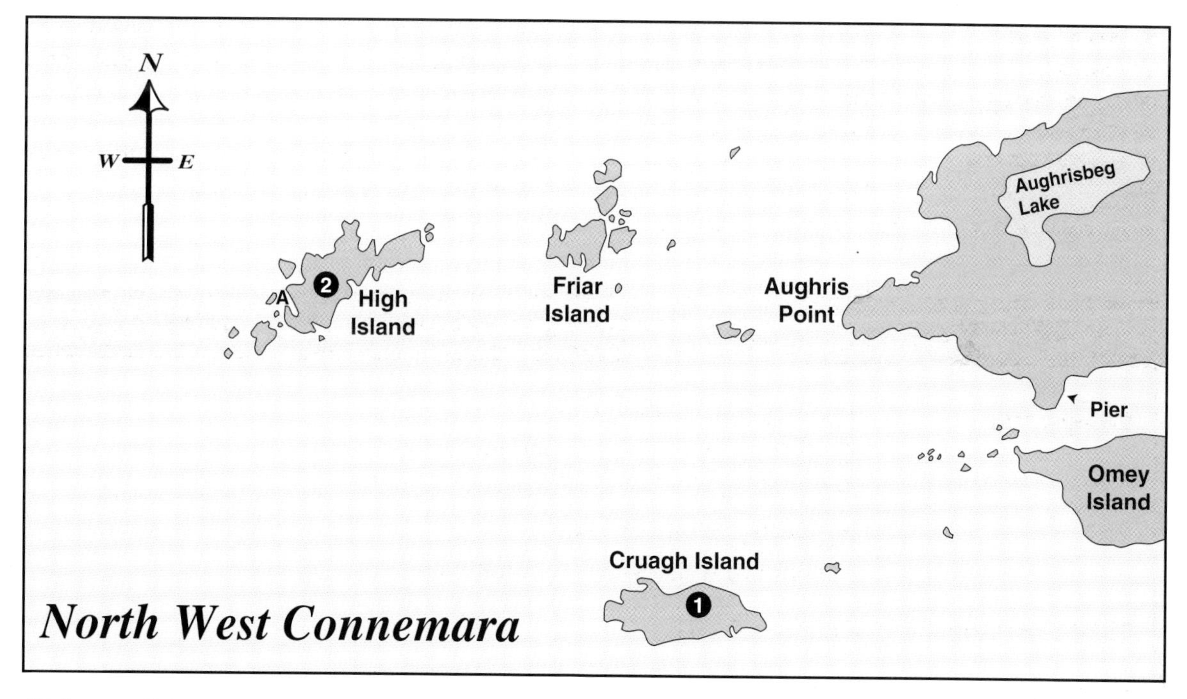

Dive Sites

1. Cruagh Island

This island is 3km from Aughrus Pier, and has an area of 34 hectares, is best dived along its north shoreline. The bottom is mostly rock with some deep gullies which run out to meet fine sand. Depths of 24m can be achieved. There are no currents and with a coastline of 0.8km to choose from the diving is excellent, with prolific marine life and good visibility in fine weather. It is best to make your first visit to Cruagh on low water as all of the reefs from Aughrus to the islands are exposed.

2. High Island:
High Island is 8km from Aughrus Pier, has an area of 32 hectares, was once owned by the poet Richard Murphy and it is now a seabird sanctuary. In calm weather the best diving is on the southwest of the island (site 1).10m from the cliff face the wall drops to 26m with depths in excess of 40m if you dive in a NW direction from the cliff face. The marine life is abundant with shoals of mackerel (in season) swimming above you. This side of the island is very exposed to westerly swells and winds so only dive this side in calm weather.

The east coast of High Island is nearly 1km long and has some good varied sites and the bottom is not as deep as the SW side. There are rock gullies which run NW–SE to the coast. This whole area is a photographer's dream with prolific and varied marine life and visibility, in good weather, in excess of 30m.

NB: These dive sites are well out to sea therefore all standard safety measures for offshore diving should be observed.

Local Facilities and Information

Compressor:	Scubadive West Lettergesh, Renvyle, Co. Galway Tel.: 095 43922 Fax. 095 43923
Tidal constant::	Dublin +06 05 min.
Local VHF station:	Clifden radio ch. 16, 67, 26.
Chart:	2707

Rossroe Pier, Killary Harbour

Killary Harbour is a fjord situated on the Galway-Mayo border. Surrounded by mountains it is an excellent 'weather safe' diving location. To get there, travel 5km west from Leenan on the N59 towards Letterfrack, turn right and follow signs for the youth hostel. Diving is usually limited to The Mouth of Killary and it can be dived in most weather conditions except in strong easterly gales.

Freshwater run-off from the mountains after rain produces two distinct detractions. The first is the early absorbent of light, leaving even shallow depths almost black and secondly surface water can be much colder than the underlying seawater particularly in winter or early spring. Typically the halocline reaches a depth of 2–5m. However, in the dry season, if one exists in Connemara, light penetration to depth is very good.

Launching a boat at Rossroe is not easy as there is no proper slip at the pier. Smaller inflatables can easily be manhandled in and out of the water but larger inflatables and RIBs are best launched and recovered at the slip at Leenan and brought down. Beware of the rocks 30m off the corner of the pier.

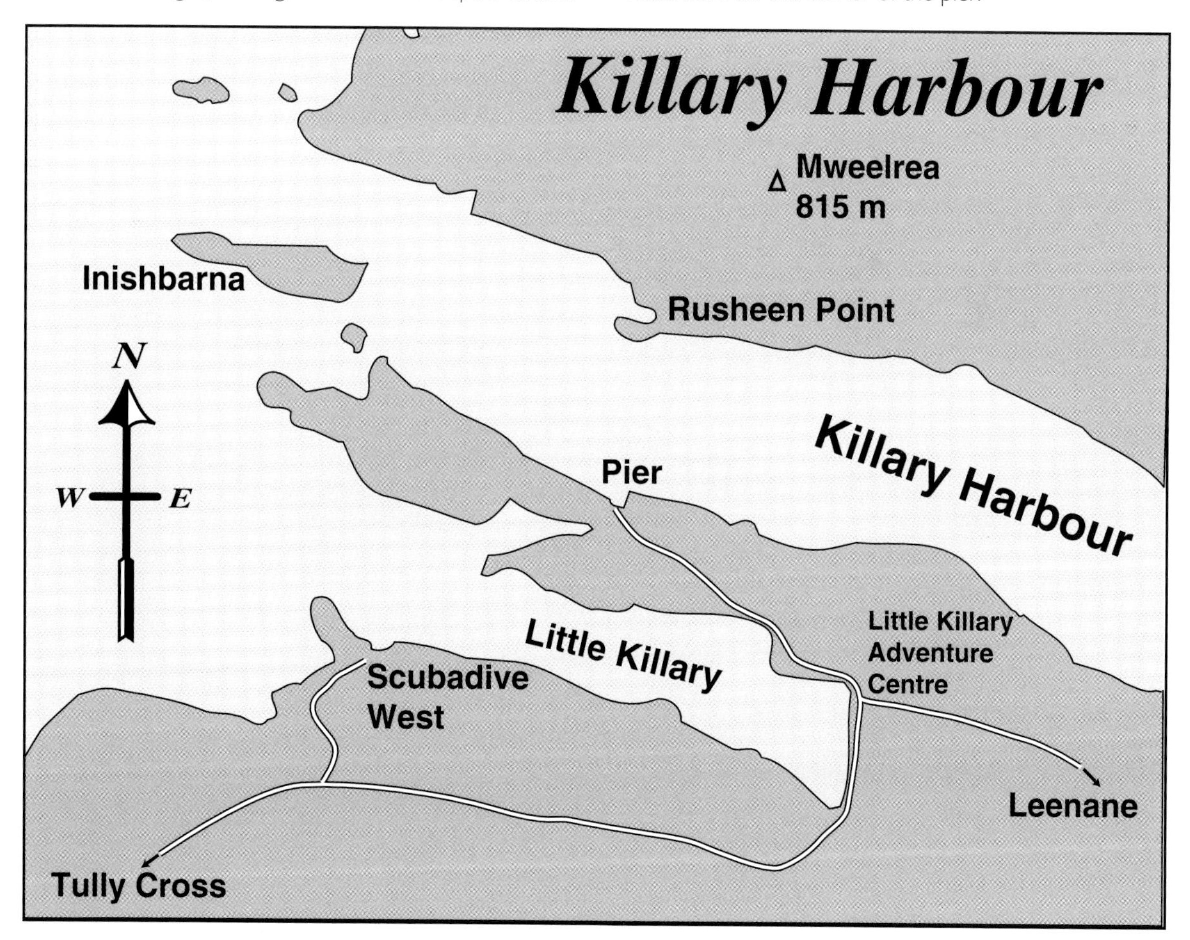

Dive Sites

The Shore Dive

The dive can be approached as a shore dive or boat dive. Shore diving is usually done in a west–east direction at a depth of 15–25m. In this direction there are several small reefs with a variety of flora and fauna. There are exit points east of the pier, if required, walking back to the pier over the hills. Diving north from the pier leads to the centre of a V shaped valley with depths in excess of 40m. However, there is very little to see at depths greater than 25m. The more interesting way to dive Killary is by boat with several good sites within 20 minutes from the pier:

1. The North Shore

The dive is directly opposite the pier under Mweelrea, the highest mountain in Connacht. Start the dive at Rusheen Point where a spit of land runs into the water. Follow the rock face underwater to a depth of 15m and continue along the rock face. Keep off the bottom as the silt will very quickly limit visibility! If you do stir up the silt, rise above it and swim against the current leaving the silt cloud behind. To minimise silt avoid diving at mid tide.

2. The Island Dives

There are several islands at the harbour's mouth, Inis Barna being the largest. Conditions around the islands are superior to those inside the harbour but the variety of marine life is not as good. Both islands can be dived on either side depending on the prevailing weather conditions. Depths of 30m+ are easily achievable but there is very little to see when deeper than 25m. For the more adventurous, there are several offshore islands, including Crump and Inis Degil, which can be dived using Rossroe as a sheltered base, particularly if mooring boats overnight.

FAUNA

The harbour area is littered with scallop (*Pecten maximus*) and cockle (*Glycymeris glycymeris*) in the shallows and, after about 15m, the sea bed changes dramatically to a carpet of brittle stars (*Ophiothrix fragilis*). Millions of tiny arms waving from the bottom give the appearance of a huge meadow blowing in the wind. A closer look reveals the great range of colours of these amazing creatures, spiny starfish (Marthasterias glacialis), which grow up to 8cm in diameter living off the huge quantities of bivalves upon which they feed.

For the Non Diver

There is a sandy beach at Lettergesh 1.5km back from the pier over the mountain road. There are several scenic drives, and a myriad of mountain walks. It may be possible to hire bicycles from the Little Killary Adventure Centre, 1.5km before the pier. The Adventure Centre also runs week and weekend adventure courses covering canoeing, sailing, board sailing, rock climbing, hill walking etc.

Local Facilities and Information

Compressor:	Scubadive West Lettergesh, Renvyle, Co. Galway Tel. 095 43922 Fax. 095 43923
Tidal constant::	Dublin +06 05 min.
Local VHF station:	Clifden radio ch. 16, 67, 26.
Chart:	2706, 1820

Inishbofin
Co. Galway

Inishbofin Island, just west of Killary Harbour, is one place you have to go to fully prepared, with boats, engines, compressors, spares, oil, finstraps etc.

The island ferry leaves from Cleggan, a small harbour near Clifden on the T71 Galway to Westport Road. From Cleggan there is a daily mailboat to and from Inishbofin. On occasions they have been cut off for long periods at a time due to bad sea conditions. It is advisable to check the weather before making a day trip.

Stepping ashore the "Island of the White Cow", freedom is the first thrilling sensation. Even the birds are less afraid than on the mainland. You have come to a world of heady, leisurely beauty where there are no laws, only courtesies and conventions, beyond the clutch of the troubles left behind. The world suddenly is something to contemplate from a distance, or ignore.

At the harbour stands Day's Hotel, one of the two hotels on the island, both being on the south end. The other one is Murray's Hotel, only 15 min. walk distance away, and they will transport your gear for you. The jeep used is one of only about half a dozen vehicles on the island.

The inflatables are easily managed by mooring or bringing them ashore at the harbour area or at the sheltered stony beach near Murray's Hotel. Some care needs to be taken when using the inflatables inside the protective peninsula due to some rocks and lobster pots.

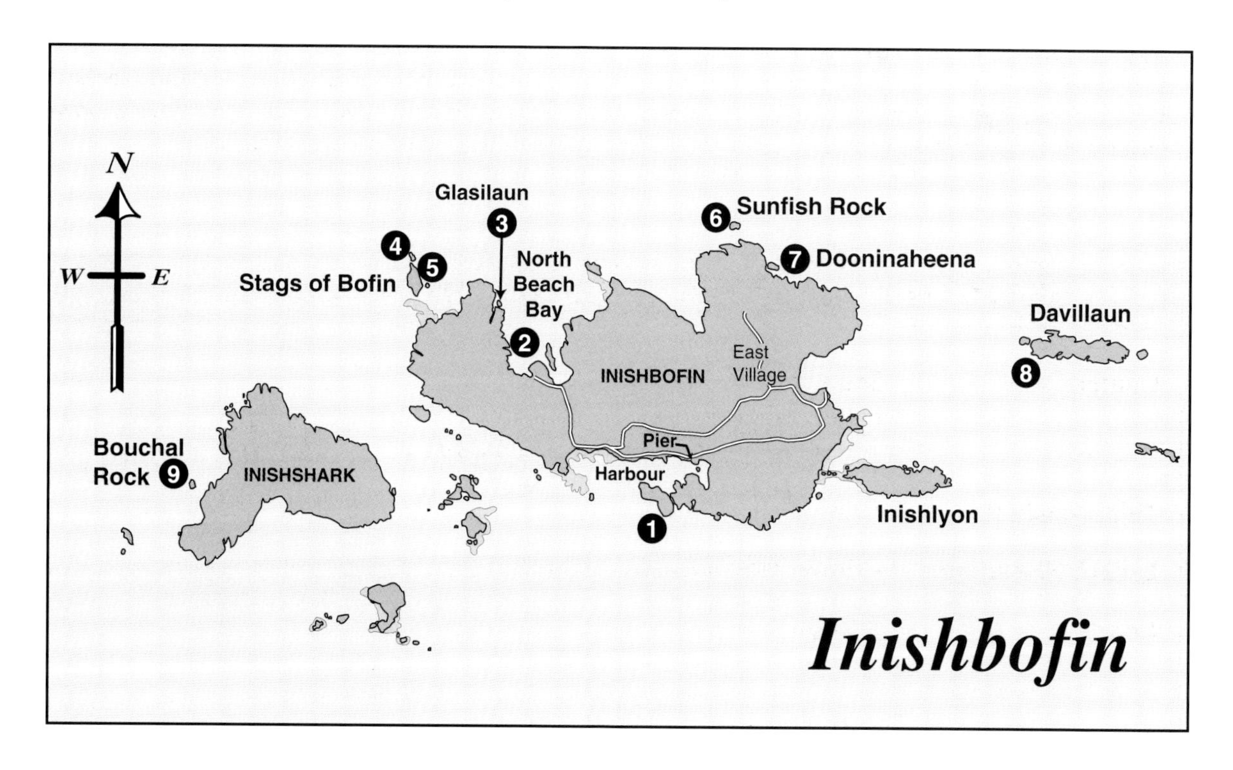

Dive Sites

1. Harbour Peninsula

A good first acclimatising dive for trainee divers is just in behind the peninsula under the ruins of the old castle which dominates it. You will find a flat sandy bottom, with lots of small rocks and sea life, at a depth of 5–8m. The area is sheltered from southerly winds.

On the outer side of the peninsula there are many little gullies to dive, with one dive being quite different from the next ranging from 5–30m with some marvellous reefs. The one thing you appreciate is the amount of fish life around the island. Visibility can range of course, according to weather conditions, from 5m to crystal clear waters with seemingly endless visibility.

Most of the better diving is found on the northern side of the island, move your boats to North Beach Bay. They can be brought around by sea going to the west between Inishark and Inishbofin, taking about 30 minutes. Take care when rounding the Stags of Inishbofin on the northwest as the seas can suddenly become very heavy with a large swell but, once passed, calm down again. The inflatables can also be transported overland using the jeep or just good old sweat and guts. The walk is about 800 m long.

The boats can be moored near an anchorage used by currachs or beached on the stony beach there. It is important to note impending weather conditions as you can choose which side of the island to dive, or whether to leave the boats moored or beached overnight. All movement in and out of North Beach Bay should be done on the western side of the rock in the middle of the bay.

North Beach Bay itself is a good dive site, see Fig. 1, at point A, Here you get lovely 20–25m dives. The bottom is a mixture of large and small reefs with patches of sand. The kelp is well scattered and causes no hindrance to the diver.

Care should be taken to dive within 50m distance of point B, a small outcrop, to obtain 20m depth or less. Divers have been known to hit 45m a little further out without reaching bottom. There appears to be some sort of a deep hole or ridge further out near point C. Finish your dive by taking a bearing towards point B and swimming into the gully or along the rock face behind it. The depth here is only about 9m but the fish life is abundant in the whole area.

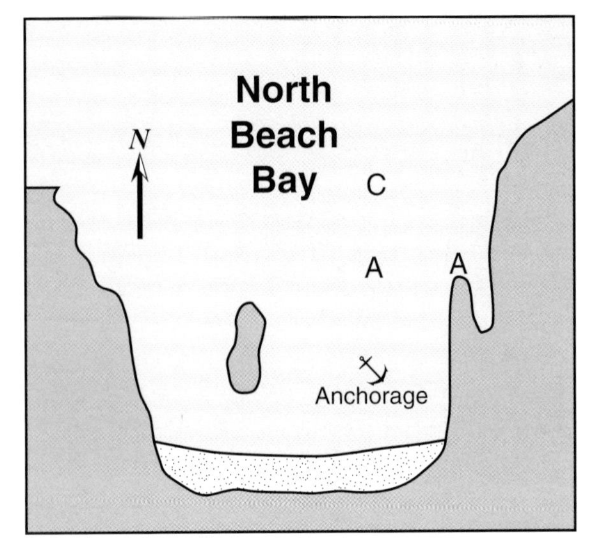

Fig. 1

2. Glasilaun

Glasilaun is situated to the northwest of North Beach Bay and is truly one of the better shallow dives of the island. It is also a good site for a night dive. Glasilaun is the name of a rock at the mouth of a gully, see Fig. 2.

Point A shows where you could start your dive, in about 20m, where the bottom is very rugged. If you take a southerly bearing, you will be brought between Glasilaun and the cliff face going towards the arch. The depth lessens as you progress along a gully to the side of Glasilaun, to point X, which is a safe anchoring location if you wish to do a night dive here.

The gully is only about three times the width of an inflatable and a boat can easily clear the arch at all tide levels and navigate towards point B approximately 35m in. At point X the depth is about 12m at low water, and as you proceed into the gully which is almost spotlessly clean from kelp, you would be in a depth of about 9m. Proceed to point B which is the entrance (or exit) of a completely submerged tunnel, and bending a little southwards.

It is approximately 15m long and leads you to the bottom of a cave on the other side of the rock face. A torch is required on this dive as no light penetrates to a section of the tunnel. It is approximately 6m high and 3m wide and can be negotiated easily, there is also little discomfort felt by the small swell, if any.

A good night dive may be had in the cave. The depth at its entrance is 12m at low water and about 10m at the back.

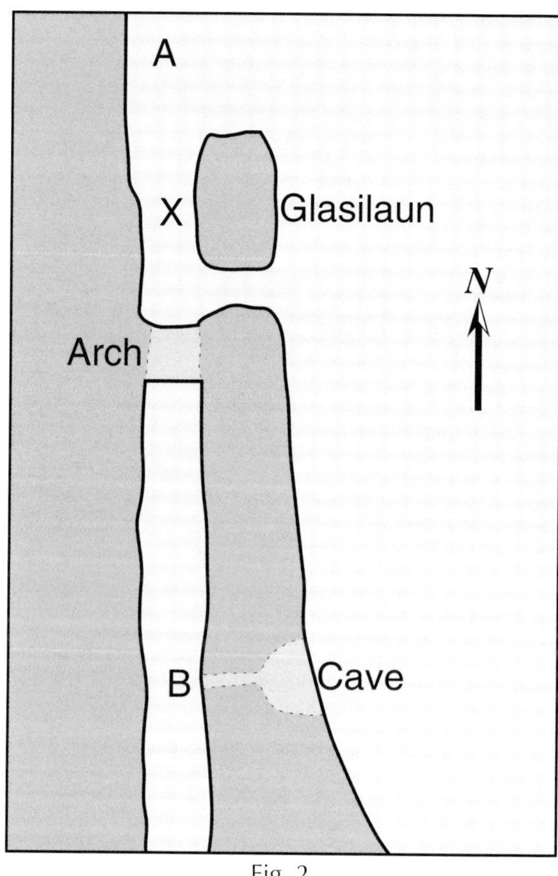

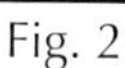
Fig. 2

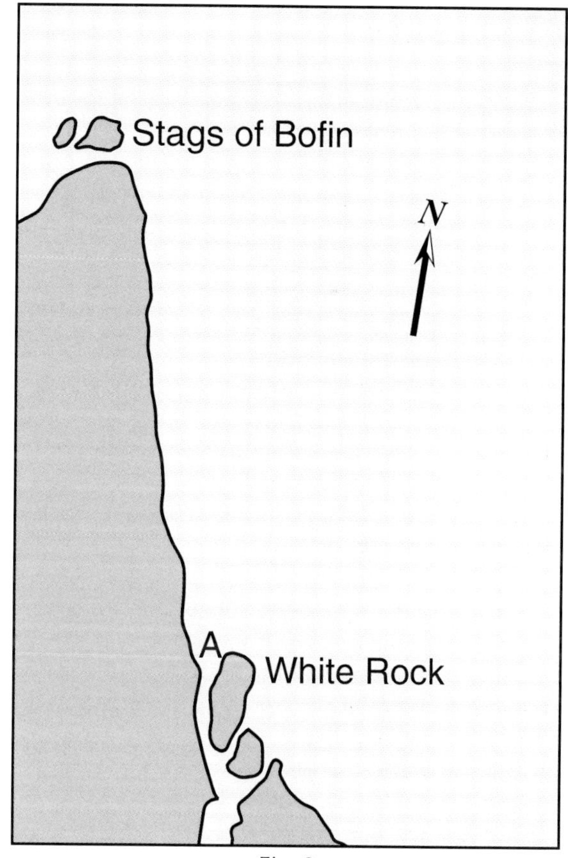

Fig. 3

3. The Stags of Bofin

The Stags are at the northwestern tip of the island and provide for a fabulous dive with whatever depth you want. They can only be dived comfortably in calm conditions as the particular area is prone to a heavy swell making it unsuitable for less experienced divers. An alternative site to this one is White Rock, shown on Fig. 3.

4. White Rock

Not a very spectacular site compared to the Stags. The channel at point A is about 10–15m deep gradually going out to any depth you wish. The bottom is rocky with plenty of fish life and small reefs.

5. Sunfish Rock

A 15 minute boat journey to the east from North Beach Bay will find Sunfish Rock. The tip of the rock is covered at high water and it is found by lining up two outcrops of land from Inishbofin and the northern tip of Davillaun Island. It is at the mouth of a long narrow gully and careful study of your chart, or diving at low tide, will help you locate it.

It is like a thumb of rock sitting on the bottom, the top of it only 3–4m wide and widening as it goes down to 30m or more at high water. The rockface is decorated with reefs, overhangs and small tunnels made by fallen rocks.

6. Dooninaheen

This is a little bay between Sunfish Rock and the north eastern tip of the island. The best site is a sheltered cove at the eastern side of this bay where the water appears to be flat calm no matter what the weather conditions. Dive to 15m and swim out along the rock face, and along the spectacular bottom. Take an east bearing around the corner at about 24m. Ascend to about 17m and continue east for about 15–20m distance until you come to an opening in the rock face of about 5m wide.

At the end of this crevice you ascend and surface to find yourself inside a chimney in the rocks which cannot be seen from the outside, although a small crack does let you see out. To get out you need only dive about 3m to fit out. The crack in the rock face runs from top to bottom. If your orienteering is "dodgy", it is simply found by counting to the third crack in the cliff face from the corner. See Fig. 4 at A.

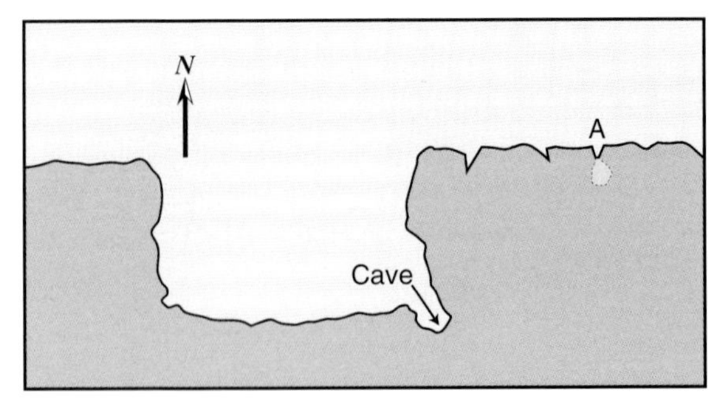

Fig. 4

7. Davillaun

The Spanish galleon "El Falcon Blanco" is reputed to have struck Davillaun at its westerly end. This has not been proven but there is a large Spanish anchor about 50m off the "sunder" (the large split in the rock). A pile of large ballast stones was also located about 100m east of the anchor. The bottom is sandy and 25–30m deep.

There are many more sites available around the island, but one must not forget its deserted neighbour, Inishark. To walk through the deserted village is, to say the least, eerie. Up to a few years ago each house still had the furniture and fittings as they were when its inhabitants left after a drowning disaster some 40 years ago.

8. Bouchal Rock

Bouchal Rock is situated on the western side of Inishark and can only be reached by a relatively long boat journey from either the north or south of Inishbofin. The dive itself is worth every single minute of it. The rock stands about 30m off the island, perfectly erect and round like a giant finger pointing to the skies from below. You have to enter the water very close to the rock as the bottom drops away very quickly. There is a great deal to be seen, small crevices in the wall, fish life is abundant and the anemones which make their own Persian carpets on its wall.

Local Facilities and Information

Compressor:	Murray's Hotel Dive Centre
Tidal constant:	Dublin +06 03
Local VHF station:	Clifden Road Ch. 16, 67, 26
Chart:	2707, 1820
Maps:	½":1 mile No. 10 1:50,000 No. 37

Clare Island
Co. Mayo

Six kilometres from the Atlantic coast of Connaught (Ireland's westernmost province), Clare Island guards the entrance to Clew Bay like a sleeping whale. Approximately 15 sq. miles in area and with a wealth of natural beauty, Clare Island offers its visitor the opportunity to experience the friendly carefree and a healthy lifestyle led by its 200 native islanders. Clare Island is a wonderland for the young with sandy beaches, clear unpolluted bays and rock pools that team with fish and other sea life.

There is a magic combination here for the walking enthusiast, walks as gentle or as challenging as you seek. From the top of Knockmore (450m), a panoramic view of 120km of mountains and mainland coastline unfolds before you. Recent archaeological surveys have established that human habitation on Clare Island dates back to 2,500 BC and many sites from that period may be seen.

The Bay View Hotel was first established by Chris O'Grady in response to demand from French and English sea anglers. Accommodation is available ranging from grade B hotel, farm houses, guesthouses and self catering hostel facilities. There is a compressor at the Bayview Hotel and boats may be hired locally.

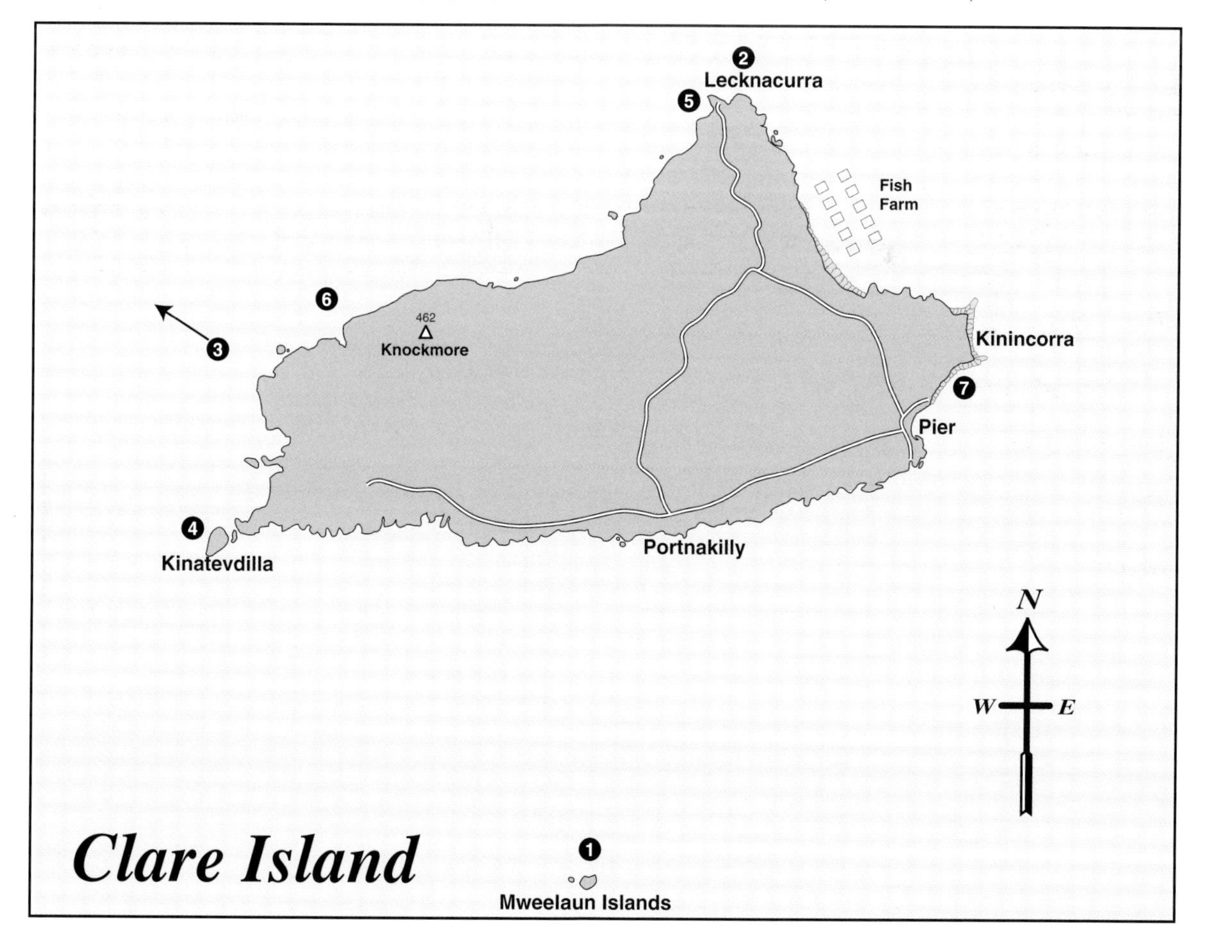

Dive Sites

1. The Mweelauns

The Mweelauns comprise two main rocks rising 20m from the sea and lying about 4.5km southwest of the Harbour. It is usual to start the dive on the south side of the gap unless there is too much swell from the Atlantic which is possible even on the best days. It is difficult to get much more than 28–30m but, once below the kelp, the bottom is strewn with boulders and the sea is filled with life.

2. Deace's Rock

Deace's Rock never quite covers, though there is invariably a swell there. It is located off the north tip of the island no more than 400m from the old disused lighthouse. There is a tidal set of about 2 knots in this area and consequently it is advisable to dive there either at high water or low water. Deace's Rock has huge underwater cliffs, gullies and ledges around it with depths up to 35m to the west.

3. The Bills Rocks

The Bills Rocks are probably one of the most renowned diving locations in Ireland. They are located about 12km WNW off Clare Island and rise forty metres above the sea. If you dive close to the north face of the eastern most rock you will have 45–50m before you hit the bottom. The way down if fantastic, with ledges, cliffs and an unbelievable variety of colours from the sea-anemone which cover the rock face. The sea, in season, is alive with mackerel, pollack, wrasse, etc. The Bills Rocks were used as a firing range before 1918 and the brass rings from the shells are still to be found.

4. Kinatevdilla Head

Kinatevdilla Head is on the southwest corner of Clare Island and it is possible to swim between it and the mainland. The passage is shallow and the seabed to the north of the main island is only of fair interest, especially if you have already been spoiled by the Bills and by Deace's Rock.

5. The Lighthouse

The northwest shore of the island under the old lighthouse and south of it, is an interesting, if shallow, dive. The area is sheltered from SW winds.

6. Two Fathom Rock

Two Fathom Rock, which lies a little more than 800m north of Lecknacurra Head, is another popular dive. Many have swum south from Two Fathom Rock towards the island in search of a German WWII aircraft, which has never been found. Every time the story is told the aircraft is "reliably" positioned in a different location.

7. Shore Dive

It is possible to dive from the shore, but, without transport all but the very enthusiastic are limited to the shore which lies between the Bayview Hotel and the harbour. The water there is clear and the bottom mainly sandy with depths which are seldom in excess of 10m. Nevertheless, a night dive from this beach can be most rewarding.

Local Facilities and Information

Compressor:	Bay View Hotel, Clare Island Tel. 098 26307	
Tidal Constant:	Dublin -05 50	
Local VHF station:	Clifden Road Ch. 16, 67, 26 Belmullet Radio Ch.16, 67, 83	
Chart:	2667, 2420	
Maps:	½":1 mile OS No. 10	1:50,000 No. 30

Pogge photographed at Tralee Bay, Fenit ***Photo: Nigel Motyer***

Common prawn reflected in air bubble ***Photo: Nigel Motyer***

Anenomie *Photo: Costello*

Velvet swimming crabs mating *Photo: Nigel Motyer*

Diver and crawfish – Valentia ***Photo: Eddie Dunne***

Compass jellyfish – St. John's Point   *Photo: Nigel Motyer*

Puffin ***Photo: Nigel Motyer***

Shag
Photo: Nigel Motyer

Turnstone
Photo: Nigel Motyer

Fulmar
Photo: Nigel Motyer

Herring Gull
Photo: Nigel Motyer

Cormorant *Photo: Nigel Motyer*

Grey seal at the Skelligs *Photo: Nigel Motyer*

Sleive League cliffs, Teelin, Donegal *Photo: Nigel Motyer*

Achill Island
Co. Mayo

Achill Island lies 5km north of Clare Island at the entrance to Clew Bay and is a prime tourist location with fine beaches, good pubs and thriving craic. Though an island, it is linked to the mainland by a bridge. Petrol supplies on the island are ample with several garages. The flood tide travels towards the east while the ebb goes west. There are strong tides approaching the headlands and in the shallow areas.

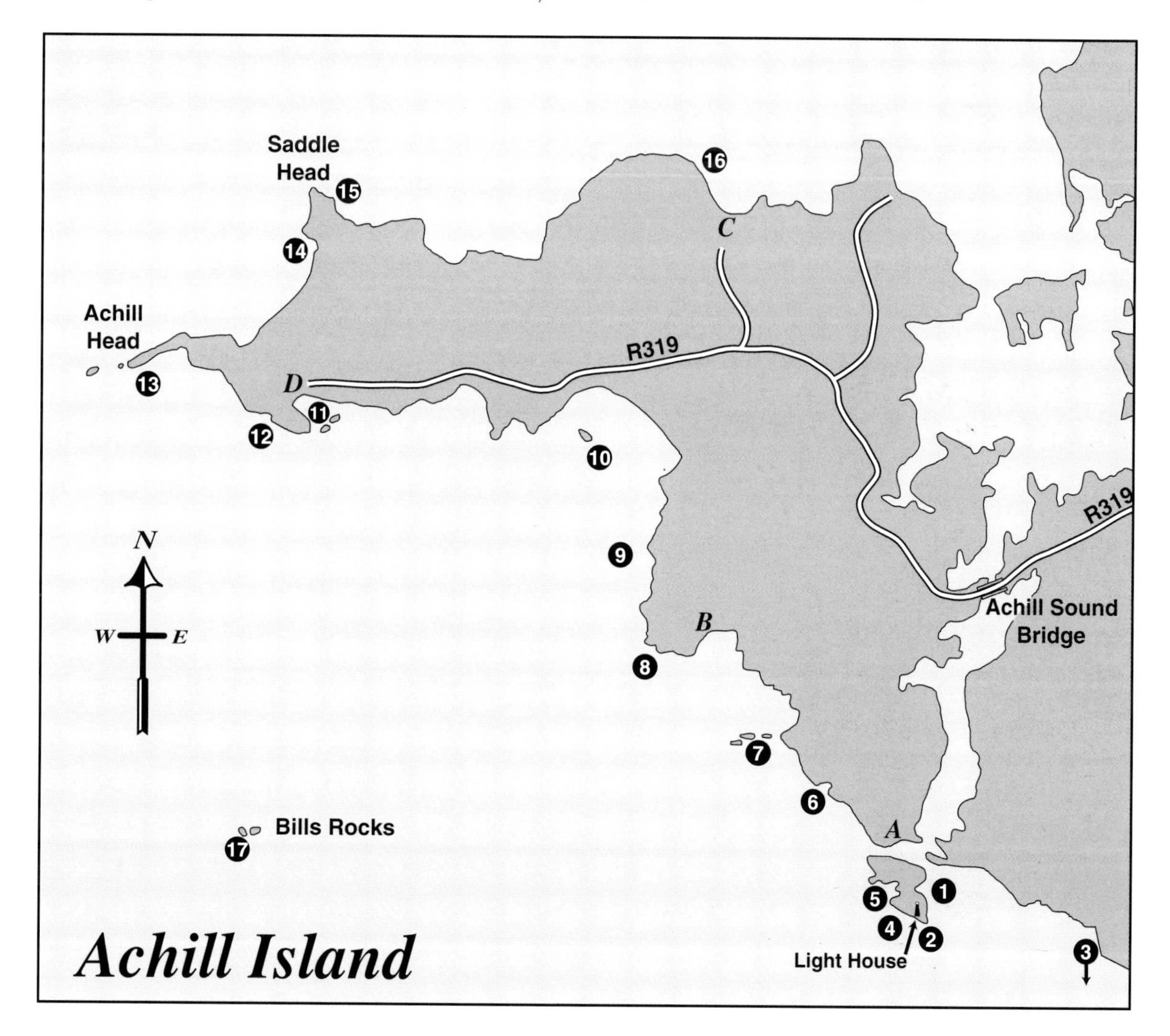

The Launching Sites

A. Darby's Point
This slipway leads to a solid beach with easy access for cars and a good launching site. A freshwater tap and a power point are available.

B. Dooega
This is the best launching point on the island. A long slipway leads to water at all stages of the tide. There is however little parking for cars.

C. Dugort
This is a steep slipway with no room for errors unhitching. The winch works and is useful.

D. Bullsmouth
This is a good slipway which reaches well into the water. There is no problem launching. Care is necessary when recovering as strong tides and currents rush over the slip which can push a trailer off.

E. Porteen
This is next door to the Achill SAC clubhouse. Both the slip and harbour are very rough due to storm damage. This makes it very hard on cars when launching. Fresh water and a power point are available.

Dive Sites

1. Achill Beg East
A safe and pleasant area for trainees which can easily be accessed from Cloughmore Pier. A sandy bottom varies in depth from 5–10m. The area where the sand meets a rocky reef, running parallel to the island shore, contains fish life ranging from wrasse and pollack among the kelp to squid, blenny, place and dogfish on the sand. The beach offers a safe anchorage and picnic area. A small pier halfway between the beach and the lighthouse can be used from half-tide to high water.

2. Lighthouse
This is deeper than dive no. 1 ranging from 9m in an interesting gully down to 25m close offshore. The area between the big rock close to the lighthouse and the shore offers shelter for kiting up and starting the dive. Options on this dive include staying in the gully where the depths range from 9–15m and the steep sides offer a wide range sea life growing from surface to bottom. The deeper area outside offers a variety of diving with the deeper water to the southwest and west going down to 25m. The area to the east is more even in depth ranging from 15–18m depending on the state of the tide.

3. Deace's Rock
Deace's Rock is about 3km south of Achill Beg lighthouse and 400m north of Clare Island. Well worth a visit for a deeper dive with depths up to 40m. See description in Clare Island chapter.

4. Achill Beg West
West of Achill Beg lighthouse is an area rich in fish life, wrasse and pollack being the most prolific. There are many interesting gullies and holes down to 25 m, choose your depth. A dive can begin close to the lighthouse going westwards with the ebb tide and eastwards with the flood tide. Generally the current is not a problem on this dive, the wall is north of the main flood tide.

5. Achill Beg Bay
The bay area is rich in fish and plant life with depths ranging from 10–22m. The wall to the south side has many gullies and drop-offs with pollack and wrasse. Lobster and spider crabs (look, photograph but don't take!) can be seen here.

6. Greek Freighter
This wreck can be located 2.5km northwest of Achill Beg in a big cove on the Atlantic Drive. The winch used in salvaging this wreck can still be seen above the cove. The remains of the freighter, torpedoed in WWII, lie in water ranging from 12m at the north to 18m at the south end. This wreck harbours a wide range of fish life of the "round" variety, cod, pollock, wrasse and conger eels. Moving south from the wreck the water deepens to 20m with ledges and dropoffs rich in sea life. This area is subject to tidal movement, westerly on the ebb and easterly on the flood. The wreck site is north of the main tidal movements.

7. Corcaigh Rocks

The Corcaigh Rocks can be seen 800m offshore from the Promontory Fort car park. The area all round the rocks offers very varied diving with a range of depths down to 25m. As tides are generally strong here, dive west of the rocks on ebb tide and east on a flood tide.

8. Dooega Head

The area around Dooega Head has a wide range of depths and fish life. There is 15–25m depth to be found on a rocky bottom. The deeper area is to the south and west. The many coves to the north of the head offer good diving without current. There are many conger eels here. Stronger currents run past the head so good surface cover is essential, again easterly on the flood and west with the ebb tide.

9. Minawn Cliffs

Steep slopes descend from the cliff leading to sand at 20m. There are a lot of underwater peaks.

10. Inishgalloon

Here kelp leads onto sand at 15m. This is a good snorkel location and is close to shore.

11. Keem Bay

A boulder type bottom lies at 15–20m. There is profuse kelp and fish life. If you are diving from the shore (a long swim) make sure that you do not get swept around Moyteogue Head with the flood tide. Inflatables can be manhandled down to the beach and launched if the surf is not too bad.

12. West Moyteogue Head

Here steep cliffs drop to the seabed at 20–30m. Rocky crevices hold plenty of fish life. It is a very good dive. Suitable in good weather.

13. Achill Head

Visibility is especially good here. A cliff leads to the seabed at 20–30m. This is the best of the Achill dives. There is loads of fish life.

14. South of Saddle Head

This is a very exposed site and seas can be rough. Good weather and boat cover are essential. The bottom is at 30m.

15. Saddle Head

Here there is a boulder bottom with plenty of kelp and sea life.

16. Dugort

There is an ideal snorkel along the shore towards the beach. A boulder bottom leads to sand at 10–15m.

17. Bills Rocks

The north side of the Bills Rocks descends to 50m. On the south there is very good diving to 25m. Inside the Bills there are shallow spots and loads of lost lobster pots. Only diveable with good boat cover and fine weather. The nearest launch sites are Dooega and Purteen. See also description given in the Clare Island Site Guide.

Local Facilities and Information

Compressor:	Dol-Fin Divers Cloughmore Pier, Achill, Co. Mayo Tel. 098 45473 Fax. 098 45473
Tidal Constant:	Dublin +05 50
Local VHF station:	Belmullet Radio Ch. 16, 67, 83
Chart:	2420, 2704, 2667
Maps:	½":1 mile No 6 1:50,000 No. 22, 36

Belmullet Penninsula Co. Mayo

The Belmullet/Blacksod Peninsula is a very extensive and largely untapped diving area providing spectacular and very deep diving around the offshore islands and very sheltered weather proof shore dive sites. One reason why the area has largely been ignored by divers is that it lacks a popular resort town and is somewhat off the main arterial routes. These, in fact, are advantages for a large group planning an expedition. The roads are uncluttered and you can certainly get away from the crowds (and diving compressors) to enjoy peace and solitude in an area which provides plenty of beaches and beautiful and dramatic scenery.

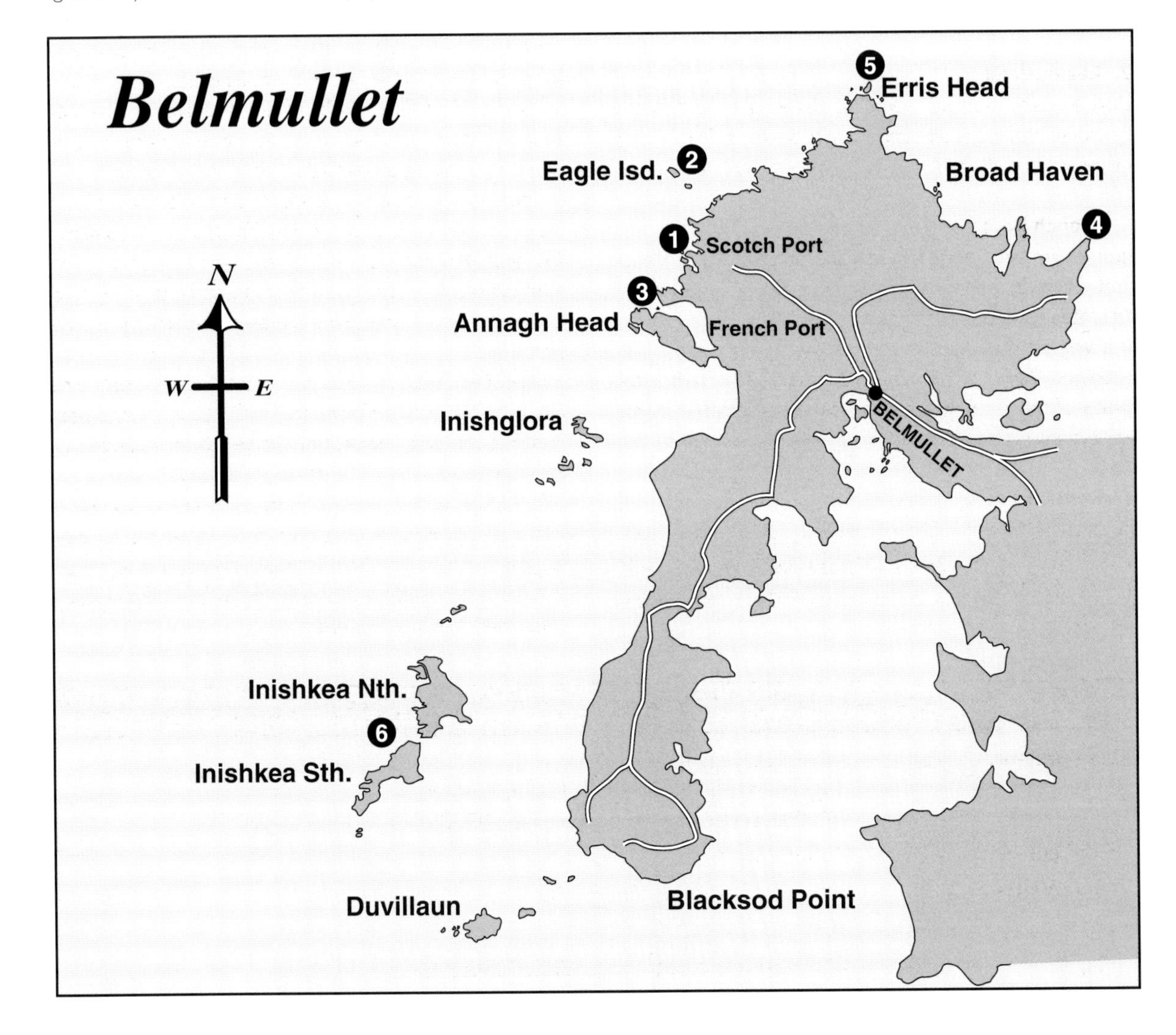

Dive Sites

1. Scotchport

Scotchport, just west of Belmullet, is a beautiful bay extending about 1km seaward to a very narrow entry making it extremely sheltered. The shore line is stony and free of sand. The water is crystal clear and provides the sort of colourful marine life you see in the pollack holes at Kilkee. The advantage here is that the inner bay extends several hundred metres across and up to 10m in depth making it perfect for snorkelling and training dives.

Just further out towards the mouth but still sheltered from the open sea there is 25m, good reefs and rocky scenery. Inflatables can be safely moored in this bay overnight in summer time.

In good sea conditions a 10–15 minute boat trip out into the open sea gives access to excellent diving north and south of Scotchport along the cliff faces and small bays. Depths of 30m may be found close to shore.

2. Eagle Island

Easily accessible from Scotchport, this isolated island with its lofty lighthouse provides spectacular diving with sheer cliff faces falling off very quickly into deep water, not an area for the novice.

3. French Port

Just to the south of Scotchport is the far larger bay of French Port. There is shelter here for hard hulled and bigger boats and a good slipway for launching.

Diving just north and south of the mouth of the bay is very good and like Scotchport up to 25m is available within the shelter of the bay. Eagle Island and its smaller "satellite" islands are also accessible from here.

4. Broadhaven

Because Ballyglass in Broadhaven Bay faces north it gets shelter from southerly winds and is a good base for a trip to The Stags of Broadhaven in suitable weather. There are a very good quay and slipway here.

The lighthouse at Broadhaven provides a very good shore dive for novices. There is easy access to a sheltered cove via stone steps and though the depth is only 10m the area is colourful and full of fish life.

5. Erris Head

To the west juts into the Atlantic but a road and a slipway have been hewn out of the rocks giving access down a steep incline to a delightful gully. This is an ideal location for a small group and gives easy access to very good diving around the head. The dive boat does have to be heaved up the steep slip afterwards however!

6. Inishkea Islands

The Blacksod Peninsula to the south of Belmullet opens on to a magnificent view of Achill Island, Blacksod Bay and the various rocks and islands to the west. Chief of these are Inishkea North and Inishkea South whose Irish speaking inhabitants have recently moved to the mainland and abandoning the islands to the seals and their intrepid defenders Greenpeace.

There is a good slipway at Blacksod Point and the islands are within reasonable travelling time. The trip can be considerably shortened for the divers by arranging to pick them up from the beautiful white sandy beach to the west of the head to which they can drive while the boats are brought around by sea.

The Inishkea Islands provide an ideal location for a well organised diving holiday. There is a good harbour, empty houses with excellent diving on both east and west shores and access to other offshore rocks, and no distractions like pubs!

The Belmullet area abounds in good dive sites, is reasonably "weatherproof" once you are prepared to drive to alternative dive sites, is away from the "madding crowds", provides rugged and spectacular scenery and is served by an excellent hotel which caters specifically for divers.

Local Facilities and Information

Compressor:	Cuan na Farraige Dive Centre, Aughoose, Pullathomas, Ballina, Co. Mayo Tel. 097 87800 Fax. 097 87800
Tidal constant:	Dublin -06 09
Local VHF station:	Belmullet Radio Ch. 16, 67, 83
Chart:	2420
Maps:	½":1 mile OS No. 6 1:50,000 No. 22

North Mayo

Starting at Ballycastle, a small village of 14 pubs overlooking Bunatrahir Bay, the North Mayo coast is one of Ireland's last unknown diving areas. As you look out to sea Doonbristy (a spectacular sea stack) on Downpatrick Head, rises from the ocean and promises an exceptional dive that completely lives up to expectations.

Downpatrick Head is about 3km from Ballycastle on the R314 from Ballina. One and a half kilometres outside Ballycastle on the Belmullet road, a side road signposted for the "Stella Maris" guest house leads down to a wide slipway with plenty of parking.

Boats may be launched at any time, all diving is by boat and north winds can cause problems. It is also advisable to watch out for fishing nets here and all along this coast. This is a very remote area of Ireland, barely touched by the outside world and divers have a responsibility to respect and tolerate the local people.

It takes about 30 minutes to get to Downpatrick Head by inflatable which offers a range of truly spectacular dives.

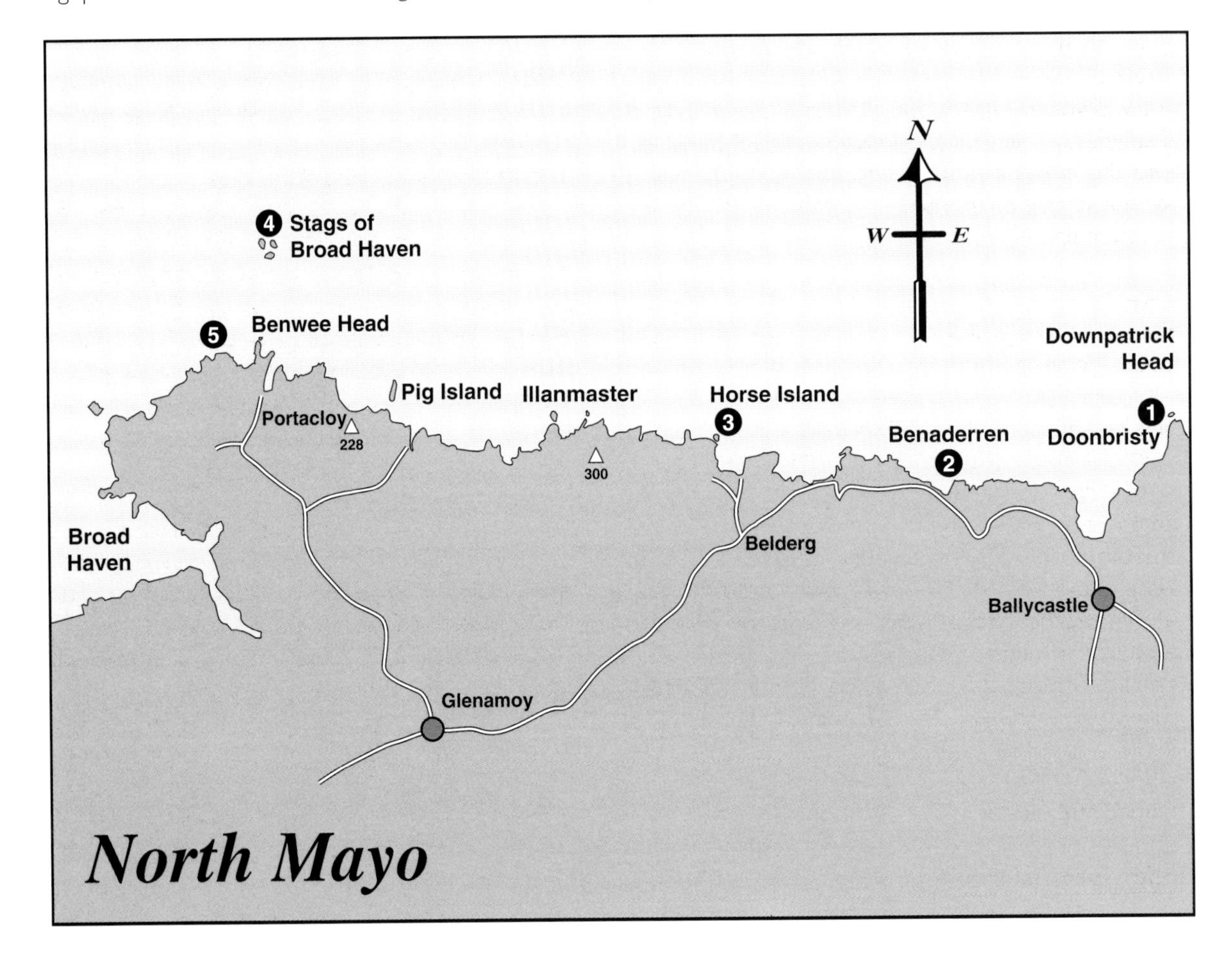

Dive Sites

1. Doonbristy

Doonbristy, a sea stack, starts at 3–4m on the inland edge, a flat, kelpy plateau with plenty of swell. In the immediate area of Doonbristy there are four or five superb dives, generally the cliffs are covered with anemones.

Dive 1

Start at the seaside of the head and work your way in towards the land, compass SW, depth 35m+. At the start of the dive go down the head wall, keeping the wall to your right which will bring you to a split in the cliff. The wall continues for another 100m. The height of the walls varies between 10m and 24m and there are gullies and ridges.

Dive 2

This dive is on the inner side of Downpatrick Head. Start on the second finger and again go in a SW direction to a max. depth of 30m. Descending down the wall you will see the ridge go to the right, this will lead you to a very large opening which will bring you into the cliff under the headland. Coming back out keep a straight course and your dive will finish at the northern tip of the Head.

Dive 3

Start at the beginning of the third finger, which is a good sheltered place for kiting up. Dive down the wall where you will find many openings in the cliff and kelp down to 15m with some very large rocks.

At the bottom, depth 28m, go along the wall in a southerly direction and you will come to an amphitheatre. It is very hard to describe its beautiful smooth rock, it is as if someone designed it (God?). As you exit keep to your left, which will bring you along another ridge. This is a suitable dive for advanced trainees.

Behind Doonbristy there are a number of caves that go right through the cliff and come out up to 200m away, however they are very shallow and boulder filled so they are not suitable for diving.

Immediately to the east of Doonbristy there is a series of headlands with deep cut bays. These cliffs offer spectacular diving, the biggest wall has a

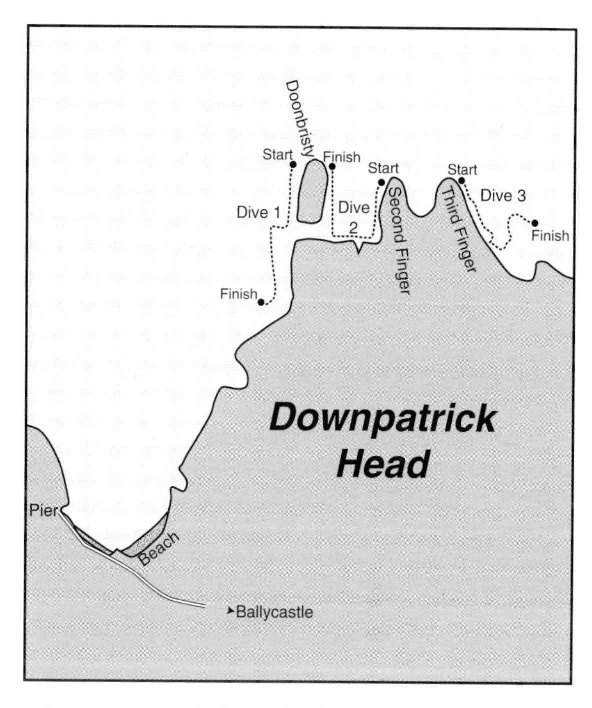

window through from the bay to the sea at 18m. At the point nearest Doonbristy this large wall has a number of caves with very large boulders at 12m through which it is possible to dive.

The depth is in the 20–25m range but the point of Doonbristy goes down to 40m+. Just around the corner from Doonbristy in the bay there is a dive which can be reached by car (the only one along the whole coast). It goes down by a series of large steps to a depth of 25m. As this area gets the full brunt of all the NW storms, there is not much marine life but there are always plenty of fish.

2. Benaderren Head.

Just 3km to the west is Benaderren Head, one of the best dives in the area. A cliff rises 60m straight out of the water, is 300–400m long, and drops vertically to a sandy bottom at 20–25m. This cliff has many deep horizontal cracks with abundant plant and fish life. As you head out to sea, the bottom is covered with large boulders. One sea cave through the cliff terminates in a huge open pool and in another the water appears to flow up hill. Visibility here is generally good, it is possible to see a boat on the surface from 20m.

3. Horse Island

Leaving Ballycastle on the Belmullet road the next hamlet is Belderg, a crossroads with an inn, a grocery shop and telephone. Just after the inn a road on the right leads down to Belderg Harbour, which is a small pier with crowded parking.

Heading out of the harbour Horse Island, to the west, has good diving on more stepped terrain. Plenty of seals around here and a sea cave large enough to hold a few trawlers. From here to Porturlin the coast is only accessible by boat (large).

The road out of Beklerg swings inland along the beautiful, barren valley of the Glenamoy River. Turning off at Glenamoy you cross Annie Brady Bridge after a few miles and then you are in one of the remotest parts of Ireland (or Europe for that matter). Follow the road to Carrowteige and turn for Portacloy. A beautiful fjord like bay about 1km deep, a silver beach, two piers, loads of parking and camping and the best diving in Ireland. Up to a few years ago this place was deserted, except for the odd lost tourist. Since British and N. Ireland divers discovered Portacloy in 1990 it is seldom free of divers. Fortunately there is enough diving for everyone but there is now a certain lack of shellfish!

4. The Stags of Broadhaven

Go straight out of Portacloy and the Stags of Broadhaven rise majestically about 1 mile offshore, a group of seven rocks rising more than 100m above sea-level. Any of the seaward sides of the Stags provides superb diving. As you approach from Portacloy a large white quartzite patch on one face is a landmark for a 40m plus dive.

On the eastern-most reef there is a spectacular canyon dive 10m deep going for 200m or more but it is very hard to find the entrance, you are usually so overawed by the rest of the reef that you miss the entrance. The western most stag has a face which is looking towards Portacloy, which has a most spectacular display of jewel anemones, whose profusion and colour are breathtaking.

To the wes,t out of Portacloy, as far as Bendee Head, offers a huge choice of dives, none of which will disappoint. However, at the mouth of Portacloy under spectacular 600m high cliffs, is the only disappointing dive of the area – 12m of kelp that just goes on and on.

5. Benwee Head

The terrain towards Benwee Head is very varied. The cliffs and bottoms have deep gullies 5–6m with crests 2–3m apart. When the weather blows in from the N or NW it is worth going to Porturlin, several kilometres to the east, from where dives on Pig Island may be made. Here the bottom is stepped at 20–30m with a profusion of Devon cup coral. As always there are lots of fish and plant life.

Local Facilities and Information

Compressor:	Cuan na Farraige Dive Centre, Aughoose, Pullathomas, Ballina, Co. Mayo Tel. 097 87800 Fax. 097 87800
Tidal Constant:	Dublin -06 00 min
Local VHF station:	Belmullet Radio Ch.16, 67, 83
Chart:	2420
Maps:	½":1 mile OS No. 6 1:50,000 No. 22

North Sligo

Ballyconnell Dive Sites

Ardboline Island

Heading north from Sligo on the N15, turn off to the left at Drumcliffe Cemetery, under Ben Bulben, where Yeats is buried. Follow the third class road towards Ballyconnell, passing the famous Ellen's Pub, if you really must, on the way. Find the part-sand, part-shingle beach where inflatables can be launched. The beach should be the base for some very easy diving, with short boat rides to the best sites. Be careful of encroachment on local lands and check with the nearest householders, if in doubt.

There is a long underwater reef running in a great arc for about 1000m from the low headland north of the beach, all the way to Ardboline Island, which can be seen to the SW. Straight out from the beach, the reef is only about 800m offshore, while it is possible to have a good shore dive under the headland itself.

Once located, the reef offers an almost continuous drop-off, from 20 to 30m, depending on the area, so the dive site is a matter of choice. The sea-life is varied and plentiful, and the visibility normally is good.

Steamer Wreck

Off the centre of the island, on the western side, there are the remains of a steamer which sank some 80 years ago. The dive site is very exposed to winds from all quarters but offshore easterlies.

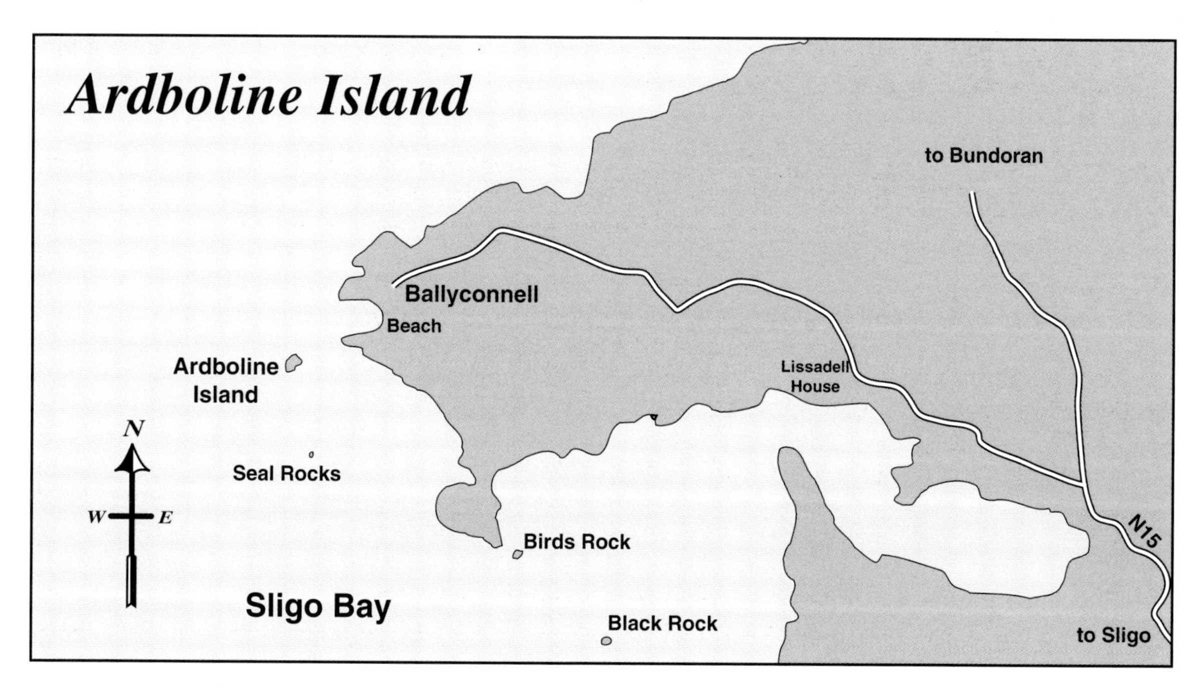

Mullaghmore

The Mullaghmore headland is situated in North West Ireland, on the south of Donegal Bay. It is a couple of miles from the main road linking Sligo and Donega (N I5). The final approach depends on whether one is coming from the north or from the south. Follow the signpost either from Cliffoney village on the main road or from a junction a couple of miles to the north of Cliffoney.

There is a beautifully built stone harbour on the east side of the headland. At the end of the harbour below the Pier Head Hotel there is a slipway which allows launching and retrieval at all but very low spring tides. The slope of the slip is quite shallow and depending on the trailer, wheels may need to be submerged. Do not obstruct the slip area with unattended trailers.

Car parking is not permitted on the northern part of the pier that leads to the breakwater. The running of compressors near the harbour has raised objections from other users so please locate them well out of ear shot.

A stroll along the road around the headland at low tide can show many of the features needed to find the dives and identify some of the features on the map.

In good conditions, a 10 minute boat journey will bring one to the most distant dive locations. The area outside the harbour mouth and along and beyond the breakwater is often very busy, with water-skiers, sail boats, fishing boats, etc., so slow speeds and a watchful eye are needed here.

Many of the dives may be reached from shore by the energetic, but keep in mind the possible difficulties in exiting which can be difficult in swells. Currents are not usually a problem in the area. The main route for boats between the head and the harbour passes over the deep end of Thumb and Crumb, so care is required diving these areas.

THE DIVING

The diving is in the 10–30m range, and wall and reef diving predominates. The geology of the area has tilted the sandstone in places to give a slope on one side and a vertical face on the other. These faces are seamed with cracks, often to a depth of a few metres, running horizontally along and into the rock. A torch, especially one with a narrow penetrating beam, can greatly add to one's enjoyment. These cracks are full of various types of marine life. The visibility is usually good.

The Thumb area is fairly sheltered from prevailing winds and any swell has less effect here. There is however a sewage outfall in this area (see map), and at certain stages of the tide, and especially when the village is busy, sewage can be encountered close to shore to the south of Thumb Rock. There is evidence of some pollution on Thumb itself in the form of a dust like deposit. Crumb Rock, 100m to the north, tends to be cleaner.

Mullaghmore Dive Sites

1. Thumb Rock

The Thumb Rock area is about 500m from the harbour (see map). This rock runs roughly perpendicular to the shore. At low tide the top of the shallow end can be seen breaking. A descent can be made down a steep slippery slope from the road near the old post office. Care is required, and a safety rope attached to a car and dangling over the steep step at the bottom can be useful.

After crossing the rocks, a fin of about 100m will bring you to the top of the rock. The direction to follow to the rock is roughly that of the shallow gully that you will see below you. The bottom depth at the start of the rock is about 10m.

If diving from a boat various marks can be used, the rock face curves a bit however, so different marks are needed for various parts of the rock. The south side of the rock is a slope rising from a sandy bottom fairly gradually, and the north side is vertical and the main attraction.

Approximately 100m to the north of Thumb is a very similar rock, known locally as Crumb rock. The area between the two rocks is a boulder field that runs out to a sandy bottom to the east. At high tide at the deep outer end of these rocks one will be in nearly 30m of water.

2. Pidgeon's Cove

To the north of Crumb there is an interesting area of a quite broken bottom with small reefs, and one quite large reef with a wall a bit lower than Thumb, and not as long.

Unless a long fin out and back is acceptable this area is best accessed by boat. The dominant feature from the boat is a large cave in the cliffs below the road. Enter the water about 75m out from this cave. The depths here tend to be about 10–25m. There is a deep depression a bit further out where depths in excess of 30m can be found.

3. The Head

The Head is the area of the rock island, offshore from the north of the headland, that is split by gullies running perpendicular to the shore (see map).

This area can be dived from either shore or by boat. These gullies vary in width and depth. In the larger ones the feeling is as if one were passing through a street of two story houses. The walls are cracked, with cracks of varying depths. At the shore end the depth can be as shallow as 6m, while at the outer end 25m can be reached.

It is possible to travel out one gully, turn 90° at the end and, and intercept an adjoining gully and return by that. This area is more exposed to swells than the previous two, and can sometimes only be dived from a boat.

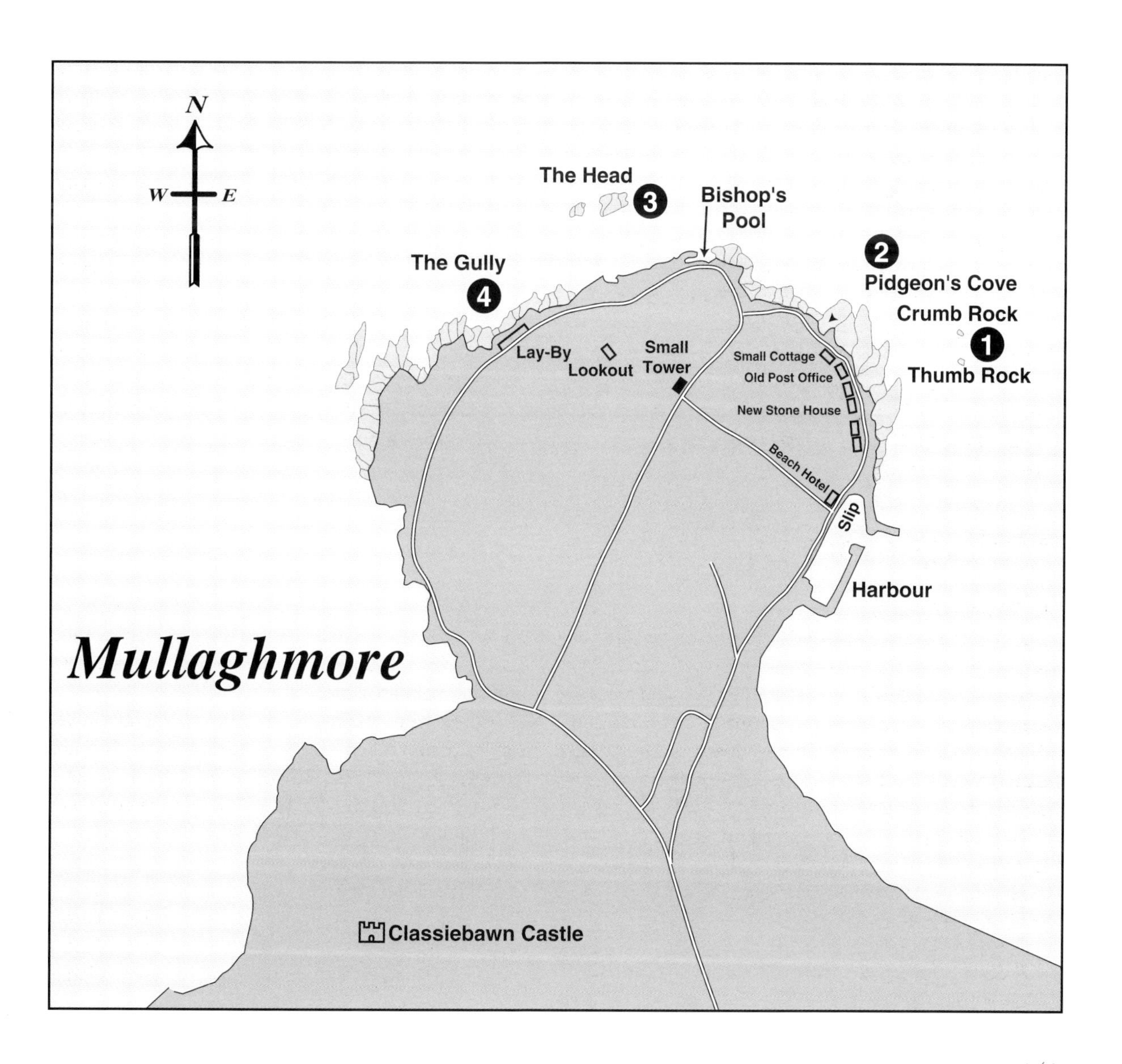

At the western end greater depths can be reached, 30m approx. and the gullies are not as regular in shape, but open out into large bowls. The Bishop's Pool (see map) at high tide and in good conditions can provide an ideal sheltered, nearly enclosed area for Snorkellers and trainee divers.

4. Beyond the Head

A few hundred metres beyond the Head there is a rocky spur that runs down from the top of the cliff. There is a gully out from the bottom of this spur. Access can be gained from the road, parking cars in the layby beside the cliff. Apart from this gully, the bottom around this area tends to be fairly shallow and uninteresting, compared to other areas. There is a headland farther over to the west beyond Classiebawn Castle. This is Rosskeeragh Point and is not dived very often as there is better diving closer to the harbour. The bottom is rocky and may be worth a visit in good conditions.

Local Facilities and Information

Compressor:	Harbour View Dive Centre Bunduff, Cliffoney, Co. Sligo Tel. 071 66366 Fax. 071 66366 E-mail: danboyle@iol.ie
Tidal constant:	Dublin +06 00
Local VHF station:	Glenhead Radio Ch.16, 67, 24
Charts	2702
Maps:	½":1 mileNo. 7; 1:50,000 No. 16

South Donegal

The South Donegal coastline is varied and dramatic, embracing, as it does, sheer cliffs, rocks, tiny islets and sandy beaches. The sea offers clear water, choice of depth, colour, beauty, a wide variety of sea life and, on occasions, the sun. The main difficulty, however, is accessibility. There are few harbours or roads along this length of coastline and it also faces into the prevailing weather. That been said there are some access points which are well worth a visit.

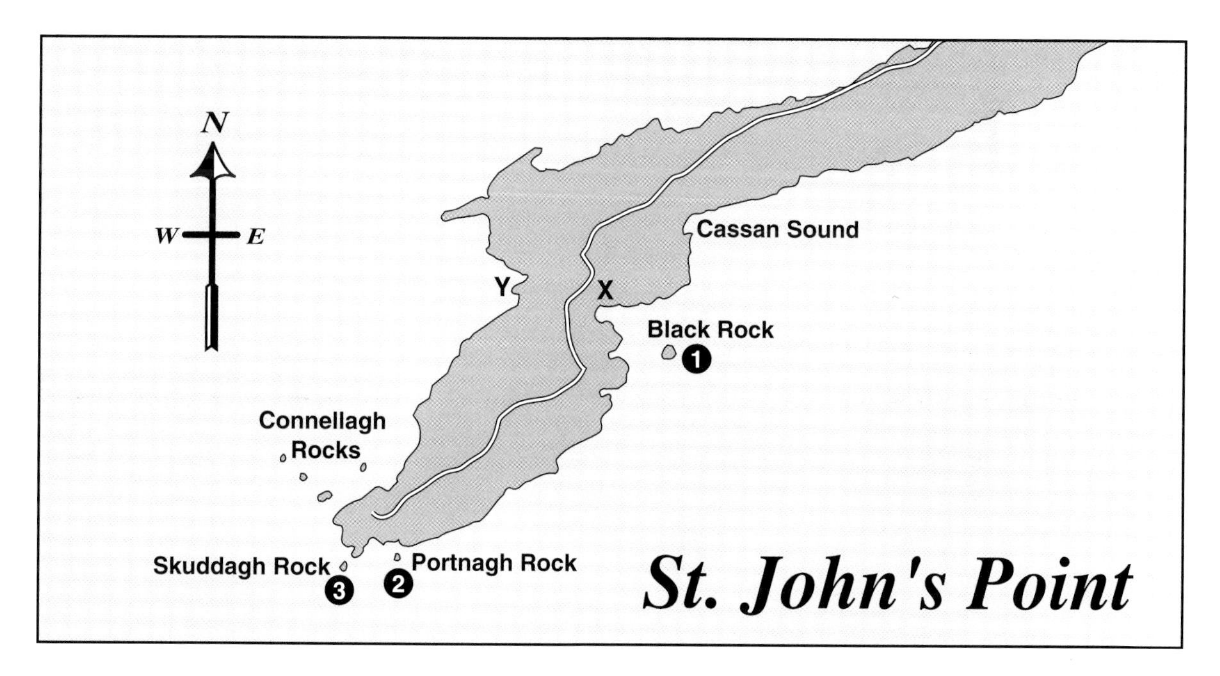

St. John's Point

St. John's Point is a peninsula situated in the eastern end of Donegal Bay. To reach the point proceed west on the N56 from Donegal town through the villages of Mountcharles and Dunkineely. Approximately 500m past the village of Dunkineely take the first turn left and continue out along this road which runs through the middle of the peninsula.

St. John's Point offers a variety of dive sites, both shore and boat. The most suitable location for launching a boat is from the small beach marked X. Keep to the right-hand side of the beach when launching as there are some stones. However, a van or four wheel drive vehicle will allow you to take the boat and trailer right down to the water's edge.

There is also a pier at Ballysaggart but it is very restricted, in particular there are no parking facilities and the road leading to it is extremely narrow and in bad repair. It is also possible to launch from Cassan Sound but it is equally restricted.

Alternatively, in the case of a large RIB, the boat crew could launch it with ease from Killybegs Harbour (approx. 8km along the N56 from Dunkineely) while the dive party proceeds directly to the point.

The diving on the south (left side) of the peninsula is well protected from north and north west winds. Alternatively it is possible to dive on the north side where the diving is shallower (especially from shore) and more "kelpy". In general this side is more suitable only as the alternative dive site. For shore diving, access to this site is marked at point Y.

The most popular dive sites are, Black Rock, Portnagh Rock and Skuddagh Rock, the first is a boat dive and the others are excellent shore dives.

1. Black Rock

This is a very accessible boat dive. Boats may be most easily launched from the beach marked X. It is a very short trip to the dive site. The best diving is on the southwest end of the rock. This dive offers a nice sheer rock face which shelves to the bottom at 20m. There is always an abundance of marine life and plenty of crevices to tempt the curious diver.

The general area of the Rock offers deeper dives. From the chart it is evident that 40m is easily obtained. As this is a particularly sheltered side of the peninsula, it is ideal for training purposes.

Again working from the beach and moving out past Black Rock there is plenty of boat diving along the SW of the peninsula and along the point.

2. Portnagh Rock

This is the most popular shore dive in the area. It is accessible from a set of steps leading down into the water. Again it is well sheltered from the prevailing winds and diving is possible all the year round. This site is at the very end of the road beside the lighthouse. The rock is nearly always visible and the snorkel out to it only takes a few minutes.

This site offers a sheer face down to 30m with plenty of fish life and crevices. At the bottom of the face is a very interesting area of large rocks and boulders offering plenty of holes, gullies and small ledges. The rocks extend down to 25m.

On a full tide it is relatively easy to acquire a 30m dive, just continue out from the rocks onto the sand where a small ledge is reached. As you move out from the point there is a current on the flood tide (see the chart). Overall the general area of this rock offers a range of depths and underwater terrain to suit the needs of most divers. It is very suitable for small groups of divers without boat facilities.

3. Skuddagh Rock

This is also a shore dive, accessed from the same point. The divers can snorkel out through the gully between the Rock and the mainland. The best dive is a circum-navigation of the rock. It is a slightly more challenging dive than Portnagh Rock.

Fintragh Bay

Fintragh Bay is 1.5km past Killybegs on the road to Kilcar. It offers a wide range of diving from 5–10m snorkel dives to 40m+ scuba dives.

On leaving Killybegs, take the first road to the left which will lead to a small sheltered bay. Here a good slipway gives access for boats and parking can be achieved without causing any annoyance to locals.

On leaving the slip the coast runs to your left and the bay widens the further one goes. The first cove you come to, just past Rosscorcan Head, gives a dive to 20m. Here a wide variety of fish and plant life can be seen in visibility which is normally 10–15m. It is common to see ling, ballan wrasse, pollack, pouting, congers and John Dory with an abundance of brittle and Bloody Henry starfish. Sea

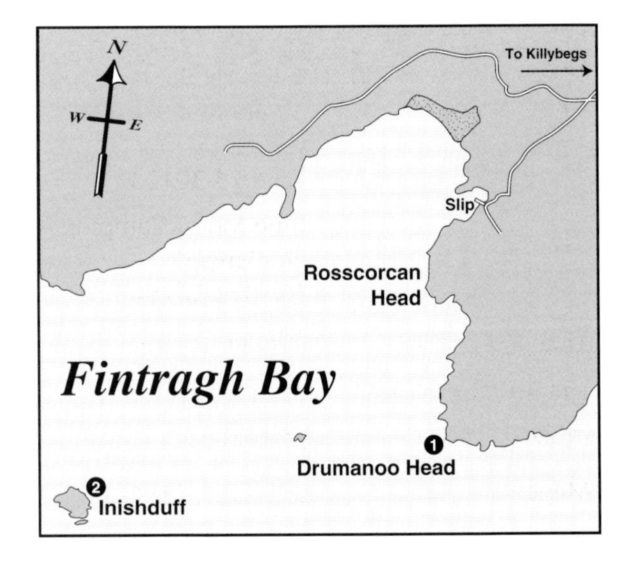

anemones are also quite prolific, seen on nearly all dives are: jewel, plumose, snakelocks and beadlet. Sponges again are very common with a wide variety. The common sea urchins are in numbers and sizes not seen elsewhere. Do not collect them!

1. Drumanoo Head
The headland is an exceptional dive, for the experienced diver. All the fish and fauna mentioned before are again in greater abundance but the terrain is quite different. About 300m from the point a dive of 20m is achieved on a plateau, and swimming in a southerly direction there is a wonderful drop-off to 30m. Going down the cliff face there is a chance to view crevice dwelling fish and a variety of fauna. The bottom is sandy with very large boulders strewn about which gives shelter to many congers and bottom living crustaceans.

2. Inisduff Island
Further out to sea this is a small island which has interesting diving with depths ranging from 10–30m and a kelp forest where greater pipefish and octopus have been seen.

All in all there are a lot of good dives in the bay but unfortunately it is exposed to the SW winds.

Teelin Pier

Teelin Pier is situated approx. 50km west from Donegal town via Killybegs, Kilcar and Carrick. Teelin has a lot to offer divers. Boats can be launched easily and quickly with plenty of parking space for cars and trailers. A boat is a must if you want to dive here, because the terrain and high cliffs makes shore diving impossible.

When leaving the estuary go west (turn right), along here you will find some of the best diving in Ireland, 40m+ can be found within 100m from the shore. There are 9km of coastline for diving from here all the way down to Malin Beg. Halfway between Teelin and Malin Beg you will come to Sleive League the highest sea cliffs in Europe. Here you will find a cave big enough to take a boat for a distance of 40m. This cave is also the home of many seals.

With such a rugged coastline it is hard to imagine the beauty that lies beneath these Atlantic waters. Visibility on a normal day is between 10–15m and on a good summer's day it is possible to see the boat from 30m. All along these cliffs, with horizontal cracks and ledges, there is an abundance of fish and plant life

It is common for divers to swim with what seems like a never ending shoals of pollack and mackerel while deeper down the large boulders, gullies and kelp offer an ideal hiding place for lobsters, crayfish, crabs and a multitude of small fish.

Local Facilities and Information

Compressor:	Malinmore Adventure Centre, Glencolumbkille Tel. 073 30123	
	Blue Moon Camping & Hostel, Dunkineely Tel. 073 37264	
Tidal Constant:	Dublin -05 50	
Local VHF station:	Glenhead Radio Ch. 16, 67, 24	
Chart:	2702, 2725	
Maps:	½":1 mile OS No. 3	1:50,000 No. 10

Malinbeg and Rathlin O'Birne

Malinbeg Harbour

This is a natural inlet with a small quay on the Slieve League Peninsula at the most westerly point of Donegal and close to the island of Rathlin O'Birne. There are many dive sites in the region of which those listed is a sample. RIBs and large dive boats must be launched at Teelin further east and driven by sea to the harbour. In good weather conditions RIBs may be moored overnight in the harbour. The Malinmore Adventure Centre run their scuba-diving courses in this sheltered place.

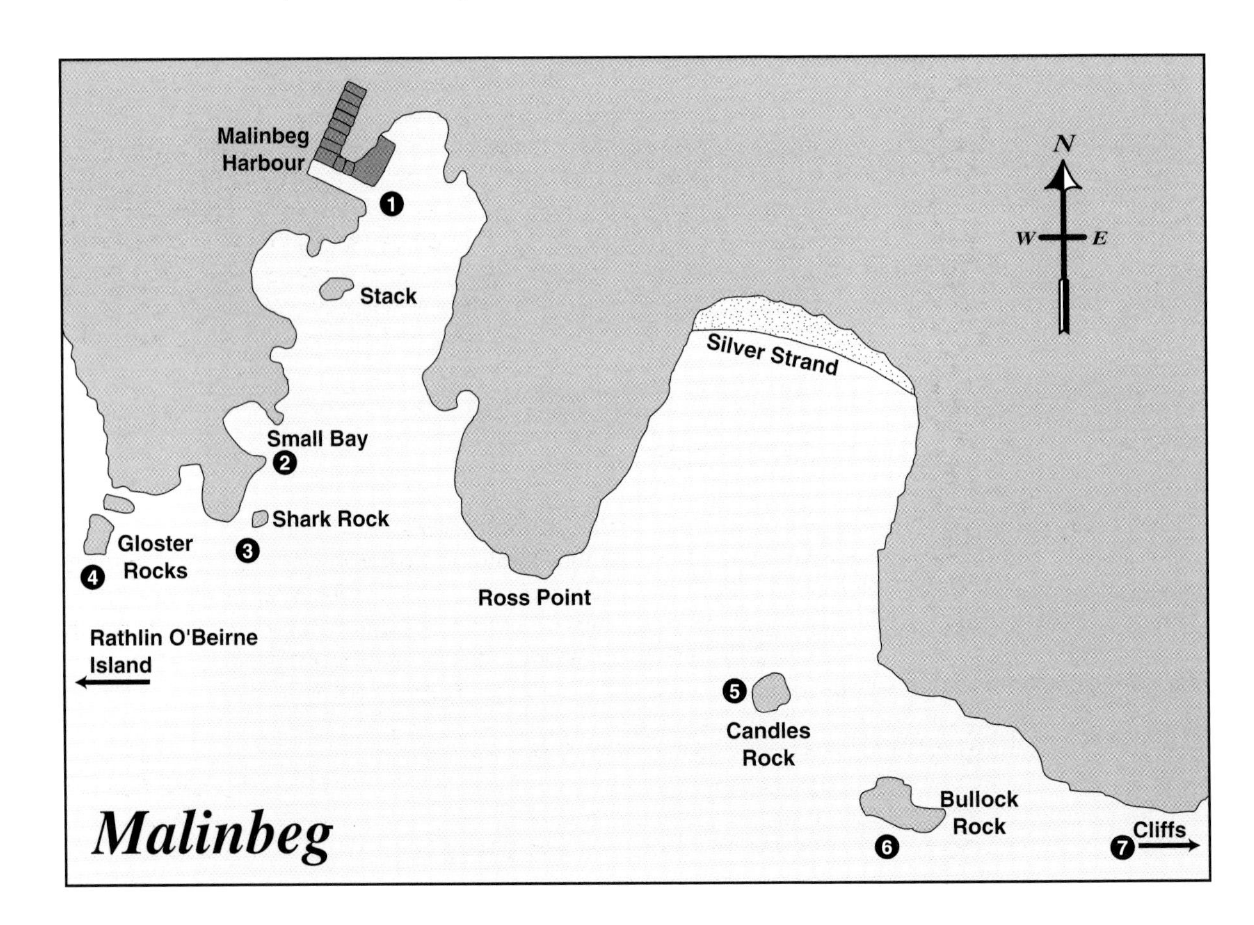

Malinbeg Dive Sites

1. Malinbeg
It is a beautiful but shallow, 5m shore dive with crystal clear water, lots of life and sheltered in most weather. The stack in the middle is an interesting habitat for a wide variety of North Atlantic life – octopus, eel, shrimp and wrasse. It makes a world class night dive, easy access and control and teeming with life.

2. Small Bay
Small Bay at the entrance to Malinbeg Harbour is a beautiful 18m dive over white sand with large rocky outcrops. The light here is excellent for photography. There is a shallow cave at the back of the bay in the centre of which is a sandy hollow, a spawning ground for a variety of fish in the spring and early summer.

3. Shark Rock
Shark Rock is a covering rock at the entrance to the harbour which offers beautiful dives through two rocky gullies. Enter the water just to the north of the rock and drop down into a large bowl, which because it is sheltered is always full of fish, swim SW into the corner which looks dark but opens out to an exciting overhanging swim-through at 20m. Passing through this swim east ascending to the 14m mark and following the rock round, you come into a 2m wide gully heading north. There is always a selection of lobster and cray in the holes in the rock walls (look, don't touch!). You can finish out the dive by swimming north and entering Small Bay.

4. Gloster Rocks
Gloster Rocks offer several dives. Enter the water to the east of the rocks and swim through the gap between the rocks and then turn either north or south and follow the rock, or again entering to the east swim south into deeper water (up to 35m).

5. Candles Rock
Candles Rock is an excellent dive where you can swim right round the rock or head SW into deep water (40m). Inside (NE) the depth is 8–14m and offers lots of broken rock. Leading away to the NW is a ledge at 18–20m.

6. Bullock Rock
Bullock Rock (Thor Lee Bullig) is a submerged reef which breaks in a heavy swell. The top is about 4m and the bottom is about 27m with shear drops and deep cuts in the rock. The inside (north side) is the most interesting but it is just possible to swim all round it. Excellent life and colours.

7. Slieve League Cliffs
The cliffs at Slieve League are the tallest sea cliffs in Europe with a height of 600m. They tower above some of the most beautiful dive sites in Ireland. Silver Strand to Carrigan Head is a distance of about 8km. Dives range from drop offs to shallow reefs, small coves and caves big enough to take the boat into. For the non-diver there is a very good viewing point from the car park on Carrigan Head but the drive up there is something else, not for the learner driver or the faint hearted.

Rathlin O'Birne Dive Sites

Situated about 5km off Malinbeg, Rathlin O'Birne island offers several worthwhile and interesting dives. The visibility of the water is usually fabulous. The island is dominated by a lighthouse marking the north of Donegal Bay. On the south side of the island is a deep cleft leading to the landing pier for the lighthouse. This pier is a convenient place for kitting up or mooring a boat. The reefs on either side of the island are ideal for snorkelling provided the sea is calm. Steps on the west of the island allow access to explore it and its unmanned lighthouse.

8. Amphitheatre
Amphitheatre is a natural underwater bowl. It starts with a cave at the back at about 18m and opens out to either side in a curve of rock. The water deepens out to 35–40m. There is an abundance of fish life for which it seems to act as a natural shelter.

9. Crane
Just out from the landing steps and round the corner dropping down the reef, you come into a gulley, which is a spawning ground for fish in the early part of the year.

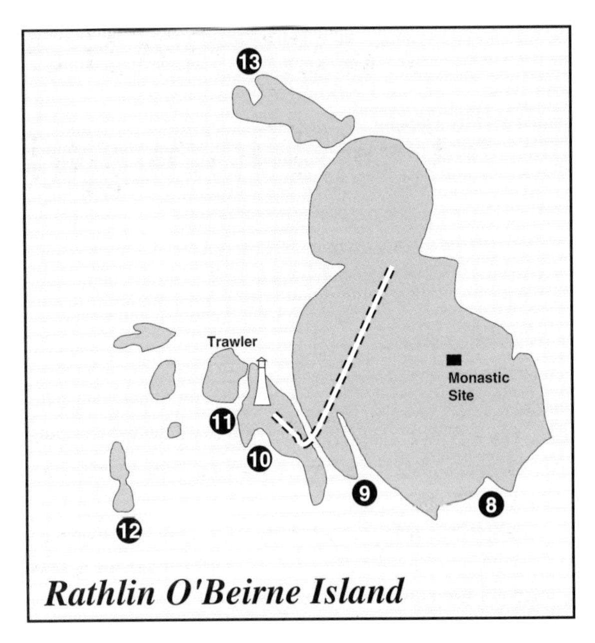

Rathlin O'Beirne Island

At the back of the gulley is a crane which fell from the headland where it was used to lift supplies from a tender to the lighthouse. You can carry on into the cut between the rocks or swim out into deeper water. The gully can dry at its shallowest point at low tides. There is a great variety of plant and animal life in beautiful colour.

10. Bays

There are a number of bays on the south side of the island offering excellent dives with a variety of terrain and depths. All have a large number of inhabitants who are all friendly and offer a unique opportunity to get close to North Atlantic fish and shellfish.

11. Wall

There is a wall running SE from the small bay where the landing steps are. The best dive here is to enter the water off the southern end of the wall, you can pick your depth, from 10–35m, then swim NW onto and along the wall. This leads you into the bay by the steps where there is an excellent open cave which offers brilliant photo opportunities.

12. Trench

The trench outside the SW corner of the island has to be experienced to be believed. Entering the water by the rocks which are about 14m deep, you swim south or southwest and over the edge of a drop-off to 35m. You can then cross the trench and rise up the opposite wall or swim west into deeper water. You can get all the depth you want here.

13. Gully

There is a gully on the northwestern corner of the island which offers a magnificent dive, with large rocks and deep cuts in the rock. Pilot whales have seen at this point. Some of the other dives are close to the rocks where the seals bask. Dolphins are also a common sight off the island.

Wrecks

The remains of two trawlers wrecked on the island with tragic loss of life lie scattered on the west side of the island. These were the "Carraig Una" and the "Evlyn Marie" wrecked in 1975 and 1976 respectfully. There is another wreck lies between the island and Teelin, the "Rostellan", a coal boat holed in 1934 while landing coal for the lighthouse.

Local Facilities and Information

Compressor:	Malinmore Adventure Centre, Glencolumkille Tel. 073 30123	
Tidal Constant:	Dublin -05 50	
Local VHF Radio:	Glen Head Radio Ch. 16, 24	
Local Chart No:	2702, 1879	
Maps:	½":1 mile No.3	1:50,000 No. 10

Aranmore
Co. Donegal

Donegal has many fine dive sites but none better than the sites around Aranmore Island near Burtonport. Have a look at the chart of Aranmore and you will see that there will always be sheltered shores. Burtonport has a lot going for it. Accommodation is relatively plentiful and the large slipway is good at any state of the tide. There are white sandy beaches for the kids and the local establishments certainly know how to cater for hungry and thirsty divers.

As a general rule if you can get access to the exposed western side of Aranmore go there!, keeping the sheltered sites for when the westerlies blow.

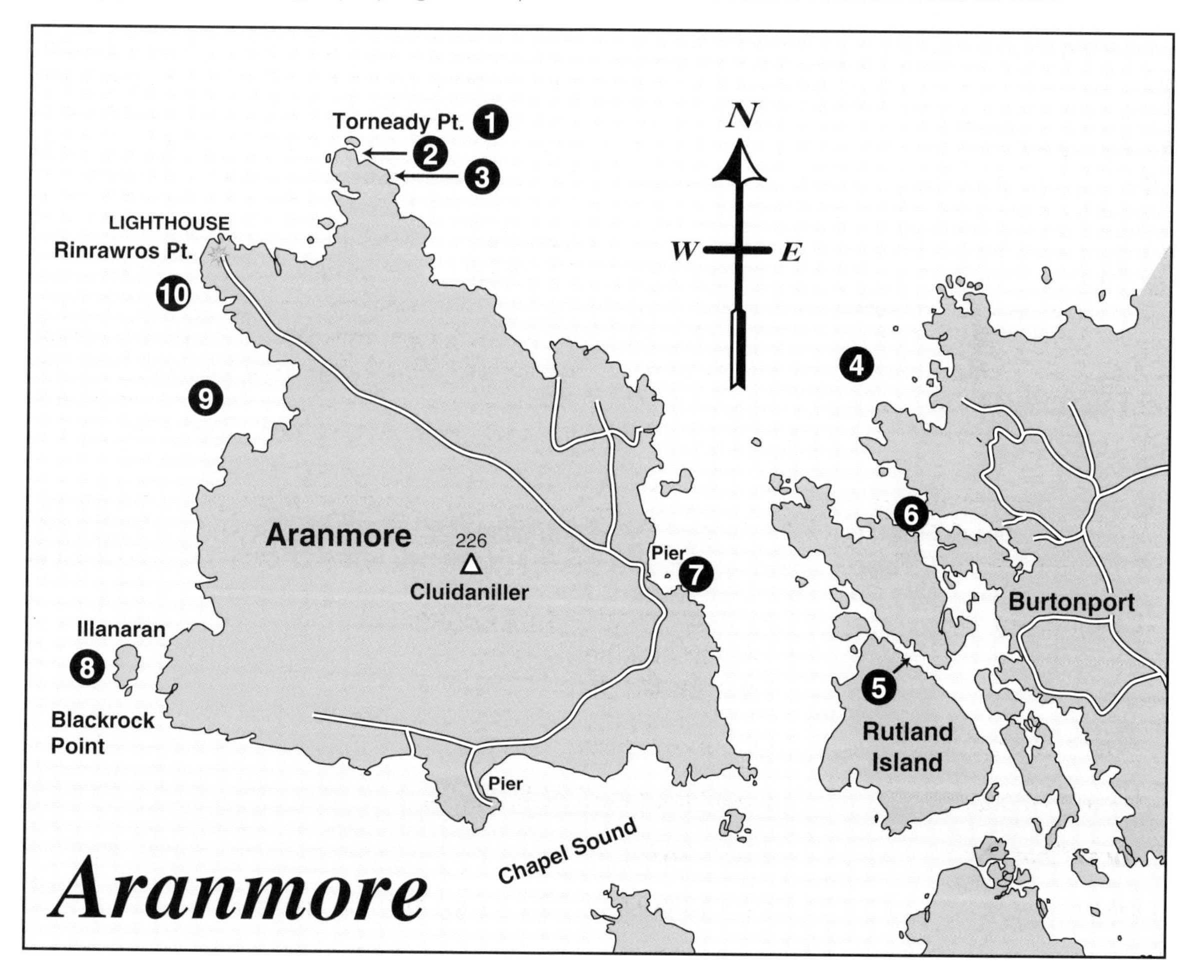

Dive Sites

1. Tomeady Point
Plenty of sheer faces and overhangs coupled with lots of fish make this a popular dive. The north face with depths of 35m is the more dramatic side, keep an eye out for Alcyonium glomerutum, the red dead man's fingers which are quite scarce this far north.

2. Paradise Cavern
Halfway along the narrow channel between Tomeady and Avonmore is an entrance to Paradise Cavern. The other entrance is just south and is more suited to mooring the boat (which should never be left unattended). Divers, snorkellers and photographers who love stunning marine life will appreciate the name. The walls and overhangs are absolutely smothered in anemones of many species and colours and in the spring the sea firs are prey to hundreds of nudibranches. If anyone knows of a better cavern please let us know.

3. Pinnacle Rock
Here there are steep rocks which slope down to 20m with plenty of fish including friendly cuckoo wrasse. You can circumnavigate the rock and finish off the dive in the sea cave to the southwest. As with most areas around Avonmore, the best displays of anemones are in shallow water.

4. The Skiford
Just east of Bullignamirra Rock lies the Skiford, a trawler which went down in a storm only a few years ago. Tragically all hands were lost. The wreck lies listing to starboard in 26m with a reef a few metres to the north. Visibility is usually good and from amidships the whole intact ship can be seen. Trawl nets festoon the stern section and marine life is sparse, apparent from plumose anemones which clothe the fore and aft masts. A dive you'll never forget.

5. Rutland Sound
This is the main thoroughfare for traffic between Burtonport and Avonmore Harbour and is over 20m deep in places. The channel sides drop steeply to 10–15m and there is a pleasant swim through on the southern side. Bring a good torch to light up the nooks and crevices.

The rock walls are dominated by tunicates such as Ascidia aspersa which is indicative of strong currents but no wave action. Kelp stalks are smothered in bright yellow and orange sponges and the shingle, sand and rock sea bed offers a variety of habitats to keep marine biologists and photographers happy. The currents in the sound are strong with upward and downward eddies to the south caused by spring tides. An SMB normally used on drift dives can be a hindrance here particularly when the ferry is bearing down on it, so use common sense. Rutland Sound provides good diving by itself and because it is so sheltered can be dived even in the foulest weather.

6. Inishcoo
There is a shallow drift dive here, max. depths 10m, however, access is a bit dodgy due to rocks and the shallow approaches.

7. The Greek Wreck
Just out from Avonmore Harbour in 6m lies the gutted remains of a large cargo steamer. It is the "Eliosthevous", known locally as the Greek wreck. There are lots of nooks to explore and there is a swim through at the stem with the large propeller at the entrance. A long drive shaft, rather like a pipeline leads to the engine, boilers and condenser which still has a large stack of brass pipes. This wreck makes a good third or fourth dive of the day.

8. Ullanaran
At Ullanaran and Blackrock Point there are some tremendous gullies on the western side of Ullanaran and under the cliffs of Avonmore to the east you will find interlinking caves. In one of these caves two of our divers nearly died of fright when a large grey seal slid between them in the gloom.

9. Sharp Rock
A steep rock pinnacle going down to 20m. The scenery around the pinnacle looks interesting and to dive across to the shore would probably be very good.

10. Lighthouse Steps

Rock walls, gullies and overhangs to 20m make this a varied site. However, it is typical of the whole western coast so choosing a reasonable dive for your buddies need not be a risky business.

Do make sure that your boats and your divers are properly equipped. A chat with the local fishermen about local tides, currents and salmon nets is usually a good idea.

Local Facilities and Information

Compressor:	Lawrence Strain, Forguar, Milford, Co. Donegal Tel. 075 53686
Tidal constant:	Dublin -05 51
Local VHF station:	Malin Head Radio Ch. 16, 67, 23, 85
Chart:	1883, 2792
Maps:	½":1 mile OS No. 1 1:50,000 No.1

Malinbeg ***Photo: Nigel Motyer***

North Donegal

The neighbouring villages of Gortahork and Falcarragh lie in the centre of Cloughaneely Gealtacht (Irish speaking area) in North West Donegal. An area of unsurpassed beauty, notable for its numerous mountains and jagged coastline which combine to present some of the most spectacular coastal scenery in Ireland.

This is an area of particular appeal to divers with young families and to accompanying non divers. There are miles of safe sandy beaches as well as many points of interest in close proximity. These include the resort areas of Portnablagh, Marble Hill, Dunfanaghy, Doe Castle, Ards Forest Park and Sheep Haven Bay. Tory Island, (see below), some 14km off the coast is clearly discernable from the shore.

Along the entire length of this coastline the diver enters a world of giant caves and sheer cliff faces. Even though it is necessary to dive from a boat, any point of entry offers a dive site worthy of exploration. The unusual variety of sea life one encounters includes seals, squid, shark and porpoises as well as exquisite plants and sea anemones.

The principle diving area extends from Dunfanaghy in Sheep Haven Bay to Bloody Foreland, including Horn Head, where the spectacular cliffs rise straight out of the water to a height of 180m.. Within this span of 16km there are innumerable diving venues a few of which are listed below.

The area's weather is dominated by the North Atlantic depression and receives the full force of the strong westerly winds preceding these depressions. Gales are frequent and can blow up in a short space of time. There is also a strong tidal flow. Thus, good dive planning is necessary. Well-equipped boats with VHF radios and SMBs are essential.

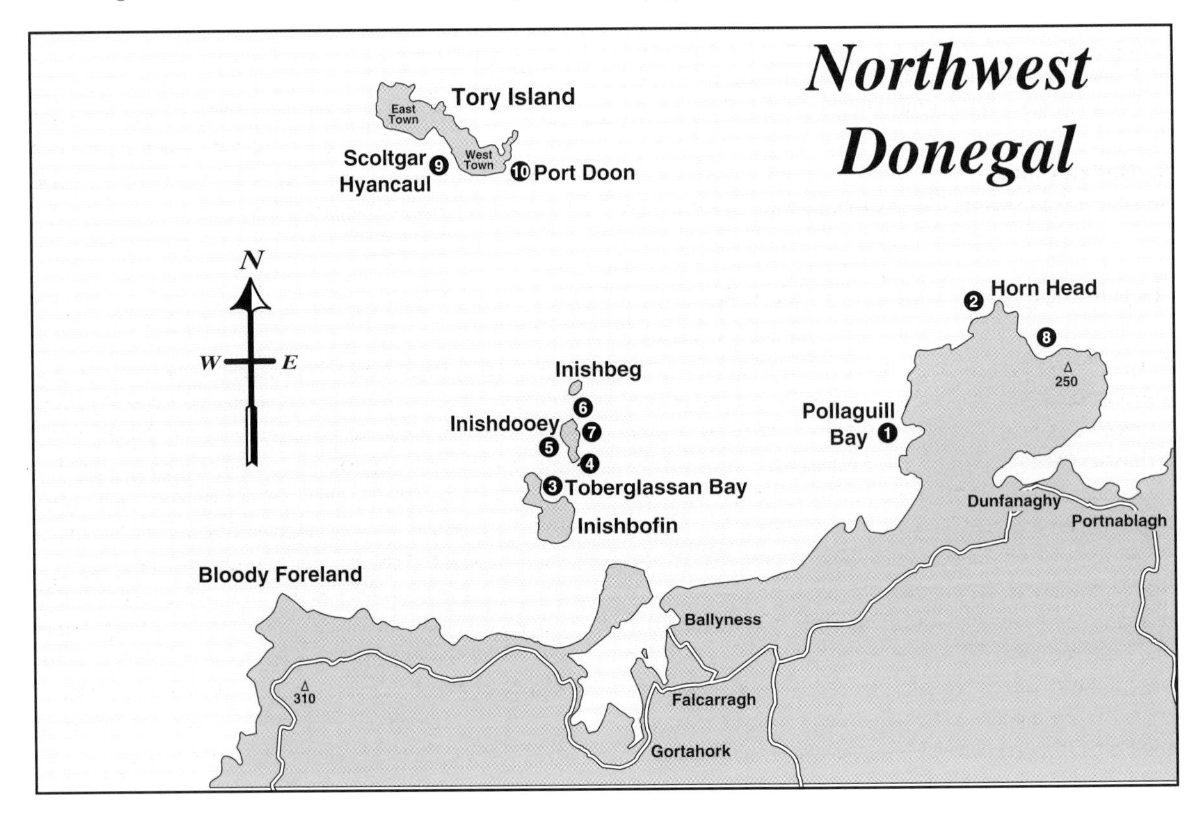

North West Donegal Dive Sites

1. Carricknaherwy
This site is located, off Pollaguill Bay, some 10–15 min. from Ballyness Pier. It consists of a rocky bottom with deep gullies and good sea life including many species of fish and shell fish. This area is also very interesting as there are a large variety of bird life and porpoises to be seen.

2. White Vein Point
Off Micky's Hole (ask directions locally) on Horn Head conditions include a tidal race which makes for a good drift dive. The bottom is sand and rock with a depth of 25m and the visibility is usually 6–10m. Flatfish, dogfish and porpoises are frequently seen.

3. Toberglassan Bay
Located on the north side of Inishbofin, this site is not as good as could be expected but is sheltered from westerly winds. The bottom, which reaches a depth of 12m at the mouth of the bay, is broken rock with sandy gullies.

4. Doon Beg Rocks
Located on southern end of Inishdooey this area is quite shallow with a maximum depth of 10m. The bottom is rocky with gullies, sand and kelp. Sea life is plentiful and varied and there is a small beach on which to land.

5. Binlahan Bay
Situated on the west side of Inishdooey. Entry is at the south side of the bay which has a depth of 15m. This is an excellent dive as the terrain is most interesting with underwater caverns, arches and holes. Sea life is plentiful and many species can be found here. Of particular note are the seals which can be seen underwater. The vision of huge seals darting swiftly and gracefully through the rocky crevices is truly magnificent.

6. Carricknacruboge
This is a reef located on the north side of Inishdooey. It is a good area for a snorkel or shallow dive, on the south side the rocks deepen to the east. This is a good area where two or three seals may be seen swimming along together. A very fast tidal race exists between the reef and Inishdooey. Caution must be observed but it should be diveable during slack water.

7. Seal Caves
There is a series of interconnected gullies and caves much loved by seals. It is possible to get close enough to even photograph them. However, the caves are shallow being only 10m deep.

8. Skate Bay
Between Duncap Isle and Horn Head there is a wide shallow bay which has a varied rock and kelp bottom up to 20m deep with plenty of life, particularly skate. Good for a snorkel or long, shallow dive.

Tory Island Dive Sites

Tory is the most remote and exposed of all the inhabited Irish Islands. It lies about 14km off the coast. Its outline provides a striking contrast against the background of the Atlantic Ocean. This unsheltered isle suffers the destructive effects of the wind and sea and it is because of these elements that Tory Island is so barren.

The island is only about 5km long by 1.5km wide and is mainly composed of granite. The shelving nature of its coastline allows extensive rock beaches to be exposed in the sheltered bays of the northern side of the island. On the southern side, sandy beaches appear at low tide and these can be utilised as landing places – Camusmore Bay and Port Doon are two of Tory's few landing places.

The northern and north-eastern coastline is more irregular, being carved into a multiplicity of minor headlands and many inlets, gullies and coves. The best way to dive the island is to hire a half-decker for a day and use an inflatable as a dive tender. This can be done quite easily from Portnablagh which is approx. 20km from the island, where several half-deckers are available for hire.

The local community is close knit, living in two main villages, East Town and West Town, and fishing is one of the island's principal industries (particularly lobster fishing) and for this reason the islanders are rather suspicious of divers – unfortunately rightly so, in some cases! So please don't strain relations any further by taking the abundant lobster and crayfish. Look, photograph, but do not touch! .

Tory's insular position and distance from the mainland explain the retention of many aspects of a life similar to that practised on the mainland several decades ago.

The diving around Tory is a matter of personal preference, because the island is one of those unique places that has no poor dive sites. It is virtually undived and the marine life is breathtaking. Lobster and crayfish are in abundance, fish are inquisitive and too numerous to try and catalogue here. A photographer can happily spend hours in these waters.

9. Scoltgar-Hyancaul

Particularly spectacular dive sites are at Scoltgar-Hyancaul which has some of the most spectacular underwater scenery, alternating deep gullies with long sloping plains all covered in exquisite marine life and sloping off to 30m.

10. Port Doon

Another site warranting particular mention is between Port Doon and Tormore. This site provides some of the most extensive gully systems on the island, some with sheer walls 15–20m high and only a couple of metres wide, all covered in marine life and providing truly exotic diving.

These are only two of the numerous available sites. As you will have guessed, the landscape underwater is as stunning as it is above. Cliffs drop away to 30m and slope out into 40m, there are reefs and drop-offs all around the island with numerous overhangs and it is a case of not knowing what you are going to see next.

However, there are some strong currents so it is advisable to use a surface marker buoy, particularly at the eastern and western tips of the island and on the more rugged and exposed northern side. The visibility is often 20m or more and all this adds to the pleasure of diving the area. On going to press there are rumours that a compressor station is being considered for Tory.

Tory Island ferry:
Tel. 075 31991/31340/31320
Fax. 075 31665

North East Donegal Dive Sites

11. Mulroy Bay

This is a very sheltered bay surrounded as it is on almost four sides it can be dived regardless of the weather. You can always get a dive there. Depth from 3–50m. Launch from the picnic area at Woodquarter or (the more difficult boat entry) at Cranford.

12. Campbells Bed

Is a nice little reef stretching quite a long distance – Depth from 15–27m. Just opposite Carlan Bay there's not too much animal life, but it's varied and there is a nice conger there. Animal life seems to be on the increase, and there are always the seals on the surface. Beautiful place for a night dive – landscape is crying out to be photographed.

13. Massmount

Lovely shore dive (depth 7–20m) with striking plant life. Night diving here is something special, try it out. **N.B.**: The road here is narrow, please be very cautious with your vehicles, also check that you don't block any entrances to the houses. This is a shore dive but if you want to use boats you can launch from across the bay.

This is a busy bay with plenty of people using it. Divers have never caused the locals any problems (makes a change, doesn't it!). Watch out for marker buoys and shellfish farming areas. Keep your speed down.

14. Downings

There is a fine slipway here. Don't block it. Head out of the harbour, turn right and keep going. You will soon see the Wearyman Rock by the water crashing over it. Depth 15–20m. Interesting rock face.

15. The Black Rocks

Big majestic rock in 25–0m. Head about 30m to the seaward side, and then drop down. Clear water, fish, fine rockscapes, clear white sand and congers. When the weather permits, this is a fine dive.

16. The Narrows

An underwater garden in 21–24m. You have to get this one dead right. Usually crystal clear, but the current is

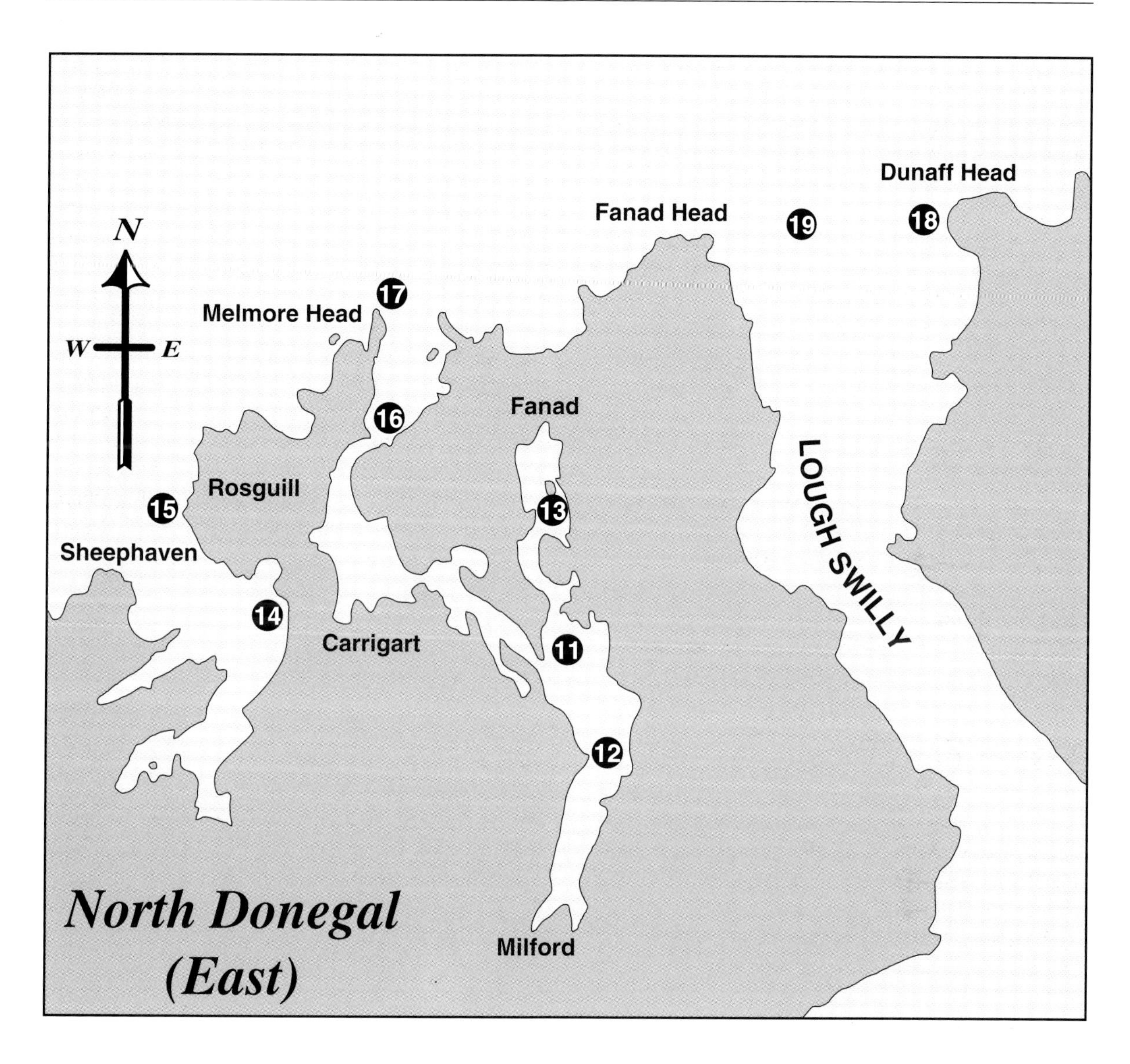

quite strong. If you get swept off the rock race, watch yourself. Bruised arms and legs are not unusual. This is a drift dive, not for the faint hearted, but God! it's exciting! Launch from the boatyard at Neevagh.

17. Melmore Point

With depths of 20–30m this is a nice area and a favourite spot for local divers. Go down along rock face and keep to the inside of the point. There are large shoals of fish in a very large rocky area. You never know what you'll find here. If you start your dive at the point and head along the reef, you will find a lovely unspoilt rugged area.

N.B.: As this dive is along the outside of the point, pay particular care to the weather conditions and the use of SMBs for each pair of divers is recommended.

18. Dunaff Head

Dunaff Head is at the Eastern side of Lough Swilly. There is a series of gullies running north–south between Portbane Island and the Head, narrowing in the centre to an inverted keyhole swim through. The general depth is 15–25m. Launch from the slipway in Rockstown Harbour, just around the head.

Donegal Wrecks

19. SS Laurentic (GPS 55.18.250N 07.35.528W)
Rockstown is also suitable for those who wish to dive the SS Laurentic which lies 20 min. away by RIB in 40m of water. The 14,892 ton SS Laurentic, an armed merchant ship, was torpedoed during WWI and sank in the mouth of Lough Swilly. On board were 43 tons (3211 ingots) of gold bullion most of which was salvaged from the wreck, but 25 gold ingots have still not being accounted for. Permission to dive this wreck must be sought from the owner Mr Ray Cossum, 61 Malin Gardens, Derry City, Northern Ireland.

20. William Mannell (GPS 55.18.452N 07.04.514W)
A fishing trawler built in 1917 and used as a mine sweeper during WWII. She was converted back to fishing after the war and was wrecked in 1946 after hitting rocks near Glangad Head. She is named after a crewman who served with Lord Nelson on the Victory at the Battle of Trafalgar. Max. depth is 28m to sea bed and because of the strong currents can only be dived at slack tide. Launch from slipway at Bunnagee Pier, Culdaff Bay.

21. Castle Eden (GPS 55.19.286N 07.03.280W)
This is the wreck of a trawler sunk by a U-boat while carrying a cargo of coal. The wreck which lies 33m deep is well broken up and can only be dived at slack water. Launch from Bunnagee Pier, Culdaff Bay.

22. U-boat (GPS 55.24.064N 07.15.125W)
One of the surrendered U-boats taken out from Lisahally Harbour on the outskirts of Derry city after the war. She was sunk by the RAF in the sound between Malin Pier and Inishtrahull Island. She lies in a gully on the sea bed at 43m and can only be dived at slack water because of the very strong currents. This is a dive which should only be attempted by the most experienced and well equipped divers. Launch from Bunnagee Pier, Culdaff Bay.

23. HMS Audacious (GPS 55.28.311N 07.45.157W)
This 23,000 ton Royal Navy battleship struck a mine behind Tory Island during WWI. She tried to return to Lough Swilly with the help of the Olympic but sank approximately 22km off Fanad Head Lighthouse. She is huge, rests in 65m of water and is well broken up. Another wreck only for the best equipped and trained diver. Launch from Downings Pier or Rockstown Harbour, Dunaff Head.

24. Unknown Wreck (GPS 55.17.900N 08.01.580W)
This wreck was thought to be the "Fern" but later proved not to be. Lying at a depth of 57m she is well broken up. Launch from Portnablagh Pier.

Local Facilities and Information

Compressor:	Lawrence Strain, Forguar, Milford, Co. Donegal. Tel. 074 53686
	Marine Sports, 119 Spencer Road, Derry. Tel. (08) 01504 345444
Tidal Constant:	Dublin -05 49
Local VHF station:	Malin Head Radio Ch. 16, 67,23, 85
Chart:	2752
Maps:	½":1 mile No. 1, 2 1:50000 No. 1, 2, 3

Malin Head Co. Donegal

Malin Head is easy to get to, just keep going north on the R242 from Malin village. This is as far north as one can go on the mainland. Where the tarmac runs out there is an old tower and beyond that a massive cleft bisecting the headland. This has high vertical sides plunging straight down to 20m at the western end and to a modest 2m at the eastern end. The western end of the gully is about 5m wide. The sea bed here is covered in massive slabs of rock. The scenery is stark with splashes of colour provided by hundreds of large daliah anemones. Higher up the walls are covered with sea firs and anemones associated with high energy sites. Kelp can only survive in the top few metres.

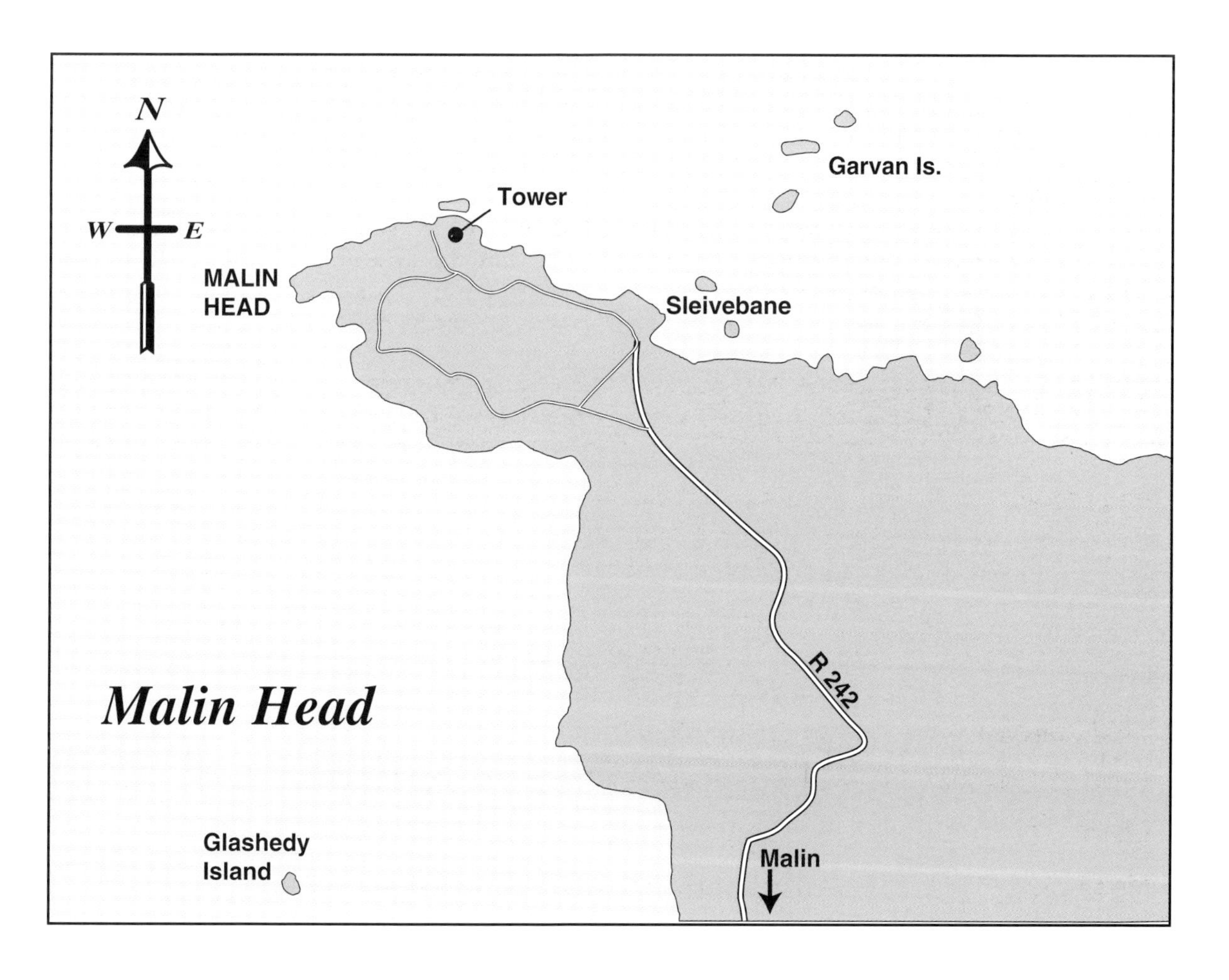

Dive Sites

1. Caverns

A short swim into the gullies will reveal the first of two large caverns. The entrance to the first is at 7m, dropping down to 15m. It gets quite dark inside and a torch is a must. The solid rock bottom is totally devoid of marine life. The roof, unlike the floor, is covered with a thick blanket of sponges and red turnicates.

The second cavern is bigger and has a forked entrance at the seaward side. Here, amongst the weirdly carved rocks, is a pot hole full of edible crabs. This natural trap had probably been the final home and resting place to thousands of crabs over the centuries.

Back in the gully the sides narrow to around 2m wide and huge blocks of stone stand in the way. You can fin under these in near swimming pool visibility. A cave two-thirds of the way along the gully displays superb rock formations. The fact that the roof is not under water makes it a little less exciting than the two caverns. However, the smooth rock indicated one thing clearly . . . an awful lot of the Atlantic ocean hits this site.

Continuing eastwards, the gully gets narrower and shallower and the swell, barely evident at the west end, becomes quite noticeable. The exit at the east is easy and the walk back to the car park much easier than the trip down . . . no holding onto blades of grass for balance on the two-inch sheep trail.

Malin Head is probably one of the most dramatic shore sites in the country. But with a westerly swell it can be hazardous. It is a 'calm' site only and the dry suited diver might be as well using a boat for entry to avoid over heating on the long slog to the site. Slievebane Harbour is only about a mile to the east and boasts Ireland's most northerly pub.

2. The O'Doherty Rocks

There is an underwater reef running for hundreds of metres to the east of the Garvan Islands which lie about 1,500m to the north of the fine harbour at Slievebane, which is close to the Malin Head Marine Radio Station.

The Malin area is subject to frequent and sudden changes of weather, so care must be taken in assessing the forecast for the dive. Very severe tidal currents sweep around Malin Head in both directions depending on the tide, and divers must be very wary of these. Once divers go down, they should not surface for trivial reasons, as the tide will carry them swiftly from their chosen dive spot during ascent and descent. It is not a suitable dive site for trainees and cox'ns should be experienced. Two boats are recommended and diver pickups must be swift and efficient, otherwise the surfaced divers will be halfway to Inishtrahull Island in no time! SMBs or other means of signalling is a must for at least the dive leaders.

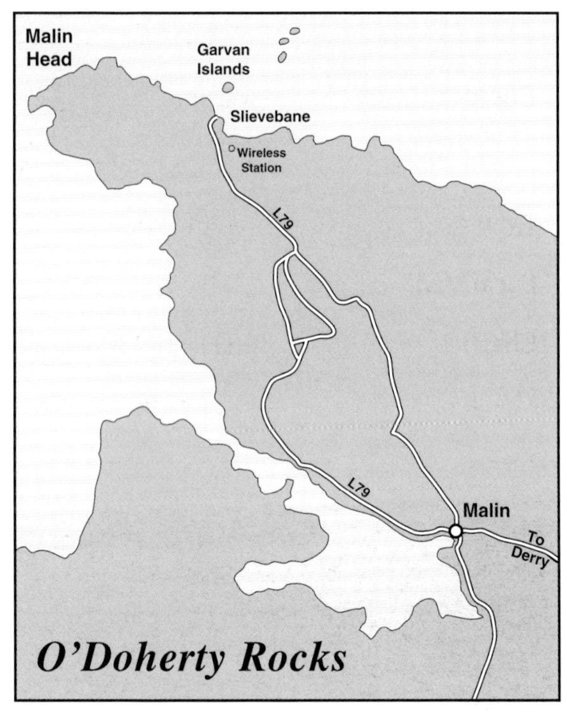

What makes this site so special is the underwater terrain. There is a large system of potholes in the reef, at an average depth of about 20m. These holes were formed by wave action rotating large boulders on a softer base rock. They can be up to six metres in diameter and some have joined up to make canyons. You should plan to get into and stay within the system for the entire dive moving from one pothole into the next. By staying in the steep-sided canyons divers are sheltered from the powerful tidal currents. The visibility is better than in open water and the sea life is excellent and varied. There is a fine diving watch there belonging to this writer, if found pleased contact the editor!

Local Facilities and Information

Compressor:	Marine Sports, 119 Spencer Road, Derry. Tel. (08) 01504 345444
Tidal Constant:	Dublin -05 40
Local VHF station:	Malin Head Radio Ch. 16, 67, 23, 85.
Chart:	2811, 2723
Maps:	½":1 mile OS Nos. 1, 2. 1:50,000 No. 3.

Basking skark at Tory Isd. ***Photo: Eddie Dunne***

Rathlin Island
Co. Antrim

Rathlin Island lies just 10km north of the pretty seaside resort of Ballycastle and 22km from the Mull of Kintyre, Scotland.

The island is L-shaped; one side 6.5km long, the other 4.8km, and nowhere is it more than 1.6km across. It is almost treeless and most of the coastline is cliffs, much of it 60m high.

To reach the island, take the ferry from Ballycastle across Rathlin Sound to the harbour at Church Bay. The trip takes about 1 hour. As you motor along, you can identify the main features of the North Antrim coast, with Fair Head towering above the sea, marking the topmost corner of Ulster. Slough na Morra, 'swallow of the sea', is a whirlpool in the sea south of Rue Point, the southern tip of Rathlin, which arises when two tides flowing in opposite directions meet and form pyramid waves.

You don't have to do the round trip in one day: there is a guest house and a restaurant at the harbour, and a pub, and you can pitch a tent in the campsite with permission.

Rathlin is popular with birdwatchers, geologists, botanists, divers, sea-anglers and anyone with a love for wild and rugged scenery.

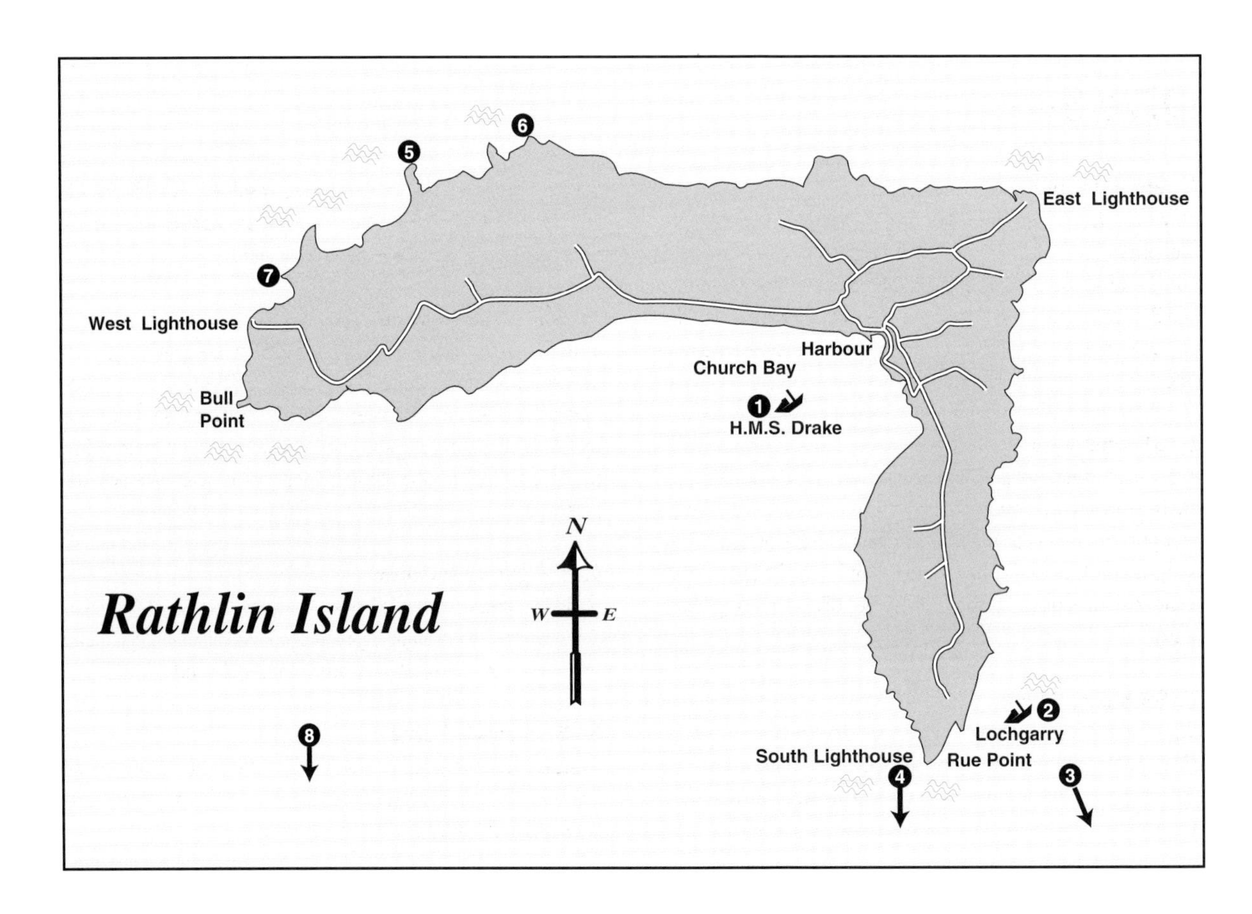

Marine Life

Considered unique by marine biologists, Rathlin contains species at their most northerly existence. One explanation for this is the little temperature fluctuation as a result of the Gulf Stream plus strong tidal mixing around Rathlin. A plankton-rich flood tide has created a great diversity in marine life with many sponges, some extremely large and along the east side, many hydroids.

Underwater cliffs off the north side are lime stone and basalt layered to 180m deep. The underwater scenery is breathtaking with caves and arches illuminated with the clarity and visibility for which Rathlin is famous. Diving with the currents in these areas can be thrilling, making it an area for experienced divers only.

Accomodation

Situated beside the harbour is the Richard Branson Activity Centre which has been especially designed with divers in mind. This fine building is the tithe barn of the old landlord's residence and was renovated by the Rathlin Island Trust. It has wet rooms and showers, a fully equipped self-catering kitchen and a dining room which can also serve as a lecture room. There are 26 beds in hostel form, outside drying racks for wetsuits, and a launderette attached to the building.

The Diving

The choice and variety for the Rathlin diver are quite phenomenal. With some of the deepest underwater cliffs in these islands, and some of the most famous wrecks, it has something to offer everyone. Rathlin has become established as a diving special, and now with increased facilities and accommodation created with divers in mind, it is a diving opportunity not to be missed.

Wrecks

Rathlin has more than 40 recorded wrecks around her shores. Some are more or less gone but there are several very exciting wrecks which prove extremely popular with divers, some shallow dives some deep. For a more detailed account of the wrecks of Rathlin read the late, and sadly missed, Tommy Cecil's book "The Harsh Winds of Rathlin" where full details of all the Rathlin wrecks may be found.

Dive Sites

1. HMS Drake

A WWI heavy cruiser torpedoed by U-79 on 2nd October 1917 sank in Church Bay. With a length of 40m, a draught of 8m and 14000 tonnes, the wreck lies in 18m of water, but still contains some live shells. It is an excellent night dive and tides are not a problem. A wreck buoy marks the site.

2. SS Lochgarry

A popular deep dive. A troop carrier in WWII, she sank off Rue Point in dense fog. She has a length of 80m, a draught of 5m and is 1600 tonnes. The Lochgarry sits upright on the sea bed at a depth of 30m. Because of its exposed position, it may only be dived during slack water.

3. SS Santa Maria

US registered oil tanker torpedoed by U-19 on 25th February 1918, Lying in 66m of water off Fair Head. The wreck lies on her side intact 50m to the top rail. Strong tidal streams ensure excellent visibility but restrict diving to slack water periods, only recommended for experienced divers.

4. SS Templemore

The Templemore sank in Ballycastle Bay on 6th December 1911 in heavy weather. She lies in 18m of water and is well broken up. This wreck is inhabited by several tame conger eels which maybe hand fed by divers. Diving conditions are good with weak tidal streams.

5. Farganlack Point

A drop-off starting at 20m and descending to 200m with a swim through arch at 30m. A slack water dive which can only be dived on the last 2 hours of an ebb tide.

6. Skerriagh Point

A steep rocky slope to 20m, sheer drop-off to 40m+ all dramatically covered with abundant life. Drift dives are possible along this and other cliff faces.

7. Derginam Point

Tremendous dive, 40m cliffs topped with pinnacles and archways.

8. Carrickmannon Rock

This is a large shoal which rises from great depths to within 5m of the surface near the mainland northwest of Ballycastle.

Local Facilities and Information

Compressor:	Atlantic Dive and Surf, 102 Main Street, Portrush. Tel. (08) 01265 823273
Tidal Constant:	Belfast -03 20
Local VHF station:	Belfast/Bangor Ch. 16, 67
Chart:	2798
Maps:	½":1 mile, No. 2 1:50000, No.5

Diver and cray ***Photo: Nigel Motyer***

Co. Antrim's Wrecks

If the West of Ireland has its "jewels", the Skelligs, The Aran Islands, Inishbofin, etc. the North of Ireland has its "pearls" – wrecks. From battleships to MTBs, from great liners to tug boats, wrecks litter the sea floor – in some places stacked on top of each other and easy to find. However, to take maximum advantage of their existence local knowledge is essential. Peter Steele of the North Irish Lodge Dive Centre who supplied this wreck information would be only too happy to assist any diving group.

The following shipwrecks are all within easy reach of the Islandmagee area. The majority of them are easily found, however, some of them have yet to be located. The area is well known for its superb diving and if you are not interested in wreck diving there are plenty of scenic dives, drift dives, shore dives and drop-offs ranging from 15m to more than 60m at the Maidens.

The Maidens, a group of nine rocks some 9.6km north of Larne hold the most spectacular diving of all. Its isolated location and strong tides have led to the area being rarely dived. With local knowledge and neap tides the clear waters of the Maidens are a must for visiting divers. All of the wrecks lie between 5 and 18m of water with one, the "Housatonic" extending down to 35m.

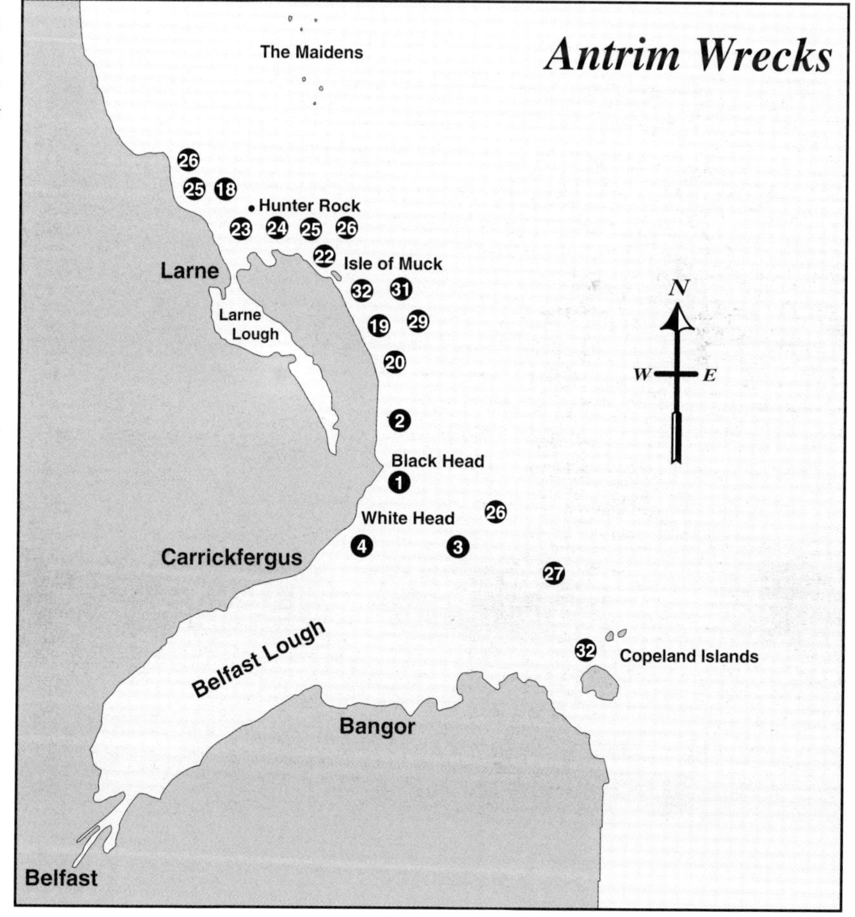

Shipwrecks of the Islanmagee, Maidens and Belfast

1. Chirripo (GPS 54 45.938N 05 40.651W)
The Elders and Fyffes cargo liner of over 4000 tons was torpedoed and sunk about 800m southeast of Black Head Lighthouse on the 28th December 1917. She is lying on her starboard side in 28m of water – 16m to the hand rail. She lies northwest-southeast direction and is a great dive for lobsters. The screw was raised in 1970. Best time to dive her is 1 hour before high or low water at Belfast. Boats can be launched at Whitehead up to 2 hours before and 2 hours after low water. Visibility can be up to 15m. Average 8–10m. An excellent dive for the more adventurous. Launching facilities at Whitehead up to 2 hours before or 2 hours after high water Belfast.

2. Tiberia (GPS 54 46.476N 05 38.653W)
The Anchor Lines cargo liner Tiberia of nearly 5000 tons was torpedoed and sunk 2.4km NE of Black Head by UB-19. She is lying in 63m of water, 50m to the bridge and 39m to the top of the forward mast. She is sitting upright on the seabed in a south-north direction. Best time to dive her is 45 min. before high or low water Belfast. Visibility can be up to 20m – average 8–10m. This is a great dive only for experienced divers. Beware there are a few monofilament nets on her superstructure. Launching from Whitehead up to 2 hours before and 2 hours after low water Belfast.

3. Lagan (GPS 54 43.049N 05 35.243W)
The Kelly's vessel Lagan was in a collision with the steamer Elmfield at the mouth of Belfast Lough in March 1946. She is lying on her side in a west-east direction in 30m of water. Quite a nice dive for the more adventurous. Best dived one hour before or after high water Belfast. Launching at Whitehead up to 2 hours before or after low water or at Carrickfergus or Bangor at any time.

4. Normandy Hall
Motor Coaster - sunk 8th October 1965.
The Normandy Hall of Chester foundered 800m south of Kilroot in the early hours of 8th October 1965 after a gallant 15 hour effort to tow her to safety. She had grounded in fog at Torr Point on the Ards Coast on the 6th October while bound from Birkenhead to Belfast. She was re-floated and taken in tow by the tanker Oarsman. She slowly settled in the water and sank 800m from shore. She is badly broken up as she was dispersed by explosives due to being a shipping hazard. Visibility in the area is poor 3–8m. Launching from Carrickfergus or Whitehead.

5. Housatonic (GPS 54 57.255N 05 44.805W)
The Housatonic, a steam tanker of 4041 tons, was owned by the Anglo American Oil Company and was in ballast from Barrow to New York. She grounded at 11pm on the Russell Rock north of the Maidens. Rockets were lit and fired but one fell back on board ship and started a fire. Thirty minutes later there was a huge explosion and the Housatonic slid off the rock and vanished. Two of the crew were lost. The wreck lies against the northeast side of the Russell Rock with the bow in 7m of water and the stern in 35m. She is badly broken up due to her exposed position.

Can be dived at either high or low water – Belfast. The last of the ebb is best. Launching facilities at Ballylumford Harbour, Islandmagee. A good dive to gain experience on wrecks. Visibility can be up to 25m with an average 10–15m.

6. Albia
Spanish tramp steamer of 1806 tons carrying ore, she ran aground on the 28th September 1929 on the south side of the Allen Rock, north of the Maidens. She is lying upright in 5–10m of water, bow towards the rock and is easy to locate. The stern section is intact, however, the bow and amidships are broken up. The propeller and rudder are still in place. A lovely dive for the beginner Best dived from low water Belfast on, as she is sheltered by the rock – cannot be dived on the ebb tide. Visibility – 10m average. Launching at Ballylumford, Islandmagee.

7. Large Smuggling Cutter
On the 7th November 1781 the London Chronicle reported a large smuggling cutter of Kintyre wrecked on the Maidens laden with contraband from Gottenburg. She had on board 1400 chests of fine tea, 100 ditto silk and 60 ankers of spirits. Out of 47 hands,

31 were saved. The captain, mate and cargo were lost. The same cutter had fought Captain Crawford in the Bay of Benluce 8 weeks previously. The vessel, her name unfortunately lost to us, was described as of 250 tons burden and mounted with no less than 16 guns. This ship was no doubt engaged in full time smuggling and bigger than many deep sea traders of the day. She had a very large crew and formidable armour to repulse a HM Revenue cruiser. She now lies badly broken up on the north side of the Allen Rock in 5–15m of water. She can be dived during neap tides, however, is best dived at slack tide half an hour each side of high water Belfast. This wreck is rarely dived. Launching at Ballylumford, Islandmagee.

8. Large American Trader

A large American Trader, a sailing ship, was lost with all hands at the same point as the smuggling cutter in March 1798. She is badly broken up and is also on the north side of the Allen Rock. There is very little left, however as this wreck is rarely dived there is bound to be a lot more to discover. Lying in 5–15m of water.

9. Dalnada

The Collier Dalnada, 200 tons, was en route from Ayr to Larne with coal when she ran aground on the east side of the Allen Rock and was a total loss. She lies in 4–15m of water and is best dived half an hour before high or low water Belfast. This wreck is rarely dived. Visibility Average 10m. Easily found on the easterly side of the rock. Launching at Ballylumford, Islandmagee.

10. Sumatra

The largest square-rigger sailing vessel (1551 tons) ever lost on the Antrim Coast. She was en route from Greenock to Rangoon with a full cargo of coal when she ran aground on the east side of the Highland Rock, north of the Maidens. She is badly broken up and easily found in 8-18m of water and rarely dived. There are still artefacts to be found. Best dived _ hour before high or low water Belfast. Visibility average 10m. Launching Facilities at Ballylumford, Islandmagee.

11. Maria

Canadian Barquentine, sank 3rd July 1882. The Maria ran aground on the east side of the Highland Rock while en route from Liverpool to Pictou, Nova Scotia

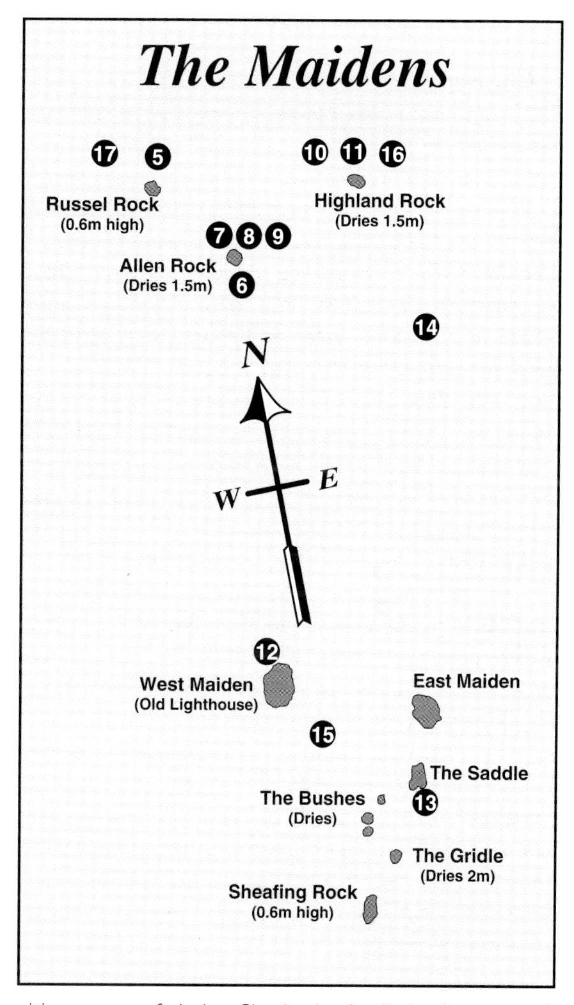

with a cargo of chains. She is also badly broken up and easily found lying in 5–15m of water beside the Sumatra. Best dived half an hour before high or low water Belfast. She is rarely dived and there are still artefacts to be found. Average visibility 10m. Launching facilities at Ballylumford, Islandmagee.

12. Norseman (GPS 54 55.780N 05 43.533W)

The 200 ton steamer Norseman was en route from Ayr to Magheramorne in December 1916 when she grounded on the north side of the East Lighthouse on the Maidens. She is badly broken up and lying in 6–15m of water. Rarely dived she is best dived at slack water half an hour before high or low water at Belfast. The last of the flood tide is best. Visibility normally is 8–10m. Launching at Ballylumford, Islandmagee.

13. Overton (GPS 54 55.558N 05 43.515W)
The 250 ton steamer Overton was carrying general cargo from Liverpool to Larne when she ran aground in fog on the southeast tip of the Saddle Rock. Attempts to dislodge her failed and she disappeared in heavy seas on 12th December 1955. She is quite badly broken up and lying in 8–16m of water. She is rarely dived and there are still artefacts to be found. She is best dived half an hour before high or low water Belfast. The last of the ebb is best. Visibility is normally 8–10m. Launching facilities at Ballylumford, Islandmagee.

14. Industry
The Sloop Industry foundered on 31st December 1821 after striking one of the rocks off the Maidens. Her wreck has not yet been located.

15. Pembury
The 383 ton steamer Pembury left Ardrossan on the 5th August 1897 with coal for Belfast. She encountered heavy fog and ran aground on one of the rocks of the southern group of the Maidens. Captain Russell and the 10 crew members quickly left her and the chief engineer had no time to blow off steam. Eight minutes after touching, her boiler exploded with a deafening report. The entire crew were saved, however, the Pembury was a total loss. As the area is rarely dived she has not yet been located.

16. Raylight
The MV Raylight (117 ton) struck the Highland Rock in thick fog at 7am on 4th August 1975. She was on her way south from Dunbegan in Skye to Kilroot to load salt. She sank less than 10 minutes after grounding and her crew were picked up by the ferry Ulidia within 20 minutes. The wreck has not yet been located as diving in the area is rare. This will prove to be a lovely dive when found. Visibility in this area can be up to 25m.

17. Zetland
The 700 Tons Steamer Zetland was lost off the Russell Rock in the early part of this century. She has not yet been located and details of her loss are very scant.

18. State of Louisiana
Bow: (GPS 54 52.911N 05 45.118W)
Hunter Rock: (GPS 54 52.913N 05 45.066W)
The State Steamship Company Liner the State of Louisiana was approaching Larne from Glasgow on 24th December 1878 with 17 passengers and 2000 tons of cargo. Unknown to Captain McGowan the buoy marking Hunter Rock off Larne had been dislodged. She grounded on Hunter Rock, and was badly holed and lay for 2 weeks before breaking into 3 parts and slipping beneath the waves. The bow and bridge sections lie on the south side of the highest point of the rock while the rear mast and stern section lies to the north of the rock (the top of the rock is 4m at low tide). The bow section is intact and lying on its port quarter in 24m of water. The bridge portion is sitting upright 15m from the rock and 15m astern from the bow. The stern section lies in 25m of water at the base of the rock. This is one of the most interesting wrecks in the area. It abounds with sea life and visibility can be up to 20m. Beginners can work their way down the rock from 5m. Best dived 1 hour before high or low water Belfast. Launching facilities at Ballylumford, Islandmagee.

19. Alcedo (GPS 54 48.695N 05 41.402W)
The Alcedo, a steamer of 200 tons was wrecked in January 1892 at the Gobbins Cliffs on her maiden voyage. She is very badly broken up and lying against the cliff face in 7m of water. She can be dived at any state of the tide and is rarely visited. Visibility is usually 5-10m. Launching facilities at Whitehead up to 2 hours before and 2 hours after low water Belfast.

20. Black Diamond (GPS 54 47.252N 05 41.315W)
The wooden hull was an oddity for a steam vessel of 259 gross tons, but she had a robust two cylinder steam engine from Coates Works in Belfast. She was wrecked 1.6km North of Blackhead. She is badly broken up and wreckage at the above position is thought to be the Black Diamond. The site is rarely dived and needs more research. The wreckage is lying in 7m of water directly opposite a blue 40ft container on the foreshore. Visibility 5–10m. She can be dived at any state of the tide. Launching at Whitehead up 2 hours before and 2 hours after low water Belfast.

21. Peridot (GPS 54 51.608N 05 45.691W)
The 200 ton coaster Peridot was en route from Scotland to Camlough on 25th November 1905 with a cargo of coal. An easterly gale forced the small coaster to run for the safety of Larne Lough. She foundered on Skernaghan Point at Browns Bay and her entire crew of 9nine were lost. The vessel had broken in two and was just visible above the waves. The bow section lies approximately 20m to the southwest of the point while the stern section lies to the east of the rock. She is badly broken up with the boiler just below the surface. The bell was recovered by divers in 1995. She is rarely dived and is excellent for beginners. Can be dived 1 hour before high or low water Belfast. Best dived at the last of the ebb. Launching from Ballylumford, Islandmagee.

22. Ailsa (GPS 54 51.204N 05 44.302W)
Built 1867, wrecked 26th February 1892, length 100ft. The Ayr Shipping Company's Ailsa was on a regular run from Ayr to Belfast with general cargo and one passenger when she ran aground and was a total loss approximately 1.2km north of Portmuck. She is badly broken up and lying in 3–5m of water. Part of her hull can be seen on the shore above the high water mark. She can be dived at any state of the tide. Visibility usually 5–10m. Launching at either Portmuck at high tide or Ballylumford, Islandmagee at any time.

Skernaghan Point Area

(GPS 54 51.590N 05 45.740 W)
The following known ships have been wrecked on or near Skernaghan Point, however they have not been located as yet.

The sloop 'Roberts' in 1811 she was carrying glass and china and was washed into Browns Bay during a snow storm.

The barque 'J.E. Hudson' in 1827.

The brig 'Alpha' in 1827.

The steamer 'Tuskar' lost on 27th November 1891 was 397 gross tons and was carrying 100 tons of limestone from Glenarm.

No less than 12 ships were lost on Skernaghan Point during the early 1800's, their names are now lost to us.

23. Harrington (GPS 54 51.124N 05 47 355W)
The Harrington (1000 tons) was leaving Larne when she got a rope entangled in her propeller. Before her anchor could bring her up she grounded at the extreme end of Ferris Point and became a total loss. Her crew were all rescued by breeches buoy and when she finally broke up her cargo of potatoes was strewn all over the island shore. She is badly broken up and rarely dived. Lying in 3-6m of water she is an excellent shore dive. There are lots of congers lurking in the wreckage. Access is best from Ballylumford with good car parking. Beware of large ferries entering and leaving Larne Harbour. Visibility usually 3–6m.

24. George (GPS 5451.052N 05 47.355W)
The brigantine George of Workington had been built in 1796 at Aberystwyth and ended her career on the rocks between Ballylumford Harbour and the present lighthouse on Ferris Point on the 20th December 1876. She is lying in 5m of water and is badly broken up. This is an easy shore dive to access from a small slipway north of the harbour. She should only be dived when ferries are not operating **and divers should not go any deeper than 7m or stray into the main channel.** Be aware that the engine noise from ships entering Larne harbour can be quite frightening if you are not used to it. Visibility usually 3–6m.

25. Ferric (GPS 54 52.502N 05 49.185W)
The steamer Ferric which was owned by H.J. Scott was en route from Ayr to Larne with coal in January 1905. She battled a southeasterly gale all the way across the channel but failed to get into Larne and ended up on the rocks at the Black Arch, orth of Larne. Her entire crew landed safely but the Ferric was a total loss. She is very badly broken up and lying in 3–8m of water. She is rarely dived and little has been recovered from her. She can be dived at any state of the tide but avoid springs. Visibility 5–10m in the kelp.

26. Rose II (GPS 54 44.307N 05 38.756W)
The Rose II was an armed trawler of 100 tons which would appear to have struck a mine and sank in Belfast Lough during WW I. She is sitting upright on the sea bed at 26m, 21m to the bridge. Lying in a eastwest direction with her entire bow blown off. This is an

excellent wreck for divers to gain experience on. However, **there are some unexploded spigot mortars lying around - DO NOT TOUCH.** There are plenty of Scallops to lift instead (legal in Northern Ireland!). Visibility 5--15m. Launching at Whitehead 2 hours before or after low water Belfast and from Bangor at any time.

27. Karanan (GPS54 42.805N 05 31.768W)
The Dutch coaster Karanan (395 tons) was en route from Liverpool to Belfast with a general cargo of foodstuffs, batteries, copper piping, anti aircraft gun parts, etc. When she collided with the steam tanker 'British Engineer'. Her starboard side was stove in and she quickly sank with two of her crew being lost. She is lying in a west-east direction on her port side, with extensive damage to the starboard side just forward from the bridge. At 34m to the highest part and 43m to the seabed she is a very advanced dive. The strong tides mean that she can only be dived at slack water. Best dived half an hour before high water Belfast. Visibility can be up to 20m – average 6–10m. There are quite a few port holes left. Launching from Whitehead 2 hours before or 2 hours after low water Belfast, or from Bangor and Carrickfergus at any time.

28. Teanua (GPS 54 49.691N 05 45.754W)
The Teanua an elderly schooner sank in 1976 while at anchor at Ballydown in Larne Lough. She can be dived at any state of the tide, however visibility is poor as the sea bed is mud. The only consolations are the lobsters living in the nooks and crannies. She almost breaks the surface at low tide and the sea bed in only 5m. Launching from Ballylumford, or from the shore at Ballydown, Islandmagee.

29. Berbice (GPS 54 51.221N 05 46.187W)
The four masted square rigger Berbice enroute from Greenock to Havana with coal was swept into Browns Bay on 1st January 1827 and broke up several days later. Her exact location is not confirmed however a large anchor located on the south west side of the bay would indicate that this is the final resting place of the Berbice. The site can be accessed from the shore. Little is left of the wreck which lies in 3–8m of water however you may be lucky as it is very rarely dived. Visibility is usually 5–10m.

30. Cannons (GPS 54 50.424N 05 46.903W)
Three sixteenth century bronze cannons were found a few years ago in an ancient anchorage in Larne Lough. The cannons were cast by a London foundry called Owens and were dated 1559, the inscription read "ELYSABETH REGYNA Thomas and John Owyn Made Thys Pese Anno DNI 1559". There is no known record of any HM Ships entering Larne Lough in a damaged state. It is known however, that around the end of the sixteenth century when there was a fear of a Scottish invasion, merchant ships landed armaments round the coast of Northern Ireland. It is possible that these cannons were lost accidentally. This site has been rarely dived after the discovery of an anti-submarine rocket in the diving area. These cannons can now be inspected in the White Tower of London.

31. Woods (GPS 54 50.773N 05 42.786W)
The brig Woods was wrecked on the southeastern point of Muck Island during hard gales in early March 1827. Remains located so far are anchor chains lying in 24m of water to the southeast of the island. She is rarely dived and no doubt more will be re-discovered in the near future. There are plenty of scallops off the east side of the island and it is an excellent area for crab and octopus. She can only be dived at slack water, i.e. 1hour before high or low water at Belfast. Visibility 5–18m. Launching from Portmuck at high tide or Ballylumford, Islandmagee.

32. Ulrica (GPS 54 41.750N 05 31.660W)
The large four masted iron square rigged ship 'Ulrica' lay hove-to off Dublin Bay in a refreshing southeasterly wind on 6th January 1897 at the end of a 137 day passage from San Francisco. She once sailed 370 miles in one day on a voyage to Australia. As darkness fell the ship was blown northwards by the increasing gale. Captain John Johnston could do nothing but to steer for shelter of Belfast Lough. At 4.30 am she grounded on Old Lighthouse Island and became a total loss. Her entire crew of 28 were saved. She is badly broken up and lying in 10m of water on the north westside of Old Lighthouse Island. She is an excellent dive for the beginner and there are plenty of scallops in the area. Can be dived at nearly all states of the tide. Visibility can be 10–15m. Launching from Bangor, Donaghadee or Whitehead.

Other shipwrecks of the Islandmagee, Maidens and

Belfast Lough

Name	Vessel	Date	Tonnage	Location
Troutpool	Steamer	20/7/1949	1000	6.2km south White Head
Annagher	Steamer	1937		Ballymacormick Point.

Islandmagee

Name	Vessel	Date	Tonnage	Location
Tobago	Barkque	7/9/1886	N/K	Skemaghan Point

Maidens

Name	Vessel	Date	Tonnage	Location
Pembury	Steamer	5/8/1897	383	Off southern rocks not identified yet
Susanna and Anna	Schooner	13/8/1873		Location not identified yet
MTB No75	Torpedo boat	8/8/1892	66	North of Maidens

Local Facilities and Information

Tidal constant: Belfast -00 05

Local VHF station: Belfast / Bangor Ch. 16, 67

Chart: 2159

Maps: ISO 1:50,000 No. 9, 15., OSNI 1:50,000 Nos. 9,15

Strangford Lough
Co. Down

Strangford is the largest sea inlet in the British Isles with a meandering shoreline of 240km. This gigantic inland sea, has about 120 small islands and is surrounded almost entirely by land. This means there is an enormous diversity of easily accessible diving sites. Quite simply, Strangford Lough is unique, a marine biologist's paradise. The appeal of the lough to marine biologists is its very wide range of seabed conditions, influenced by water movements and the enormous diversity of species which are found. The life on the sea bed and around the many islands is varied and prolific with urchins, anemones, sea squirts, scallops, crabs,

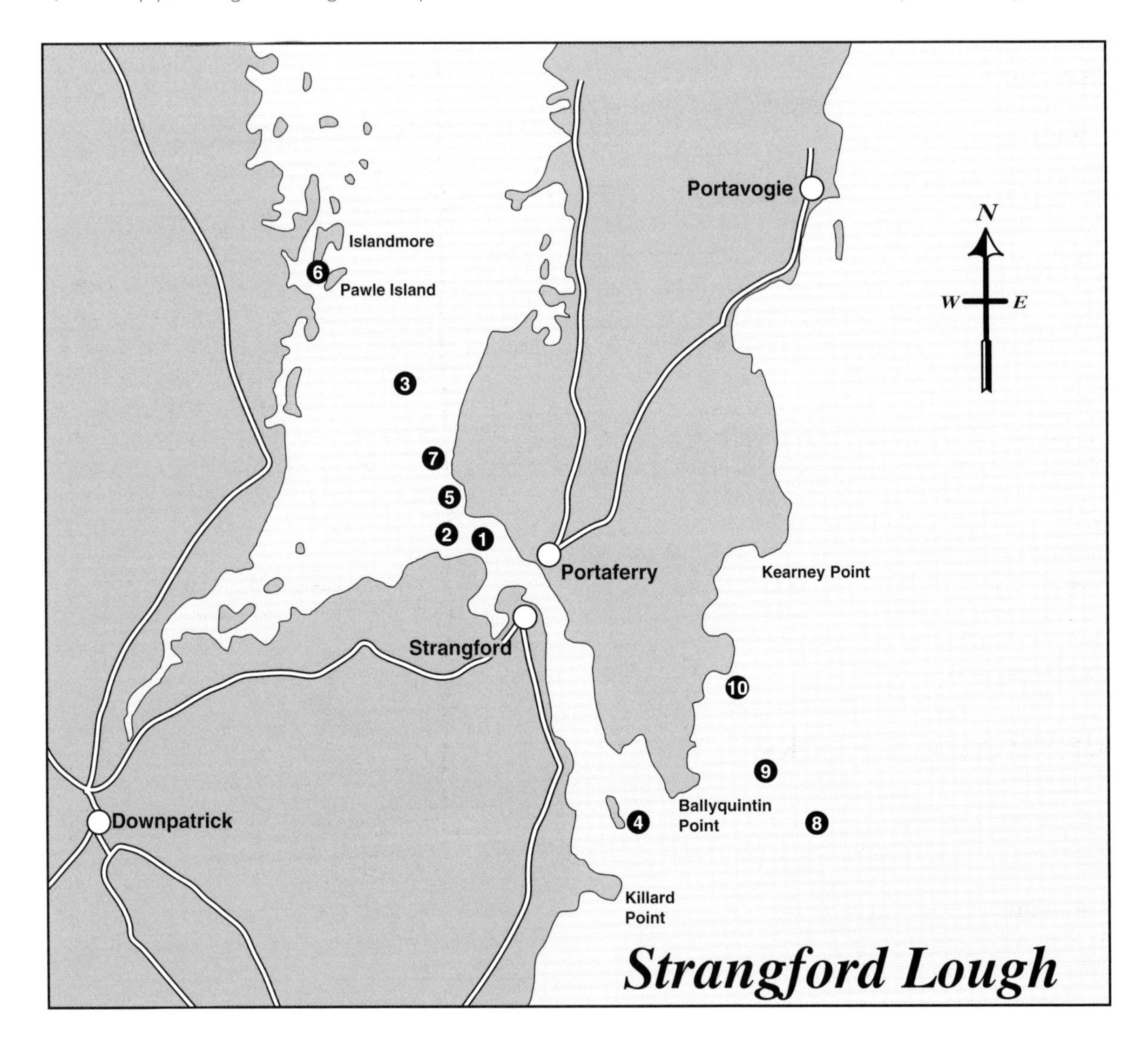

prawns and even octopus. The scampi prawn is common in the lough and can often be seen on the mud or outside its burrows.

One of the richest marine life communities is based around the big horse mussels. Its colonies provide a stable attachment for many other species including scallops. The variety of marine life and good visibility, 5–10m+, makes Strangford Lough an excellent site for underwater photography.

Strangford is very sheltered and rarely has waves of more than 1m in height, tidal streams, however, are strong. In the Narrows, they can reach 8 knots at spring tides. Slack within the lough is normally at high water or low water. These are 1 hour 52 minutes after Belfast, but there are, of course, complex tidal patterns meaning that the time of slack or maximum speed of current at different dive sites can vary quite a bit even though they're not far apart.

The lough is connected to the sea by a long narrows where the sea is usually flat and calm. This belies the fierce currents of up to 8 knots and depths of 80m which can make this as adventurous a dive as anyone could wish. Sheer cliffs are covered by luxurious growths, dead man's fingers and big sponges which, even in slack water, make the dive exciting. Outside the lough, there is a large number of wrecks, and tidal streams are not as strong, though they can be 1–2 knots so diving at or near slack water is best.

Scenic Dives

1. Ballyhenry Point

Also known as the "Drop-Off", the plateau is of gravel and coarse sand sloping gently to about 20m, with occasional rock outcrops. This is not very interesting and in most places the drop-off proper doesn't start until 25m. The steepness varies from a sharp boulder slope to sheer sections of cliff-face down to at least 50m. The bottom is mud at 66m. The marine life is spectacular including dead man's fingers, hydroids, crabs, lobsters, squat lobsters, blennies, cuckoo wrasse, balm wrasse etc. Slack water is at around high water or low water Strangford. There's hardly any slack at all at spring tides.

2. Audley's Point (GPS 54 22.98N 05 34.21W)

The plateau is narrower and the drop sharper, otherwise the terrain is very similar to Ballyhenry Point, as is the marine life.

3. Limestone Rock (GPS 54.24.30N 05.36.10W)

Rocky slope with sea squirts, feather starfish and sea urchins. Depth 5–20 m.

4. Marlfield Bay

Marlfield Bay is two bays further round from Ballyhenry Bay. It has more space for parking and on the shore at all states of the tide. The main disadvantage is that at low tide it can involve a 100m snorkel to get to a depth of 5m. The bottom is sandy and reasonably flat with brittlestars and the occasional outcrops of rock covered in sponges and deadman's fingers. It's diveable at any state of the tide, depth 10–40m with good drift up to 2 knots, usually going south.

4. Angus Rock

This is a scenic dive and a good place to start a drift dive. Depth 20–30m. Slack water at around high water or low water Strangford, but sit and wait. Calculations using the nearest tidal diamond are not valid for this site.

Strangford Wrecks

Strangford Lough has 15 wreck sites. Below are examples of the main wrecks.

5. EMPIRE TANA (GPS 54 23.36N 05 34.35W)

Also known as "Lee's wreck" this was a WWII Liberty ship which also acted as part of the Mulberry harbour at the landing beaches in Normandy. It broke away while under tow to Lee's breakers yard on Ballyhenry Island. It has broken into two large pieces off Ballyhenry Point at the sheltered end of the Strangford Narrows. It breaks the surface at low water and is in 10m of water. Once famous for its tame conger eels it is teeming with life, resembling a garden full of colour. It is carpeted from stem to stern inside and out with a huge variety of marine life. Care should be taken not to disturb the soft mud inside the wreck as the visibility can plummet to zero. Diving is best carried out after high water Strangford. Low water is okay but it is advisable to stay on the landward side. It is one of the favourite dives in Northern Ireland.

6. ALASDAIR (GPS 54 27.06N 05 37.71W)
A large motor yacht in Ringhaddy Sound, Strangford Lough. The wreck apparently sank after a fire, but is largely intact, and its sheltered location makes it an excellent beginners wreck (17–23m). Both the sea bed and the wreck are teeming with marine life. Fish species which can be expected to be seen in the vicinity include large ballan and goldsinny wrasse, pollack, poor cod, congers, Yarrell's blenny, gunnels and gobies.

7. ZARINA (GPS 54 23.35N 05 33.50W)
"The Pins" wreck is thought to be a barque which sank around 1700 in Ballyhenry Bay at the north end of the Strangford Narrows. It is an ideal beginner's wreck, and the hull is sheathed in copper with large pins holding the planking of the vessel together. There is a gently sloping bottom of fine sand and gravel with large kelp-covered rocks. The widely scattered wreckage lies in 8–12m of water when the tide in full.

8. HUNSDON (GPS 54 19.13N 05 27.30W)
Large wreck, 2899 tonnes, depth 35–39m. Visibility is often poor but slack water is available over a fairly wide period of the tide, perhaps an hour either side of high water or low water Strangford.

9. BANGOR (GPS 54 19.74N 05 26.60W)
This is a cargo ship carrying stone blocks, depth 30–40m. Slack water the same as the Hunsdon but the currents are stronger.

10. ARANTZAZU MENDI (GPS 54 22.46N 05 26.49W)
Wreck of 6600 tonnes lost on Yellow Pladdy in 1939.

Local Facilities and Information

Compressor:	DV Diving, 138 Mountstewart Road, Newtownards, Co. Down BT22 2ES. Tel. 01247 861686 / 464671 E-mail: dvdiving@dial.pipex.com Norsmaid Sea Enterprises, 152 Portaferry Road, Newtownards, Co. Down BT22 5ED. Tel. 01247 812081 E-mail: salutay@btinternet.com
Tidal constant:	Belfast +01 52
Local VHF station:	Ch. 16 Belfast Coastguard
Chart:	2159
Maps:	IOS ½" No. 9 1:50,000 No. 21, OSNI No. 21

Lambay Island
Co. Dublin

Lambay Island is situated 16km north of Dublin. There are three possible launching points for access to the island, Howth Harbour (beside the yacht club), Rush Harbour and Loughshinny. The shortest route is from Rush, with a 4km journey, where there are good launching facilities.

Rush is located 27km north of Dublin on the N1, turn off at Blake's Cross onto the R127 after 5km at Lusk turn right and continue for another 3km until you see on the right a sign for Rogerstown Harbour. Follow the signs.

Lambay is a private island of 1100 acres, of which 360 acres are arable, where one may only land with permission or during an emergency. Because it is a bird sanctuary this alone makes the trip worthwhile. The island also has a herd of about 200 deer and even a few wallabies.

The depths around the island are mainly in the region of 18–20m, but up to 40m may be obtained off the Nose of Lambay. Visibility around the island is seldom more than 6m, and can be badly affected by current and silt. There are at least four wrecks to be found off the island as well as several excellent, if shallow, normal dives.

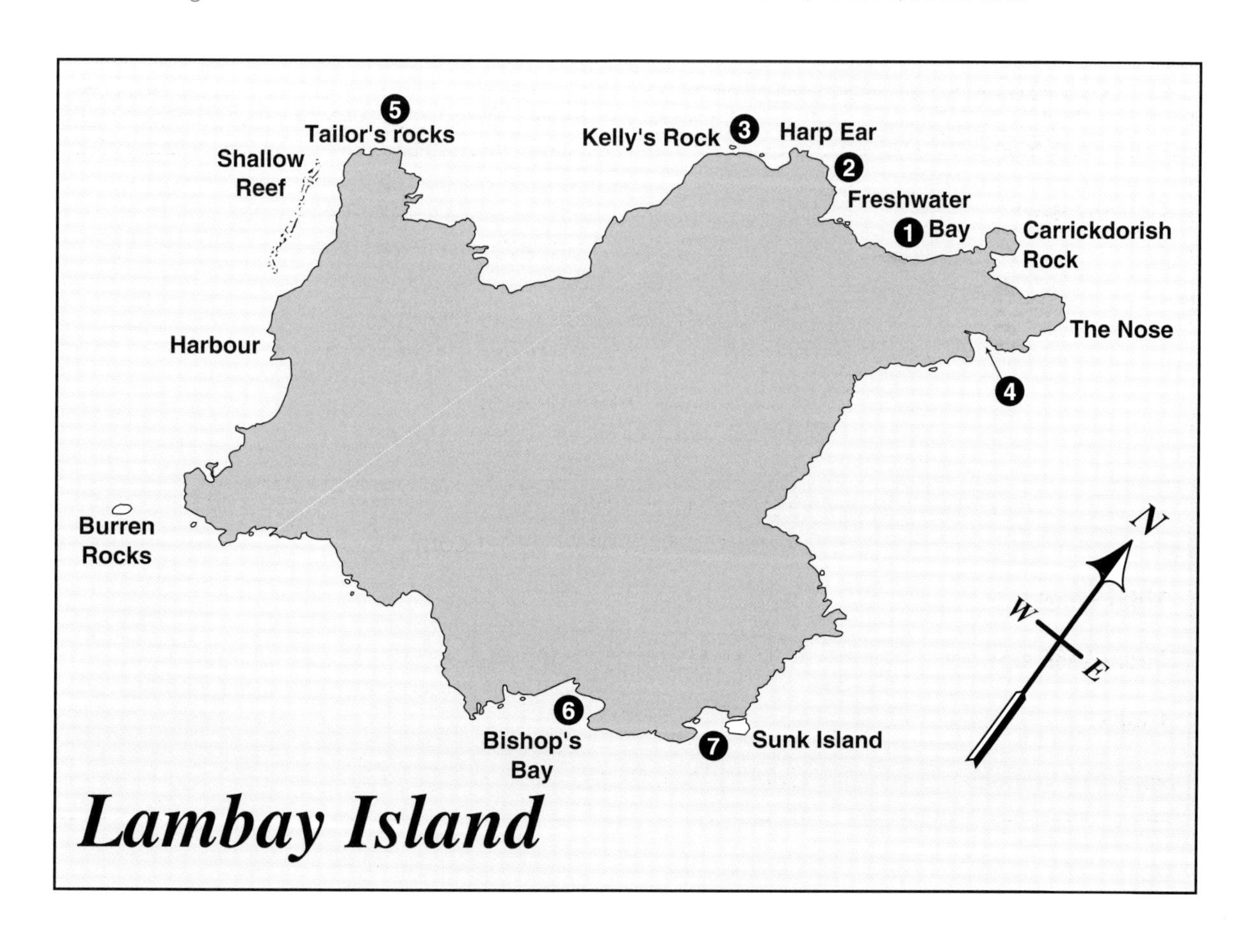

Dive Sites

1. The Shamrock

The "Shamrock" lies north of Carrickdorish Rock and under the fresh water stream. The wreck position can be identified by the steps cut into the rock face. It is in a depth of 12–16m and there are no currents as it is protected by Freshwater Bay. The "Shamrock" sank in 1916 loaded with phosphorous and high explosive shells most of which were salvaged, hence the reason for steps. However, not all shells were recovered and wedge shaped pieces of phosphorous may still be found. If you do find any, leave them in the water as it can spontaneously combust when exposed to air and cause very unpleasant burns.

2. The Stratheay

The "Stratheay", a 1900 steam ship, which is in 18m of water and exposed to the full flow of the ebb tide so that it can only be dived on a flooding tide or slack water.

3. Unnamed Wreck

Northeast from the Stratheay around Harp Ear is another wreck, sunk in the 1920s. Again this ship is in 14 to 18m which makes good diving with little current.

4. The Tayleur

South of the Nose of Lambay in the first bay below the falling rocks, about 40m out, is the "Tayleur". Wrecked in 1854 with a loss of over 400 lives she was a three decked, three masted sailing ship. One of the first iron vessels she was wrecked on her way to Australia, it is said, because of compass error. Lying in 15–18m, protected by the bay and with little tidal movement it can get silted up very quickly.

The "Tayleur" is a protected wreck, being over one hundred years old, and a licence must be obtained from the Office of Public Works, National Monuments Branch, 51 St. Stephens Green, Dublin 2, before diving on her.

5. Tailor's Rocks

A reef runs between the harbour and Tailor's Rocks about 300m from the shore line. A relatively shallow dive but with plenty of fish life and colour. There is a tidal current which runs north/south, it is advisable to dive at slack water.

6. Bishop's Bay

On the south side of the island Bishop's Bay with its stony beach is ideal for an introductory or trainee dive. The bottom, which gradually slopes to 16m, consists of large rock formations with patches of sand. There is an abundance of sea life. The bay is free from current providing that you keep away from the exposed points of land.

7. Sunk Island Bay

The next bay to the east, Sunk Island Bay, is also worth a visit although it is similar to Bishop's Bay. Again making sure you keep within the sanctuary of the bay you will encounter no currents with depths ranging from 12–22 m.

These are only a few of the good dive sites on Lambay, remembering that the advantage of an island is the ability to dive no matter which way the wind is blowing but , of course, you have to get there first.

Local Facilities and Information

Compressor:	Great Outdoors, Chatham St. Dublin 2. Tel. 6794293 Lambay Diving & Watersports Ltd., Kilmessan, Navan, Co. Meath. Tel. 046 25164 Fax. 046 26085 E-mail Walshe@indigo.ie
Tidal Constant:	Dublin -00 10
Local VHF station:	Dublin Radio Ch. 16, 67, 83
Chart:	44
Maps:	½":1 mile OS No. 16 1:50,000 No.43

Notes